KT-466-750

ALL IN ONE
BASKET

Also by Deborah Devonshire

The House: A Portrait of Chatsworth (1982)

The Estate: A View from Chatsworth (1990)

Farm Animals (1991)

Treasures of Chatsworth: A Private View (1991)

The Garden at Chatsworth (1999)

Counting My Chickens and Other Home Thoughts (2001)

Chatsworth: The House (2002)

The Duchess of Devonshire's Chatsworth Cookery Book (2003)

Round About Chatsworth (2005)

Memories of Andrew Devonshire (2007)

Home to Roost and Other Peckings (2009)

Wait For Me!: Memoirs of the Youngest Mitford Sister (2010)

Letters from Deborah Devonshire are included in:

The Mitfords: Letters between Six Sisters (2007)

In Tearing Haste: Letters between Deborah Devonshire
and Patrick Leigh Fermor (2008)

ALL IN ONE BASKET

Nest Eggs

DEBORAH DEVONSHIRE

JOHN MURRAY

First published in Great Britain in 2011 by John Murray (Publishers)
An Hachette UK Company

Counting My Chickens first published in Great Britain in 2001 by Long Barn Books
Home to Roost first published in Great Britain in 2009 by John Murray (Publishers)
An Hachette UK Company

1

© Deborah Devonshire 2001, 2009, 2011
Illustrations © Will Topley 2001, 2009, 2011
Introduction to *Counting My Chickens* © Tom Stoppard 2001
Introduction to *Home to Roost* © Alan Bennett 2009

The text of *Counting My Chickens* remains unaltered since first publication.

The right of Deborah Devonshire to be identified as the Author of the Work has been
asserted by her in accordance with the Copyright, Designs and Patents Act 1988.

All rights reserved. Apart from any use permitted under UK copyright law no part of
this publication may be reproduced, stored in a retrieval system, or transmitted, in any
form or by any means without the prior written permission of the publisher, nor be
otherwise circulated in any form of binding or cover other than that in which it is
published and without a similar condition being imposed on the subsequent purchaser.

A CIP catalogue record for this title is available from the British Library

Hardback ISBN 978-1-84854-638-7
Trade paperback ISBN 978-1-84854-639-4
Ebook ISBN 978-1-84854-594-6

Typeset in Bembo by Servis Filmsetting Ltd, Stockport, Cheshire
Printed and bound by Clays Ltd, St Ives plc

John Murray policy is to use papers that are natural, renewable and recyclable
products and made from wood grown in sustainable forests. The logging and
manufacturing processes are expected to conform to the environmental regulations
of the country of origin.

John Murray (Publishers)
338 Euston Road
London NW1 3BH

www.johnmurray.co.uk

CONTENTS

NEWLY LAID

INTRODUCTION

I was at a loss to know what I could write for the newly-wed *Counting My Chickens* and *Home to Roost* – now together in a new cover, happily honeymooning and thinking only of each other.

I always thought I had not written enough about Ireland in either book, because it played an important part in our lives. Andrew and I spent the month of April there every year, when the magnolias and mimosa we planted were at their zenith.

In the way of miracles, a couple of weeks ago I opened a letter which gave me just what I wanted; all Irish, more than anything I could have hoped for and all the better for being a surprise.

I have not attempted to embroider the tale in any way and I could never cap it. It seems too good to be true, but it *is* true. So I am indebted to my new pen-pal, Richard Baldwyn, for this unexpected bonus that encapsulates the unlikely happenings of the Ireland Andrew and I knew and loved.

The second new piece in this book was written specially for *The Lady* magazine's 126th anniversary issue in February 2011. This august publication was founded by my maternal grand-father, Thomas Gibson Bowles. His grandchildren Tom Bowles and Julia Budworth are still co-owners of the magazine.

In 1904 my father, David Mitford, was convalescing after being seriously wounded in the Boer War. He had proposed to my mother, Sydney Bowles, with the consent of her father, and in turn Gibson Bowles found my father a job at *The Lady*.

Gibson Bowles may have spotted in him a kindred spirit. Their attitudes to life were very similar. My grandfather was a Victorian maverick but clearly multi-talented, as is evidenced by his being a Master Mariner, a publisher (he also founded *Vanity Fair*) and an MP (for King's Lynn) – to name but three of his occupations.

He was very impatient with life. He took a room in a hotel near Wilbury to write in peace – or so he thought – and ordered breakfast for 6 a.m. and a fire to be lit before that. Needless to say, no breakfast arrived nor was the fire lit, so he flew out of his room in a rage and shouted 'Fire! Fire!', which brought the whole staff to his bidding. A curious but successful outcome.

There are strong echoes of my father in this behaviour. He could have done just that, but fortunately his time at *The Lady* seems to have been more serene and the all-female staff all loved him.

The titles to my books have developed a poultry theme so it is fitting that the third new piece should be a review of a book about chickens. Recently I was perusing the annual reports of some of the championship classes at several renowned agricultural shows, which are much sought after by the breeders of the poultry and eggs on show. The photographs of the winning owners make you wonder if they are really pleased with their trophies. Usually men, quite often stout with large hands that cling on grimly to the small, flighty birds, they are camera-shy – which makes them look more dour than perhaps they are. I am sure inside their jackets they are glowing with pride, but they certainly hide it from the camera and look as gloomy as pallbearers are trained to be!

Mrs X's Large Male and smaller Female are judged Best of

Breed, but sadly we aren't allowed a photo of her. Best in Show can be a problem for the camera. Sometimes the birds are so tiny they look more like sparrows than the champions they are. So intent are the expert wielders of the Box Brownies on finding the right angle to show the best of their beloved feathered creatures that, sadly, the owners are left out. Many birds pose for the photographer like supermodels with their heads at jaunty angles. But some of the prize-winning exhibits try to avoid being snapped by turning their backs like naughty schoolchildren.

To the layman the language used in the descriptions of these wonderful birds is as obscure as a Russian guidebook. For instance, a general knowledge question: what is the difference between a cock and a cockerel? Answer – the cockerel is the up-and-coming youngster and the cock is an older bird. Then there could be a real complication in the wording of some of the classes they can be entered into – for example, a Duckwing Female turns out to be a hen and even its wing has no resemblance to a duck. It is a mysterious, poetic lingo known only to the specialist fanciers of the rarer breeds of poultry.

I hope that these additions – including Richard Baldwyn's uniquely funny story about Ireland – complement the pieces gathered together in this book, all of which were written solely in an effort to amuse.

COUNTING MY CHICKENS

CHICKENS

and Other Home Thoughts

To Sophia Topley and Susan Hill
the co-editors
with love

INTRODUCTION
by Tom Stoppard

Our first house in England was a boy's bicycle ride from Chatsworth, and we went picnicking there in the immediate post-war years before the house (Chatsworth, that is, not our semi at Calver Sough) was re-opened to the public. My prep school, which seemed so poignantly far from home, and Dovedale, a frequent outing for the family and the pre-war Riley, were close to Chatsworth, too, but I never understood the geography until I returned to Okeover, Dovedale and Chatsworth some fifty years later as, respectively, a trespasser, tripper and guest. At the age of eight I fell in love with England almost at first glance, never considering that the England I loved was, in the first place, only a corner of Derbyshire, and, in the second place, perishable. This book of occasional writings by Deborah Devonshire is not intended as a panegyric but the overall effect on me is plangent with lament for a lost domain.

The effect, I must add, is achieved, not altogether inadvertently, by stories which made me laugh aloud, and by a general impatience with useless nostalgia or, especially, complaint. Debo's hands are too busy for wringing, her mind too occupied with the present (and the future) to dwell in arrears. And yet, the not-so-distant past cannot be kept out of these pages; it backlights the way we live now with our yellow lines, logos, 'consultants', quires of forms, and all the prescriptions and proscriptions of officialdom that have put the nannies and busybodies in charge; none of which is rued so keenly here as the rift between country life and town, making the one a mystery and an irrelevance to the other. Here in this book you will find the amazed and disgusted little boy who announced 'I'll never drink milk again' on witnessing the milking demonstration at the Chatsworth Farmyard, and the eco-militant who rang her neighbour in fury to demand 'Why have you poisoned all your dahlias?' after an unseasonal frost.

It's not funny – or not *only* funny – to Debo, who also knows which puffball fungi are good eating, and about trees, camellias, sheep, goats, chickens, cookery, housekeeping and shopkeeping and a hundred other things including pictures and 'the best book on retailing ever written' (*The Tale of Ginger and Pickles* by Beatrix Potter). Guided by Miss Potter and her own standards she has made a roaring success of the Chatsworth Farm Shop, whose London outpost in Elizabeth Street, a stone's throw from Victoria Station if you throw towards Belgrave Square, is the only shop I know where you can find Dovedale Blue Cheese, not to mention Derbyshire manners which are almost an anachronism in the metropolis.

There is and can be no sentence in this book which sums its author up, but two of those which stay in my mind are: 'I buy most of my clothes at agricultural shows', and (on receiving a moss tree as a present) 'I pulled it to bits to see how it was made'. So, now you think you've got her? Far from it. She's also mad about Elvis Presley. I've seldom scored such a success with a house present as I did with a signed photo of Elvis.

To be in love with Debo Devonshire is hardly a distinction, and my joining this crowded company occurred in the inaugural year of the Heywood Hill Prize for literature, which is presented at Chatsworth. I was invited by Andrew Devonshire to hand over the cheque and stay the weekend, with the added lure of fishing the Derbyshire Wye at Monsal Dale on the

Saturday. At that time of year, dinner and the evening rise happen at much the same time, so one has to miss one or the other, and Debo, mindful of the priorities, excused me from dinner. The company, in best bib, tucker and jewellery, were at the pudding stage when I tried to sneak past in my Barbour and gumboots. Debo would have none of it. I was sat down next to her, wellies and all, and my dinner, kept warm under a silver dome, appeared in front of me as if by magic. If there was a moment when the mild torture of writing this Introduction became irrefusable, that was it.

But is there nothing to be said against our author? Does she disappoint in any department? The slimness of the section titled 'Books and Company' gives a clue. As a literary moll, the Duchess is a hoot. Asked to nominate ten books to take on the Trans-Siberian Railway, she gives up after six, including *Ginger and Pickles*. Her third choice is a book by one of her closest friends, Patrick Leigh Fermor, and a very good book it is, but . . . 'I am sorry to say I have not read it'. Debo explains this by saying she couldn't bear not having it still to read. Later we learn that Evelyn Waugh cannily gave her one of his books with all the pages blank and only the title by which to identify it. But redemption is complete when we read that among the books kept in her bedroom so as not to risk being stolen by guests are *Fowls and Geese and How To Keep Them*, the Quiller-Couch *Oxford English Verse* on India paper and, 'most precious', *The Last Train to Memphis: The Rise of Elvis Presley*.

My first recommendation to browsers among the good stories and useful knowledge herein is 'Road from the Isles',* an account of taking a goat by boat and train in wartime from Mull – no, not from bustling Mull itself but from an island off the coast of Mull – to London. It's a classic vignette of the Mitford spirit; and it is also, to go out where I came in, a song to old-fashioned self-reliance and a reproach to this era of dependence when milking the goat between trains in the

Ladies' First Class waiting-room ('even though I only had a Third Class ticket') would bring down five varieties of authority on Debo's golden head. The goat behaved perfectly and was soon pruning sister Nancy's garden in Little Venice. (The story first appeared in the hard-to-find *British Goat Society Yearbook* for 1972, so we must be grateful to Debo's editors for saving it for the rest of us.)

Chatsworth, meanwhile, 'is now more alive than at any time in its history'. Well, we know why.

TOM STOPPARD

* See below, page 158.

DIARIES

The first sentence of a diary given to a nine-year-old child at Christmas, written on New Year's Day and kept faithfully till at least 10 January, was 'got up, dressed, had breakfast'. The first sentence of a book is a different matter and very difficult indeed. I have been pondering over this for some time. I asked my sister Jessica what to do. She tells me that in America, if you pay some money, you can get advice as to how to begin and then go on to be a famous author. They say put down 'the' on a bit of paper, add some words, keep on adding and Bob's your uncle (or the American equivalent), you're off and the rest will follow. It doesn't seem to work. Just try. So, hopelessly stuck and faced with the empty page, see how other people manage. Lately we have been reminded of 'I had a farm in Africa . . .' 'I had a farm in Derbyshire' somehow doesn't sound as good and anyway it would be a lie because in England things like farms seldom belong to women. Having failed with 'the', try 'and'. 'And it came to pass', too affected and you can't go on in that biblical style. When you open books to see how it is done it seems so easy, set down there in the same type as the rest as if it was no trouble at all, the second sentence flowing out of the first one like one o'clock. Believe me, the writer has suffered over those words. As 50,000 books are published every year the first sentences must add hugely to the level of anxiety in an already anxious race.

I looked at the television programme about Uncle Harold,* called *Reputations*. How strange it is to see his and Aunt Dorothy's private life trotted out like a story in a film. He would have considered the fashion for such entertainment unspeakably vulgar. And so do I. The point about Dorothy Macmillan was her charm, energy and earthiness; there were no frills. She was one of the few people I have met who was exactly the same with whoever she was talking to, oblivious of their class — something which people keep on about now almost as much as they do about sex. She gave her whole attention, laughed easily, was unread and not smart, and was a tireless constituency worker. I was always told that it was she who won the elections at Stockton-on-Tees. Her time in Downing Street was famous for children's parties, and the branches, more than flowers, which she dragged up from the garden at Birch Grove in the back of her car. When Uncle Harold was Housing Minister, Andrew, my husband, was president of the Building Societies' Association. It seemed to be indicated that Andrew should ask his aunt to the annual dinner as guest of honour. She asked, 'Shall I wear my best dress or the other one?' The thought of the other one made us wonder.

Harold was an intellectual and a politician all right, no doubt about that; but the mistake so often made of putting people into categories left him there, and did not allow for his interest in the family publishing business and many different aspects of life, including his devotion to field sports. The press called that the grouse moor image. After he married, his father-in-law expected him to go out shooting, even though he had never before fired a shotgun. Reg Roose, a Chatsworth gamekeeper and a delightful man, was detailed to be his tutor. Uncle Harold was a quick learner. Years later Reg and I watched his performance when large quantities of pheasants flew high across a valley with the wind behind them. 'Doesn't the Prime Minister shoot well?' I said. 'Yes,' answered Reg, proudly. 'I taught him and he's fit to go anywhere now.'

When Uncle Harold was ninety he stayed with us for three months. I will always remember his perfect manners. He dined alone with me often, and I am sure he would have welcomed other company. But he talked as if I were his intellectual equal – ha, ha – or another ex-prime minister, and I almost began to think I was. For much of the day he sat in an armchair in his bedroom and listened to tapes of Trollope. (It made me nervous when he dropped off, lest his smouldering cigar should fall into the wicker wastepaper basket by his side.) He once told me of a mistake made by the suppliers of the tapes. 'I think there is something wrong. They have sent a curious book called *Lucky Jim*, by a feller called Amis. Have you ever heard of him? I don't like it much. Must be a very peculiar man.' He was frail and shuffled down the long corridors at his own speed. He couldn't find the door to the hall and I heard him mutter, 'The trouble with this house is you have to throw double sixes to get out.'

His relationship with President Kennedy was worth watching. The President had never seen anything like him, and you could say the same for Uncle Harold. They struck up an unlikely friendship and were more surprised and more amused by one another at every meeting. They talked endlessly on the telephone – usually in the middle of the night. I used to hear of these conversations from both participants. It was the time when initials of organisations began to be used as a sort of shorthand. One night, after speaking of Castro, they went on to discuss Seato and Nato. Uncle Harold was stumped for a moment when the President said, 'And how's Debo?' When

Mrs Thatcher was new to the job he had had for years, she went to see him. 'Oh good,' I said, 'and did you talk?' 'No,' he replied, 'she did.'

Uncle Harold's good manners were often tested when he stayed with us. I am not good at *place à table*, and one night I saw he was sitting at dinner between my son and his friend, both in their first year at Eton. There was the usual political crisis on and the PM was preoccupied with his own thoughts, while the boys anxiously cast round for a suitable subject of conversation. After a long silence I heard Sto say, 'Uncle Harold, *Old Moore's Almanack* says you'll fall in October.' To his eternal credit, after a suitable pause, he answered, 'Yes, I should think that's about right.'

* Harold Macmillan and his wife, Lady Dorothy, née Cavendish, daughter of the 9th Duke of Devonshire.

It is strange to see your family enacted on television from an old book about them, written half a century ago. I suppose the royal family and politicians such as Bush and Mandy,* whose ancestors played a part in public life, do so continually. But for ordinary folk it is indeed an odd experience. It was also odd to read the reviews. Mr Paul Hoggart in *The Times* made me sad. I don't know what wing he favours politically, but his dismal summing-up of what was meant to be high comedy reminded me for all the world of my sister Decca's Communist friends of years gone by. They were incapable of enjoying themselves, had never really laughed at or about anything in their lives, and to be in their company for long was a lowering experience. Decca saw jokes better than anyone – it was her far Left friends' determination to see the downside of everything that was reminiscent of Mr Hoggart's summing up of the first episode of *Love in a Cold Climate*. He disapproves in a governessy way of the idea of my father hunting my sisters with his bloodhounds *for fun*. What else would he have done it for? (Alas, I was considered too young to be hunted and, by the time I was of huntable age, the bloodhounds had gone.) I know that some misguided people, for reasons best known to themselves, are against hunting foxes, but surely children are fair game? He complains, too, about a mother's reaction to the hideous appearance of her newborn baby. I wonder if, in his sheltered life, the reviewer has ever seen a newborn baby. Referring to Nancy, he goes on to say that 'she presents her cast as freaks'. Another reviewer states we were the 'lunatic fringe'. Oh dear, freaks and lunatics. Well, never mind.

* Peter Mandelson, MP for Hartlepool. His grandfather was Herbert Morrison, created Lord Morrison in 1959, Labour MP and Home Secretary in Winston Churchill's wartime coalition government.

My sister Nancy's letters have been published,* or some of them I should say, as we have got thousands here. They are kept in cardboard boxes with holes for them to breathe through. Whenever I pass by a pile of these boxes, containing papers of every description accumulated since the 1950s, I always hope they are a consignment of day-old chicks, which used to travel by train in the guard's van in just such boxes. They provide what Americans call Optimum Archival Conditions. I don't know about their conditions, but Nancy's are certainly of Optimum Archival Amusement. She had neat handwriting and the talent of filling the last page exactly, so 'love from' is always at the bottom: difficult to achieve if the letter is to make sense – and hers do. I am not the only one to think she was the supreme entertainer, both in real life (she and my father together were better than any turn on the stage) and on paper. Her letters are just as funny as her books. What would psychiatrists make of her teases? She called me Nine because she said that was my mental age. About right, I expect, but disconcerting when she introduced me to her smart French friends as 'my little sister aged nine' long after I was married.

The correspondence between Nancy and Evelyn Waugh has been ably read on the wireless by Timothy West and Prunella Scales, and listening, I was reminded of Evelyn's generosity when he was in Paris just after the liberation. (Why was he there? Perhaps he was a liberator; I can't remember.) He bought me a hat which he tried on himself in the shop to make sure. He didn't tell me what the *vendeuse* thought about that, but French people are keen when it comes to business and a sale is a sale whatever for or why, so no doubt she was delighted and probably thought all English soldiers wore women's hats when off duty. It was made of white felt with a blue straw brim on which perched two small white stuffed birds. Luckily the Animal Rights people were still *in utero* or Evelyn would have been lynched for buying it and I for wearing it. Sadly it has gone the way of old hats. Fifty years on it might be revered as a bit of heritage or a historic document, like a Dinky toy or a 1945 bus ticket. Who knows, it could even have found a home in the V & A with the rest of their jumble.

Nancy's letters often describe clothes. When Dior invented the New Look in 1947, my mother-in-law, 'Moucher' Devonshire and her friend, the Duchess of Rutland, who were in Paris for a less frivolous reason, wanted to see the collection. They arrived at Avenue Montaigne in their tweed overcoats, which had done years of war service, and ditto shoes. They weren't allowed in. Of humble nature, the two duchesses were disappointed, but not at all surprised. They sat on a bench eating their sandwiches to pass the time till they could decently return to the embassy where they were staying.

* *Love from Nancy: The Letters of Nancy Mitford*, ed. Charlotte Mosley (Hodder & Stoughton, 1993).

Diana Cooper has died. I admired her beauty and her guts. I was never an intimate friend of hers but we had many mutual friends, among them Evelyn Waugh and Antony Head. Both were tickled, for some reasons best known to themselves, because I call my sister Diana 'Honks'. As Cooper was also Diana they started calling her 'Honks' too. So the archivists who busy themselves with other people's letters have slipped up several times already and think Evelyn was referring to Diana Mosley (my sister) when it was another old beauty he was on about. Not that it matters much except it would be hard to find two more different people.

I have reached the stage in life when I wake up earlier and earlier in the mornings. The wait till breakfast time has forced me to put a kettle and toaster in my room, so I can help myself to their merciful productions whenever I like. I advise all early wakers who have fallen for this plan to buy a clock with a minute and second hand of immediately recognisable lengths, or you may have my disappointing experience of last week. Waking at 6 a.m., I made and ate my breakfast, only to discover that the clock's similar-looking hands had played a trick on me, and it was in fact only 12.30 a.m. Too early even for me, but too late to pretend I hadn't had breakfast.

A beautiful new television has been installed. Well, not beautiful, but a big dark object which is dead when turned off and spends a lot of time describing death when turned on.

But it isn't the programmes I'm complaining about, it is the difficulty of making it work. The last one was so nice and simple, you just pushed a sort of matchbox-shaped bit to turn it on and then 1, 2, 3 according to your whim.

It never failed to do as it was told. Now I have had to engage a tutor to coach me in Television A-levels. I have failed the exam.

There are so many tiny rubbery squares to press on two (why *two*?) hand-held, nameless objects that unless you have got long pointed nails (which I have not) and are dead accurate in your aim, you end up with a picture of a rowdy midnight hail storm instead of racing at Kempton Park or Jon Snow setting about his victim.

My tutor tells me to pay attention and explains that only four little bits of rubber need be pressed, two on each of the objects, which I clutch in both hands like castanets.

With this vital information ringing in my ears, I go to Bakewell and buy a lot of sticking plasters to cover the unwanted buttons. By this time I've forgotten which the right ones are and my tutor has gone home.

I shall never know what the other forty are for, and I wish to goodness that the manufacturer would resist putting them there in the first place. Oh, for a telly of yesteryear, just On/Off and Channels 1, 2, 3 and 4.

I buy most of my clothes at agricultural shows, and good stout things they are. Much better than the strange-looking garments in desperate colours at £1,000 each in the Knightsbridge shops. In the unlikely event of falling for one of those, you will find that all the buttons come off the first time you wear it, which is disappointing. After agricultural shows, Marks & Spencer is the place to go shopping, and then Paris. Nothing in between seems to be much good. I have learnt to pluck up the courage to go through the doors of the grand shops in Paris. They look at you as if you were something the dog brought home, but once inside the magic of French talent with clothes takes over and happiness sets in, until the agonising decision has to be made about what not to buy when you long for everything. At four score years plus, properly made clothes should last to the end – or that is my excuse. So forgotten French works of art come out of the back of the cupboard (mixed with Barbours and Derri Boots), still beautiful and always comfortable, which is my idea of what clothes ought to be.

We all know about old women being knocked down and having their bags snatched. It has become so ordinary that the newspapers no longer mention it unless the snatchee is famous and badly hurt, when there are a few lines at the bottom of the home news page. In London it happens in places like Cadogan Square and South Audley Street where I suppose the bag-owners are thought by the snatchers to be rich. I wonder how the victims are chosen. The older the woman, the larger and heavier the bag, but I'm not sure it is always weighed down with diamond necklaces and ruby rings. The contents seem to be stones or coal — or that's what it feels like if you offer to hold it while the owner rearranges her sticks. The snatcher may think he's got a decent reward for his courage in bashing the old soul to the ground, but he must feel let down when he finds only huge bottles of medicines with unpronounceable names. I pity the thief when it's my turn. My bag is positively septic inside, so if he's got any sense he will wear one of those things that dustmen and dentists cover their noses with when delving into unpleasantness. He will find handfuls of tiresome credit cards sliding about in their meaningless way, heaps of copper coins which don't even buy a newspaper, unanswered letters of top priority, combs in variety, scissors, rubber bands, stamps, an Old Age Pensioner's railway card and biros without tops, which all help to make it filthy. If he gets my basket as well, he will rue the day he decided to go in for stealing. It is loaded with iron rations in case of getting stuck on the M1, rock-hard bits of toast meant for the chickens, some Bonham's catalogues, a book I never read but is another insurance against the mysterious habits of the motorway, the Jacob Sheep Society's (very difficult) quiz in triplicate, plus the minutes of many a tedious meeting. He will be bitterly disappointed with his haul and I will be the reason for at least one thief who decides to go straight.

While I am on about old women and the awful things that happen to us, there is the ever-present trap of talking to yourself in a loud voice without being aware of it. You are apt to address whatever you are doing, or just speak your thoughts while mechanically getting on with something different, like knitting or making marmalade. A dog can save the day when someone comes round the corner unexpectedly because it is easy to pretend you were saying something important to Bracken or Nobby. But there are occasions when you have no props and any attempt at explanation would be pointless and would land you deeper in the mire. Last summer I was walking along a stream in a remote part of our garden. It was at the time of the evening when the people who come to see round have usually long since gone home. There is a small, but deep, concrete section of the stream about two feet square, something to do with water from the hill draining into it, I suppose, as the rest of the stream has natural banks and is very shallow. I saw a frog under the water in the concreted bit, unable to get out of the sheer sides. Thinking it would drown I plunged my hand into the cold water and picked it out. I thought I'd done a good deed and would get a lifesaving medal from the Frog Preservation Society when, in the unpredictable way of its kind, it jumped back in. 'Oh, you fool of a frog,' I said very loud, 'I've never seen such a stupid frog as you. You don't deserve to be saved.' I turned round and there were two complete strangers who stared at me, obviously thinking that I should not have been let out.

We live in a National Park, and very pleasant it is too. Planning restrictions are, rightly, fairly rigid and the planners' deliberations over relatively simple jobs like farm buildings are slow. This is as it should be and any small irritation is far outweighed by the benefits. Debate over the age-old local industry of quarrying is on at the moment. The winning of minerals from under the ground has gone on in these parts from time immemorial, from the lead mines of yesteryear to the valuable and versatile barytes, fluorspar and stone quarries of today. The grey and green landscape of the lonely limestone High Peak uplands is netted by dry-stone walls making tiny enclosures of crazy shapes. Every so often there are sudden deep clefts in the rocky soil which form the Derbyshire Dales, admired and enjoyed by all who know them. The scenery is more dramatic where the man-made cliffs of the huge quarries outdo the natural one and just as beautiful in its own stark way. The rules to do with reinstating worked-out quarries are strict, and nature sees to it that they soon begin to look like their natural rocky neighbours as the native flora spreads itself to clothe the stone faces. Quarrying is now described by the familiar single-issue brigade of protesters as 'a threat to the National Park'. Last week a television documentary hired a comedian to tell us it ought to be stopped. He wasn't at all funny and, anyway, it is a serious subject. He said, 'Allowing more quarrying in the Peak Park is like grinding up York Minster for motorway hardcore.' I wonder what material he thinks York Minster is built of and where it came from. No quarry, no Minster. He went on, 'The Peak District is a far cry from the paradise envisaged by the people who set up the parks.' I suppose he thinks that putting people out of work makes a paradise. Now schoolchildren are being indoctrinated against the industry. A friend of mine, who is a county councillor in another part of the country, received letters from a class of ten-year-olds with an identical message obviously dictated by their teacher. They complained of birds and bees being frightened away by work in a local quarry. My friend wrote back, 'Are you driven to school along a road? Do you live in a house? Has it occurred to you that roads and houses are made of stone and that stone comes out of quarries?' If the television comedian and the teacher have their way we shall soon be importing aggregate for roads and stone for building in spite of sitting on millions of tons of the stuff. Can you imagine anything madder?

The complainers complain about everything. They don't like foxhounds, crowing cockerels or quarrying, and now they say car-boot sales must be stopped. I suppose we are to be denied the chance of buying a Constable in a muddy field and taking it to the *Antiques Roadshow* so Henry Wyndham* can tell us we have bought a fortune for £2. Oh dear. Long live banned work and play.

* Chairman of Sotheby's and picture expert. Since 1986 he has appeared regularly as a valuation specialist on the television programme, *Antiques Roadshow*.

Most people in this country must have whirled along roads and past fields enclosed by stone walls. Few stop to think how (or when) they were built or to consider the skill of the people who built them.

This week the annual competition held by the Derbyshire branch of the Dry Stone Walling Association was held on a windy hill high up in the Peak District.

I took the chairman of one of the most respected antique shops in London to see how the experts do it. Not surprisingly he had never seen such a thing before.

'To be a good waller,' the Master Craftsman told us, 'you must have eyes and hands which act together: an eye for a stone of the right size and shape for its place and hands which feel the balance instinctively as soon as you pick it up. You can only teach so much, the rest is in you. You've either got it or you haven't.'

The construction of a wall is a building lesson in miniature, from the placing of the big foundation stones to the 'battered' – or tapered – sides and the coping stones laid along the top. There is no mortar or other binding agent to hold them together.

They depend on the 'throughs', stones long enough to reach right through the wall holding the sides together and acting as ties to prevent bulging. As the sides are built up, small stones, or fillings, are packed in the middle to prevent them from collapsing inwards. A well-built wall stands for many years, containing the farmstock and providing shelter from gales, rain and snow for outwintered ewes and lambs.

The membership of the DSWA is made up of full-time professional wallers and an increasing number of men and women who earn their living in totally different ways, from insurance broking to dentistry. These people go walling for the satisfaction of mastering another difficult skill in contrast to their usual work. 'It is a wonderful relaxation. I get completely lost in it,' a doctor said.

Late in the afternoon we looked at the finished lengths of what seemed impeccable work to my amateur eye, apparently identical in excellence. The expert on eighteenth-century furniture studied the twentieth-century walling and made his own judgement. 'First, second, third,' he said to me, pointing to his choices. When the real judge added up the points and announced the winners his placings were in the same order.

The point of this saga is that if your eye is experienced in recognising quality in one form of art it is often able to do so in another. And surely dry stone walling is an art.

Two foods which are prime examples of the capricious ways of Mother Nature are wild mushrooms, which taste so different from the tame kind, and grouse, which don't have a tame kind. They are both a conjuring trick – now you see them, now you don't. You can't make plans for them because they make their own rules. In one season, there can be plenty of grouse on one moor and pitifully few on another a few miles away, where the conditions in winter and spring – often blamed for a poor hatching and rearing time – have been identical. It is the same with mushrooms. We are told if fertiliser is put on a grass field, or if it is ploughed and re-seeded, there will be no mushrooms. Neither is true, but a mushroom field which is good one year and receives no different treatment the next can be barren. Why? We want rain for mushrooms, they say. The rain comes but the mushrooms don't. Then when they do appear they are so full of maggots they are inedible. But when everything goes right they are food for the gods.

The unexplained ups and downs of the grouse population are part of their fascination for anyone who is interested in what is now called 'Wild Life'. Salmon used to have the same mystique, but now they are 'farmed' and found in every restaurant in the country – cheaper than cod, they have lost the mystery of Williamson's *Salar*. But grouse are still truly wild and no attempt to 'farm' them has been successful. Even the gamekeepers, whose lives are spent on the moors, cannot always explain the swing in the numbers of grouse: from feast to famine and back to feast. The graph looks like a cardiogram of a desperately ill heart patient. After a record year, when too many birds are left on the ground, disease strikes and few survive. Such is their power of recovery that they can increase in number again in next to no time. I am glad that the ways of grouse and mushrooms remain unexplained. There are lots of books on mushrooms (but few on grouse) and the vast number of fungi we used to lump together and call toadstools. Experts arrange forays which you can join to learn about which kinds are edible and which will do you in immediately. Look out – the differences are not always as obvious as you might think.

A new treat for us is puffballs – the bigger the better – super-delicious when sliced and fried. Luckily, few English people fancy them. In the same way that our fishermen throw away pike, puffballs are kicked to bits by disappointed mushroomers – to the dismay of any Frenchman for whom both are a deli-cacy. When you are tired of blackberrying and get bolder in the search for free food, try 'Chicken of the Woods'. They are those whitish growths on the bole of an oak which look like enormous plates. You will have to carry a heavy and offensive weapon to dislodge them from their host, but it is worth the trouble when they are cooked and you discover not only a new taste but a new consistency.

Our kitchen is being repainted and retiled, so a great clearing of decks is going on. Behind a wall of receipt books in the back of a cupboard we found a box of menu cards dating from 1893 to 1939. They are printed or handwritten on stiff white card with gilt edges. Buckingham Palace, Derby House, Seaford House, Londonderry House, Devonshire House, The King's Guard St James's Palace, the Foreign Office and the Astors at 4 St James's Square evidently fed their guests very well. Some cards are tantalisingly anonymous, giving only the address. Who lived at 66 Brook Street in 1939? She gave a lavish ball supper there on 25 June. And the unknown occupier of 38 Bryanston Square* did even better a month earlier. We know the vast number of courses people ate at grand dinners in Edwardian times, but it is surprising to find such feasts were still going strong till the last war. If you had been invited to Mr Baldwin's farewell dinner at 10 Downing Street on 25 May 1937 you would have eaten *Consommé à la Sévigné, Filets de Sole Impériale, Noisettes d'Agneau Châtelaine, Petits Pois, Pommes nouvelles, Cailles sous la Cendre, Salade de Laitues, Asperges vertes, Sauce Mousseline, Mousse glacé aux Fraises, Frivolités, Dessert* and *Café*, plus five superb wines ending with *Grands Fins Bois 1820*. The indiscretions induced by so many fine wines would make any prime minister shudder now. And I don't think they would dare offer *Frivolités* today. The humble grapefruit was a luxury then. Several dinners started with them; the only English words on the menus except eggs and bacon, for which there is no satisfactory translation into French. They were fried up for breakfast at 1.45 a.m. at every ball.

At an afternoon reception given by His Majesty's Government In The United Kingdom Of Great Britain And Northern

Ireland for Commanding General Sir Kaiser Shumshere Jung Bahadur Rana KBE of Nepal, in 1937, the selection of teatime food is a child's dream, or a grown-up's for that matter. The guests were offered ices, cakes, éclairs, five kinds of sandwiches including foie gras, lobster and caviar, petits pains fourrés, wine cup and every soft drink imaginable, including *Thé*. I would love to know if Sir Kaiser went on to face a seven-course dinner at 8.30 followed by an immense supper at midnight.

A surprisingly extravagant entertainment was a *souper de bal* given by the Framework Knitters' Company at Goldsmiths' Hall in 1937. That night you could choose from twenty dishes, including consommé, chicken, cutlets, salmon, lobster, foie gras, quail, duck, chaud froid of more chicken, ham, tongue, asparagus, salad, compote of fruit, crème brûlée, chocolate mousse and meringues. This was supper. You had already eaten dinner. Lastly comes a refreshing reminder of Evelyn Duchess of Devonshire's careful ways. The menu for luncheon after the wedding of her son Charlie Cavendish and Adele Astaire (Fred's sister) at Chatsworth in 1932 lists several dishes, including French Pastries and two more puddings, crossed out. 'Need not have these' is in her handwriting. The Framework Knitters were not so economical.

---

* The occupant of 38 Bryanston Square was South African magnate Sir Abe Bailey.

The roof is forever being mended, 1½ acres of it. Last week, the men found a copy of the *Manchester Guardian* dated 29 May 1877 under the old lead. The names of all who had worked on the roof then were recorded in the margin in thick pencil. Interesting, but not unusual here. And the headline on the 116-year-old newspaper seemed familiar: AUSTRIA & THE BOSNIAN INSURGENTS. SERBIA PREPARING FOR WAR. SPECIAL TELEGRAM FROM OUR RAGUSA CORRESPONDENT. There followed a description of atrocities . . .

Windows. We have got to have them to keep out weather and burglars. As they are part of the architectural scheme of things, like walls and doors, their make and shape has changed over the centuries with fashion.

In the nineteenth century newly invented plate glass was greeted with joy but it made the houses look pitifully blind from the outside. Now we have something worse; plate glass with a narrow slit above, the only part which opens. Any chance of pleasing proportion goes west and the afflicted house is like one partially sighted, with a frightful wink.

The next door neighbour goes in for a thin brown lattice. How, or if, this kind of window opens and shuts I don't know, but I do know that these disfigurements have spread like a contagious disease through our towns and villages and are more than a minor tragedy.

They are everywhere, degrading the appearance of perfectly good buildings, whether built of stone or brick. There is no regard for the vernacular because they are just shoved in, new and uniform, from Glasgow to Glastonbury.

Now here's your chance, Mr Minister of Education. In your next curriculum do beg your teachers to add decent fenestration lessons to the indecent sex lessons so popular with the children. Not as exciting, I suppose, but windows last longer than sex whatever way you look at it.

If you fail we must all go out and live in the Sultan's palace in Zanzibar where there isn't any glass to vex the eye and the birds, bats and bees fly in and out of the rooms on the balmy air of the island of cloves.

I am fascinated by watching and listening to keen gardeners going round other people's gardens. Something strange seems to seize otherwise normal folk and, although they have probably travelled miles for their treat, they show themselves to be only really interested in what they have left at home. People who haven't got gardens of their own can stand back and delight in the big picture of someone else's work, but the real gardener fastens on some small plant, pleased if it doesn't look too well and triumphant if it is dead. They relate the plants to their own. 'Oh we've got that but ours is much bigger. I think this one is planted on the wrong wall, it can't stand east, well, wouldn't you think they'd know that?' When the boot is on the other foot and you are taken by the owner on a two-hour tour in foul weather it can be difficult to keep a continuous flow of admiration. Sometimes, before setting out, you are sized up by the hostess to see if you are worth it, and it is rather wonderful when she decides you aren't. That is why it is such a luxury to be able to go round so many gardens in your own time by paying at the door. You can dwell over what you love and hurry by the kidney-shaped beds with raised concrete edges full of orange rhododendrons. My father-in-law (who understood plants) said people go through five stages of gardening. They begin by liking flowers, progress to flowering shrubs, then autumn foliage and berries, next they go for leaves and finally the underneaths of leaves. Alpines ought to come in somewhere. They can become an addiction, and they get smaller and smaller relative to their importance. In the Wisley collection there is a weeny blob of grey leaves in small stones of the same colour. In the spring a label with an arrow says 'Please Notice Flower'. Charles de Noailles, a celebrated

34

French gardener, ended by preferring labels to flowers, foliage or even alpines. I think the attendants of the stalls of the magic displays at the Horticultural Society's shows in the Vincent Square halls are the most patient of beings. Just listen to some old trout describing to her trapped victim what has happened to her *Desfontania spinosa hookeri* and you will realise that the stall holder is taking the place of a psychiatrist for a free consultation while all is unburdened and the Desfontania lady gets rid of her feelings.

Gardening is almost too difficult to contemplate, but arranging flowers is impossible. I wonder if the arrangers get cross because their work doesn't last. My mother's explanation for the uncertain tempers of cooks was the inevitable destruction of their art thrice daily being enough to unhinge their minds. If the flower people don't get cross they must be sad when the products of hours of work end in the dustbin. It has all become too complicated. There are rules, and criticism is fierce. I marvel at the skill which goes into the feats you find in hotels, at wedding receptions and flower festivals in churches, but I do not wish to see them in my own house. Everything is too contrived and clever, the flowers spring out of squashy green stuff instead of a good old vase or pot. Since the invention of plastic flower pots it is a joy to see one made of proper earthenware but I expect it would lose points in a Floral Art competition. The whole subject needs simplifying and straightening as well. Those sideways stalks are worrying and against nature: but then, nature hasn't got much to do with it. I think the Americans are miles ahead in the art. In a long life in which I have had the luck to be surrounded by beauty I have never seen anything better than the flowers on the tables at the grand dinner given for the lenders to the 'Treasure Houses of Great Britain' exhibition in Washington. About two hundred diners sat at round tables of eight in a vast hall which goes up the whole height of the National Gallery. Some genius put tall narrow vases on plinths with equally tall flowers high above the heads of the diners so they could see the people opposite without interference. The result was stunning. Had I done them I should have had no better idea than a dreary plate with a few heads floating about in it.

I wish gardening wasn't so difficult. It is almost impossible to look with pleasure or interest at the lists of wallflower seeds to be planted now for next year when this year's are beginning to go over and look as depressing as only dying flowers can. You must steel yourself to do it if you want wallflowers next year.

Another problem is the bewildering choice. Open the catalogue at delphiniums, for instance, and you find page after page of descriptions so glamorous you want them all and need the concentration of Einstein to reduce the list to something reasonable.

Then you must wait till the year after next to see the fruits of your labour. As likely as not the supplier has sent the very ones you didn't choose, but you will long since have lost the carefully marked catalogue, so there is nothing to be done.

It is the same with roses. They all sound irresistible and you must pinch yourself in midwinter, when they are dormant, to remember how monstrously ugly the man-made orange ones are, retina irritants to a rose.

I prefer vegetables, but still there is the difficulty of choice. Pin down the best pea or bean, remember to plant a few every fortnight to avoid feast or famine, and you are indeed a real gardener.

Someone has had a jolly time thinking up names. Even the professors who have so kindly written to me to tell me what a quantum leap is may be stumped by Howard's Lancer, Black Velvet, Captivator, Leveller and Whinham's Industry – gooseberries all.

The National Rhubarb Collection, believe it or not, contains more than a hundred varieties. I won't weary you with all their names, but you might fancy Grooveless Crimson. I don't think Early White Stone is an advertising man's dream description of a turnip, but whoever christened the parsnip Tender and True was a poet of the kitchen garden.

The oddest of all is the radish called French Breakfast. I have never seen a Frenchman tucking into radishes for his *petit déjeuner*, but that is what they would have you believe.

The prettiest flowers I have ever seen in a small dining room were in a New York flat; lilies of the valley bolt upright in twos and threes in a bed of moss all down the middle of the table. The best at a dance were white foxgloves, one at a time in proper flower pots, round the floor of a sitting-out room. Trying to do as well myself, I bought some china vases made like old Crown Derby crocus pots with holes in the lids to stick the flowers in. Delighted to have found something which forced the stalks to stand up straight I showed them to a Floral Art friend who said, 'What, ten little soldiers?' Yes, ten little soldiers are just the thing. One Easter at our Devonshire Arms Hotel at Bolton Abbey I had what I thought was a good idea; birds' nests on the restaurant tables with marzipan eggs. So I asked the dried flower ladies if they could make birds' nests and along came some good tries. They looked really nice till the customers ate the eggs. As a robbed nest is the saddest sight going and looks like a cowpat with a rim, the manager soon banished them.

Moss is the thing. I have been given (by Americans needless to say) a moss tree, extremely pretty and more or less everlasting I'm told, unless you put it in the sun when it will fade. I pulled it to bits to see how it was made. It is a ball of moss about eighteen inches in diameter mounted on chicken wire and stuck into place with huge hair pins. It is supported by a stem of birch held in a basket filled with plaster – the base of the 'tree' is covered in moss of a different kind, to hide it. The Librarian at Chatsworth happens to know all about moss; he is no less than the treasurer of the British Bryological Society. Seeing this beauty he said without hesitation, 'Oh, that's *Leucobrym glaucum*, it only grows in the south of England.' So I see myself taking a van to some distant damp spot like West Sussex to get the precious raw material. I expect moss gathering is against the law, like picking primroses, and I shall have my head cut off; but if any of us here can succeed in making such a decorative object it will be worth it.

At this time of year I am struck by the racist ways of that mild section of our fellow countrymen – people who feed the birds. They go to great lengths to ensure that only the charming little birds, preferably prettily coloured and able to sing later on, get the delicacies provided. The 'country' magazines carry advertisements of complicated arrangements which keep out the big, ugly, floppy ones, or any species the bird-table owner doesn't fancy. Yet these same people are mad on raptors of all kinds, even the murderous magpie, but at conveniently far remove. It would be interesting to see their reactions if a sparrow-hawk or a merlin chose to swoop while they happened to be watching and the loved tits, robins and chaffinches were reduced to a flurry of feathers in a split second. If they saw a pair of magpies hunting a hedge for eggs and nestlings in the spring they would surely be sickened by the sight of the desperate attempts of the parent birds to distract their attention. But people don't see the balance of nature acted out beak and claw, so they follow the fashion, which is to preserve all birds of prey whatever the cost to the rest. Unless there is a change of heart soon, the bird-tables will no longer provide the pleasure that once they did.

Last week I went into the garden to look at something the hot weather has brought out. While I was staring at it and thinking of nothing in particular, there was a rush of wings and a murderous sparrow-hawk dived from nowhere and caught a blue tit which let out a small bird's version of a scream. The hawk, usually so precise in its fatal sweep, somehow entangled itself between a rose hedge and a yew hedge where my ancient spaniel was happily mousing. His reaction was to grab the hawk, thinking, I suppose, that it was that bird of very little brain, a pheasant. I nearly got to them, but, alas, the old dog realised his mistake after a vicious nip from the hooked beak, and the hawk extricated itself. It flew away to catch and *pluck while still alive* its daily ration of three songbirds plus a racing pigeon or two, so precious to their owners. Parliament has decreed that these hateful creatures are 'protected'. If the spaniel had hung on would he have been sent to prison for killing it? I must ask our policeman. It never ceases to surprise me that the same people who enjoy watching the violent and often revolting wild life films of birds and animals disembowelling one another on the telly are against fox hunting and for hawks and the other disembowellers. The Great British Public is very contrary. So are our legislators.

The pullets arrived early this year. The old hens were moved into one house to make room for the young ones, so smart and neat to look at. All were shut in for two days to make sure they went back to the proper house at night. In spite of this time-honoured way of explaining to chickens where home is, several of the old girls went back to their original houses, only to find the pullets installed. They were not pleased. They looked as puzzled as you and I would be if we returned to our bedroom to find it crammed full of strange teenagers. Some of these teenagers have started laying very small eggs of superb quality, which are not appreciated by housewives as they are a far cry from the big eggs we are told we must eat. To explain their lack of size, we put a notice in the Farm Shop saying: 'Pullets' eggs, half price', but this means nothing because few know what a pullet is. Oh dear!

If second childhood means going back to first loves in old age then I am deep in it. As children, my sisters and I kept poultry and sold the eggs for pocket money. Now I have pens of Light Sussex and Welsummers in the garden at Chatsworth, and the pleasure I get from them is enormous.

In middle age, when looking after my own chickens was too complicated, I gathered together pottery and china hens and ducks. They are less trouble than the live kind and are ever-present in my bedroom and sitting room. My favourites are a Belgian faïence pair of life-sized speckled hens with heads turned back and beaks buried in their feathers, in that expression of poultry contentment hens wear after a dust bath on a spring day. One has a brood of chicks poking out from her breast, the other an egg. They are dishes – the top halves lids, heads and necks the handles.

I bought them from one of those expensive antiques shops that catered for rich tourists in Park Lane, long since replaced by a travel agency. I remember stopping and staring at them with a great longing. The price seemed wild at the time and it certainly was. A recent valuation put the dishes at less than I paid twenty years ago, but the price is not the point when grabbed by such a longing. They have given, and continue to give, great pleasure.

A pottery nest with chicks hatching and hatched from jagged broken eggshells is also well loved. I have never seen another such group and would love to know where it was made. One chick has only its head out of the egg, another has a bit of shell stuck on its behind and the third is fully hatched, wearing the surprised look of a chick that's found itself hatched, dry and facing an uncertain world.

I have fallen for paintings of hens too. An enormous canvas of double-combed Derbyshire Redcaps by T. Benson hangs in my bedroom in our house at Bolton Abbey. William Huggins, taking time off from painting lions, is the artist responsible for another group of poultry, in which the iridescent green and black tail feathers of the cock are brilliantly painted. In Théophile-Alexandre Steinlen's lithograph of a cock and two hens (called a trio in the trade, the eternal triangle in this case) you can see from their expressions that he is portraying a prosperous gentleman, his dowdy wife in black feathers and his flighty mistress – all on one perch.

The behaviour of poultry is like human behaviour and it is just as predictable. They fight, they resent newcomers, they hate wind and rain. Some are bold and forage far from home and some hardly bother to go out of doors. They practise a bit of racial argy-bargy and their purposeful walk when hurrying into the house to lay is like that of determined women heading for the sales. They queue to use the same nesting-box (why, when there is a row of identical boxes?), and when they haven't got time to queue they climb on top of the first comer, to her intense annoyance. Some are neat in appearance and habit, but the Hi-Sex are sloppy and have no idea of chic. They seem to be permanently losing a feather or two, instead of having a good moult, getting it over and then looking smart again, bright of eye and comb. These feckless females drop their eggs anywhere on the floor of their house or on the ground outside. Our long-suffering guests are subjected to collecting the eggs, the high spot of my day. They pretend to enjoy it, but I notice a careful examination of the soles of London shoes when we get home.

I can't remember laughing out loud at anything I have read in *The Times* for years till a piece from the Washington correspondent about American nannies appeared. I thought the point of Americans was that they don't have nannies, that women are judges and all sorts of other things while the children bring themselves up. A notable example of the system, I thought, was Mark Thatcher's half-American baby, whose legs, still at the pipe-cleaner stage, were shoved into navy-blue dungarees at a month old, obviously expected to go out to work pronto. Just to complicate the issue, a woman called Ms Ireland, who is leader of a women's organisation called the National Organisation of Women, is on the prowl to discredit men who have important jobs in Clinton's administration. These despicable fellows may have employed women to look after their children. What I'd like to ask Ms Ireland is, how did these men get their children in the first place? Could it be that yet another woman was involved? Not Ms Ireland, of course. Perish the thought that she could have been in close enough contact with a man to result in a baby, who might even demand some years of luxury in the lap of an illegal nanny. Excitement mounts daily. Now we find that Ms Ireland might have bitten off more than even she can chew. Arising out of pretty Judge Kimba Wood's five-day training course as a Bunny Girl, Ms Ireland is to discover how many men in the administration read *Playboy* magazine, or, horror of horrors, went to a Playboy Club. At the tribunals, dear, sweet Ms Ireland will stump on to a rostrum and force the poor little men with important jobs to bow their heads and plead guilty to these crimes as well as getting the housework done for them while

46

they live it up in the law courts. I trust she won't come here. She would find things which would make her hair stand on end.

I have been in America and enjoyed myself enormously, but I find the language is getting difficult. An advertisement in the *Wall Street Journal* reads: 'Need a hand when figuring out where to open a Roth IRA?' I certainly would, and I bet you would too. Advertising an expensive raffle: 'See Jackie O's necklace in person at the following locations . . .' President Clinton's little local difficulty had just hit the press and produced some memorable stuff: 'Miss Lewinsky lied and lied again and thought her credibility was being questioned.' Ms Goldberg, Linda Tripp's literary agent, was quoted as saying: 'I told her to sleep on it. This is not something that ladies do, to tape each other.' I agree with Ms Goldberg, but I know I'm old-fashioned.

The purpose of my visit was to give some talks. I boldly spoke on Hardwick Hall* to a delightful audience in Los Angeles, who politely listened to the story of that extraordinary house. Afterwards I met some of the audience to answer their questions. One asked if there are facilities at Hardwick Hall. Not sure what she meant, I said 'No', in case she arrived in the summer hoping for massage, pools and hairdresser. Many were keen students of books written by my sisters Nancy and Jessica and wished to know more about the Hons Cupboard. A sad-looking lady asked me if I had been denied education. Afraid so, I said. 'And your father, Lord Rubenstein . . .'

No one told me how pretty the country is around Los Angeles. The steep valleys and immaculate gardens are very attractive but you never see anyone about. I wondered about the right to roam and if one could go for a walk through the prickly scrub on the hillsides. No one knew. Perhaps no one has tried. I was dumbfounded by the 200-acre garden at the

Huntington Library. Closely planted cactuses from the desert are within shouting distance of a valley thick with camellias as shiny-leaved as those which grow in the mists of Ireland. How is that done? In Pasadena there is an English tea-room run by expatriates, called Rose Tree Cottage. So popular is it that you must book for the twice-daily teas, where you sit surrounded by Derby china, Marmite, marmalade and pictures of Windsor Castle. What impressed me most about the new Getty Museum was not so much the building, its situation or the wonders to be seen there, but the unforgettable sight of John Walsh, the director, holding open a swinging door for ages while a torrent of people of all shapes, sizes and colours poured through, ignorant of his identity. He must be the reason for the wonderful atmosphere which hits you as soon as you enter the tram to go up the mountain. It is all the more surprising for a brand-new building. Other museum directors, please note.

* Fine Elizabethan house built by Bess of Hardwick and architect Robert Smythson between 1591 and 1597. The property came into the Cavendish family through her marriage to Sir William Cavendish and was taken by the government as part payment of death duties following the death of the 10th Duke of Devonshire in 1950.

Beware the difference in pronunciation of English and American. It changes the meaning of words which are spelt the same, so you have to pay attention when listening to someone from the New World and translate as you go. I met a Texan woman the other day who spoke at length about one Korda. I thought she must be too young to have known Sir Alexander of that ilk, then I suddenly twigged it was President Carter she was on about. Gonna meaning going to and wanna for wanting to are easy, but watch out for riders when they are talking about writers and be prepared for a waiter to turn into a wader without warning. So writers ride and waiters wade, which isn't surprising when a dot is a dart and a pot is a part. It happens here too. Last night I heard someone describe the predicament of buttered wives.

The two best days of entertainment of the year took place here last weekend: the fifteenth Country Fair. It was enjoyed by 50,000 people, watching or taking part in every conceivable country sport, skill or pastime, from clay shooting, fly casting, catapults, falconry, archery, stunt aeroplanes – too frightening to watch – terrier racing and gun dog displays. Jemima Parry-Jones brought her birds of prey. On a still day, one of her peregrines rose higher and higher till it was a speck in the sky. Jemima swung a lure of raw meat on a string round and round and the bird made a spectacular swoop, its wings folded so that it dived like an arrow at 100 miles an hour. The stars of the show were the King's Troop, which bring a lump to the throat when they gallop into the ring pulling their heavy gun carriages and making the earth tremble. They perform an intricate dance, harnesses jangling and wheels missing each other by inches, at a furious pace, till they thunder out of the ring still at the gallop. Mr Blobby marches with any band he can latch onto, followed like the Pied Piper by a crowd of children. The rows of shops here are nearer home than Bond Street, the assistants are much more pleasant and a wardrobe against the Derbyshire winter was bought in no time. The music of the pipe bands goes through the head for days after the event. Desert Orchid* was cheered and the ferret racing drew its own crowd of fans. The best notice was a sign saying: 'Lurchers' car park'. I don't know how many lurchers can read, let alone drive, but it looked pretty full and the occupants piled out of their cars and raced against each other all day.

* Outstanding and much loved grey steeplechaser, who, since his retirement from racing in 1991, makes popular celebrity appearances.

It may be the silly season in London but it is a serious time of year in Derbyshire. The opera festival in Buxton has been in full swing, the bed and breakfasts are bunged up with people enjoying the evenings in the beautifully restored Matcham Opera House of 1903 and the days wandering in the town buying picnics at Mr Pugson's cheese and delicatessen shop.

I hope they are shocked by the state of Carr of York's magnificent crescent of the 1780s, now boarded up and desolate, awaiting rescue by the local government. They can see the source of Buxton water bubbling up, surprisingly, in a room off the Tourist Information Centre.

They will be delighted by the dome of the Devonshire Royal Hospital, bigger than that of St Peter's in Rome. This extraordinary building was the stables for the horses belonging to visitors taking the waters, and the old covered ride for exercising them in bad weather is now the place for practising wheelchairs.

The High Sheriff's cocktail party, with its reassuring parade of mayors and their shiny cars, is over. So is Bakewell Show. This annual ritual draws a big crowd even in a temperature of 57° F, this year's scorcher.

The summer national dress of English country women — cotton skirts, anorak and gumboots — was the rule as the wind whipped us into the tents.

Poultry and rabbits, with their devoted followers in as much variety as the exhibits, was a good place to escape the weather. I thought I knew poultry but I was stumped by the breed name of one class — Furnace, Polecat and Salmon Blue. I bet you don't know they are types of Old English game birds.

Most of the egg classes were won by a Reverend and his

son. I like to think of those two in their vicarage garden look-ing after pens of Marans, Welsummers and other layers of mahogany brown eggs which produced the perfectly matched winning entries.

The Floral Art exhibitors must be devils for punishment and have a strong streak of masochism to be able to bear the judges' biting criticism. However hard they try there is something wrong with the strange edifices of whichever material is ordained by the show schedule, topped by a flower and a leaf or two.

I would give up after spending hours trying to shove a lily and a fern into yards of velvet, bits of glass or a straw teddy bear, only to find the judge's note saying: 'A good attempt but you should try to be flatter in front', or 'a pity there is a crease in your base'. Difficult for some lady competitors to obey the first directive and impossible for anyone to comply with the second.

Earlier this week I drove through the higher reaches of beautiful Wharfedale to give a talk to a Women's Institute. I was reminded (not that I needed reminding as I live among such people, thank God) of the quality of the silent majority who live out their lives without bothering the headlines and are the backbone of our country.

The WI allows no nonsense like letting men in. It is the female reply to White's, and the other London clubs which stand firm against admitting women members. So that's good.

But I hear there is a move to get away from the 'Jam and Jerusalem' image. If so they make a great mistake and will miss the nostalgia bus which gathers speed daily. The home-made food stall at any money-raising event is cleaned out in a few minutes.

It is what people love, so why should the WI *wish* to get away from that at which they excel? Jam is the thing and long may it remain so. As for 'Jerusalem' we sing it almost without thinking about the words. The idea of WI members being brought a bow of burning gold, a spear and a chariot of fire and their swords not sleeping in their hands fills me with terror. Even Genghis Khan would retreat in the face of this lot.

Our nearest big town is Chesterfield, and a very good place it is. A few years ago the sign announcing that you had arrived there read 'Chesterfield – Centre of Industrial England'. It has been changed to 'Chesterfield – Historic Market Town'. Why? I suppose industry is out of fashion.

We have just come back from the Republic of Ireland, staying at Lismore Castle, a house we know well, this being the forty-seventh year we have spent part of April there.

Of course, there have been vast changes after so long, but some things are reassuringly the same and happen to time, as they did half a century ago.

The great-great-great and more grand chick of the 1947 heron arrives to fish at the same spot at the same time on the river bank under the sitting room.

A familiar draught comes through the same gap where the door has never shut properly, the cow parsley and chestnut trees come into flower on the usual date whatever the weather, the wood anemone come up blue under the oaks and there are still red squirrels in the tallest yews I know.

The slow coming of the Irish spring is as pleasant as ever, starting earlier and going on longer than that of its neighbouring island to the east. The temperate climate keeps winter and summer pretty well alike.

Touring friends coming from the west coast report huge improvements to hotels and restaurants. Kenmare, in County Kerry, till lately a bit of a desert for anything more ambitious than a ham sandwich, now has two restaurants with a Michelin star. You can stay in Bantry House with the descendants of the family who built it in the 1720s and gaze at the stunning view over Bantry Bay to Whiddy Island. It must be the only bed and breakfast where the drawing-room furniture and tapestries belonged to Marie Antoinette.

Dinner at the Butler Arms in Waterville was praised more than the star of Kenmare because of the shellfish straight out of the sea, now appreciated for what it is – the best of its kind. Ballymaloe House near Cork deserves its reputation for impeccable food and comfort, and the Shanagarry Pottery next door produces the only wares of that kind I ever want to buy.

The land of a Hundred Thousand Welcomes may not have sun or snow (not enough to slide down anyway) and the sea is too cold to play in, but the beauty of the country, stuffed with history and mystery, plus the rising standards of the hotels delights people who feel compelled, as we do, to return year after year.

The beauty and the atmosphere of the place stay with me every year long after I have left Ireland. There, the local newspapers are a continual source of pleasure. Their pictures and headlines are a running commentary on current affairs which I greatly prefer to their dull English counterparts. The *Cork Examiner* can be relied on for eye-catching stuff like 'Mouse in Bottle of Stout' and 'Kerry Lady Dead in Drain', neither of which needs much enlargement underneath for the reader to take in what has happened. But 'Wives May Get Dental Benefit' from the *Irish Times* conjures up lucky husbands grinning to show off their smart new snappers while their new wives dare not smile (even if they felt like it) because of the nasty sights which would be on show. The *Kerryman* sums up the work of a hospital committee with 'Nothing Has Been Decided' while the *Dungarvan Leader*'s ' "Am I Here At All?" Asks Waterford County Councillor' poses a basic question which we must all have asked ourselves at some time or another. Even *Horse & Hound*, the trade mag of the Sloane Rangers, has got the drift when its Irish correspondent heads his column 'How to Get Farmers Back into Breeding'.

My sister Nancy loved the road signs, specially the ones on the mountain roads which have desperate twists and turns over the streams. The worst are announced in wasp black and yellow: 'DANGEROUS HAIRPIN'. More surprising is a big notice on a quiet stretch of road which says 'ATTENTION/ ACHTUNG. DRIVE ON LEFT. CONDUIRE A GAUCHE. LINKS FAHREN.' The spot where it is planted is many miles from any port or airport, so the Franco-German driver must have got the hang of how to do it or he would have met his fate long before he arrived on this remote moorland road far from the nearest village. There is a fine new dual carriageway which lets out most of Cork city on the road to the airport. 'NO PEDESTRIANS' it says, but in the middle of the road is a boy selling evening papers.

Spring and autumn are the seasons of annual general meetings. The older I get the harder I find it is to sit through them. The words which go with committees like 'minutes' and 'agenda' don't exactly send the adrenalin racing, and impatience with a ponderous chairman sometimes makes the affair nearly unbearable. The items on the 'agenda' are slowly ticked off and you pray no one will take up the chairman's suggestion of bringing up something arising out of the minutes. The obligatory thanks to the officers still come as a surprise after all these years. It is such an unsuitable collective word for a group of kindly women who spend much time and energy in raising money for whichever charity the meeting is about. My idea of an officer is anything from a second lieutenant to the Colonel of the Coldstream Guards – a far cry from the good ladies present in the church hall, who aren't the type to bark out orders on Horse Guards Parade and would look out of place in bearskins. When it comes to finding a seconder for the vote of thanks to the auditor, desperation sets in and I long to go out in the rain. 'Any Other Business' can be risky and it is a great relief when it passes quietly by. Then comes the speaker, who is, I suppose, meant to instruct or entertain and very often does neither but spins out the time till the blessed cup of tea looms and freedom is in sight. If you happen to be the speaker, of course, things are different and you are in an all-powerful position. Disappointingly soon you spot people crossing and uncrossing their legs, shifting in their chairs and searching in the depths of a bag for the key of the car. All of which makes for a general feeling of unease and means that the audience is thankful you forgot the second half of what you were going to say. If it is a talk with slides, the audience is in the dark, so you can't see signs of restlessness. Snoring is their only weapon, but they are your victims, imprisoned in rows till the last click of the projector. Their patience is an example to us all.

After the annual meeting comes the annual report. These arrive in our house by the ton, sent by every known organisation from Barnardo's to Bloodstock via the Water Board and the National Gallery. I suppose their production gives work for growers of trees, manufacturers of paper, photographers, designers, the people who write them and the Post Office. That's good, but 99 per cent of the wretched things represent a huge waste of time and money, written as they are in unreadable official language and printed on reams of shiny, expensive paper. Annual reports published for their shareholders by public companies vie with one another in richness of appearance and sheer weight. I guess the shareholders would prefer a Churchillian single sheet with the glad or sad news of the company's results so the money saved could go towards higher dividends. But it is a question of keeping up with the Joneses, so no respectable company would agree to such lack of pomp. I have discovered one exception. It is the annual report of the National Heritage Memorial Fund. If you have had enough of heritage – English, Living, Built, Landscape, World, Gardens and the Department of National – do swallow your objection to the overworked word and have a look. The beauty of it is its clarity; never an extra word, everything is straight to the point. Instead of the usual rigmarole about financial resources or funding, even the taboo word 'money' is used every now and again. The organisation itself must be unique in that it has more trustees than staff, who, believe it or not, number seven. When you have taken in that amazing fact, start reading and you will see what I mean. The descriptions of jewels, woods, paintings, manuscripts, a shingle beach, a fairground king's living wagon, a bit of the Brecon Beacons, a tractor, a colliery, drawings by Gainsborough, Raphael and Co., Somerset corn-fields, several church interiors, a trades union banner, a smashing portrait by Lawrence, a croft in Caithness, garden tools and an organ which have received grants are a delight. The accompanying photographs of such disparate beneficiaries make one pleased to be a taxpayer. No government department, no waste, no messing about; the grants they can give go straight to these diverse and needy places and things. And now their money is to be reduced from £12 million to £7 million. Remind yourself, please, that the fund was established as a memorial to those who have died for this country. Their number has not diminished. Roll on the National Lottery and may the NHMF get a whopping share of whatever is going. Meanwhile, congratulations to Lord Rothschild, chairman, and Georgina Naylor, director, for the work they do for us.

As a regular listener to the early morning programme on Radio 4 called *Today*, I am fascinated by the fact that the people who are interviewed find it impossible to answer a question with a simple *yes* or *no*. I except politicians because woolly answers are their style, but lots of people are quizzed on every subject under the sun and they all hover about uncertainly. The last few mornings, I have written down the replies which mean yes but are more complicated. Here are some of the most often repeated: 'certainly', or, to spin it out a bit, 'most certainly'; 'I agree'; 'exactly'; 'indeed', or, playing for time while they are pondering what they might be asked next, 'indeed that is so'; 'absolutely' ('absolutely' is rather new, but is getting more common); 'you're right' – 'that's right' – 'that's perfectly right' – or just the fashionable 'right'; 'true' or 'very true'; 'definitely'; 'of course'; 'very much so'; 'precisely'; and 'I hope so' with a little laugh and the emphasis on hope. How I long for someone to say yes, if that is what is meant. It would have the advantage of surprising the cruel questioner so much he would be silenced. The radio abhors a vacuum – so does an interviewer. I shall keep listening and perhaps one morning someone will manage it. But the ultimate joy would be to hear the answer 'I don't know'.

The world of consultants, which has appeared out of nowhere in the last few years, is a thriving off-shoot of whichever trade or industry it professes to know all about. Not so long ago professionals were trained in their profession and it would have been an insult to suggest that an outsider probe into the affairs of a company.

Not so now that consultants have arrived. Investing in a new enterprise, or upgrading an old one, be it a restaurant to feed visitors at Chatsworth or arrangements to ease the flow of customers round our Farm Shop, is extremely expensive, so it is thought prudent to consult a consultant before plunging into the unknown. Woman's Intuition is not to be trusted. The consultant is the one to go by.

He arrives from London, first class on the train, with a couple of acolytes, consultants in the making. Most probably he has never been this far north, so the geography and the ways of the locals have to be explained, all taking his valuable time. After a suitable pause of a few weeks (he is very busy being consulted) a beautiful book arrives, telling you what you spent the day telling him. It is written on paper about which he has consulted a consultant. The paper consultant has consulted a design consultant, and someone deep in an office has drawn a logo, without which no self-respecting consultant can practise his consultancy.

The result is a ream of paper the size of a tennis court, logo to the fore, and the address (which you might conceivably want) flanked by telephone, telex and fax number in fairy writing at the bottom.

You and your colleagues spend some time translating the book into plain English. You meet to discuss it and decide to do what you thought of doing before going to the consultant.

Almost at once a huge bill arrives topped up by first-class travel expenses and more meals than you can imagine three men could possibly eat in a day. It has all added considerably to the cost but you pay with the comfortable feeling that you have consulted the best consultant in the business.

The word luxury seems to be bandied about in a curious way these days. People's ideas of what it means vary enormously. I'm never quite sure what a 'luxury flat' is, though I believe it should have running water and a radiator or two. Better than not having them, I admit, but what is *real* luxury?

For me, a winter weekend sticks in the memory. I was staying with an artist and his wife in Dorset. I can't remember if there was central heating, but I do remember my hostess coming into my room before breakfast, her head tied in a duster like Miss Moppet, laying and lighting a coal fire for her guest to dress by. If you've never dressed in front of a coal fire you don't know what luxury is. They also had half a cow – the farmer had the other half – which meant they had not only proper cream but real butter, a rare commodity indeed.

I can't help comparing that house with many bigger, richer, electric fired households, some of which are the centre of hundreds of acres of their own farms, milking big herds of cows. But no one can be bothered to skim and churn, and thereby profit from what they own by producing what is described in old-fashioned cookery books as 'best butter'. My Dorset friends win the luxury stakes hands down. A coal fire, half an acre and half a cow, that's the thing.

A new word which is used to describe anything from houses to holidays is 'affordable'. Surely what Lord Lloyd-Webber and an unemployed miner can afford are not the same, yet it is trotted out as equally applicable to all. I imagine it means cheap, so why not say so?

The other day I went to Harrods to look for a coat for a friend who can't go shopping. After all these years I still miss the bank on the ground floor, and the green leather seats where my sisters and I used to meet and sit and talk and laugh so loudly that the other customers got annoyed. Now there is a slippery marble floor and fierce young ladies sell all the same make-up things under different names. You can't talk and you certainly don't feel like laughing. But it was what happened outside that struck me as so odd. It was pelting with rain and a gale was blowing, people's umbrellas turning inside out like Flying Robert's in *Struwwelpeter*. A smart car with a chauffeur drew up and an old, cross, rich couple got out. The woman had a mink coat slung over her shoulders, which fell into the road and the dirty water. The commissionaire dashed to pick it up, shook it and hung it on her again. He opened the door for her and her beastly husband, who didn't lift a finger to help. She walked straight through without looking round. 'Didn't that woman say thank you?' I asked the commissionaire. 'Oh no,' he answered, 'they never do.'

Packaging has gone too far and the simplest things have become impossible to open. If you buy a toothbrush or a pen or tweezers you need a strong and sharp pair of scissors to cut through the armour plating of plastic which encases them. No house has enough scissors so you go out and buy some. But they are similarly encapsulated in a thick shiny film, which human hands and nails are not designed to penetrate. You pull, drag, stamp and bite but to no avail. You can see your longed for object in its close-fitting jacket, shining and clean, which makes it all the more desirable, but there is no hope of getting at it. You buy another pair of scissors and another, till they are ranged alongside the things they are meant to open. If there is a Scissor Package Opener lurking among the terrifying objects in John Bell & Croyden you may be sure it will be aseptically sealed so only a scalpel will do the job.

A few days after this piece was published, an anonymous scalpel arrived by post and happiness set in.

Buying water in bottles to drink at home must be one of the oddest crazes of the last few years. All right, I know London water tastes horrible and Nanny would say don't touch it, darling, you don't know where it's been (sometimes they tell us where it's been, which proves Nanny to be right), but most water tastes the same as the bottled kind and is perfectly good just as it comes out of the tap. Beautiful pictures on the labels and names which conjure up moorland streams, most likely to be stuffed with liver fluke, appeal to the gullible shoppers. Once bought, the heavy bottles have to be lugged back to the car as there is not much pleasure in a guilty gulp of water in the shop. The choice seems endless. Bottles of all shapes and sizes and even colours (the blue one is very pretty) fill the shelves of grocers' shops already given over as much to dog, cat and bird food as that for humans. I suppose people will soon be buying water for pets or they will be accused of discriminating against them. Think of the number of lorries carrying this extraordinary cargo all over the country, getting in the way of things that matter, like you and me going for a spin. But the astonishing thing is the price. Please note that milk costs 43p a litre (it averages 23p to the farmer, by the way), petrol is a little over 50p a litre, and still water, would you believe it, costs up to 79p for the same quantity. As a shopkeeper, I must think up some other pointless commodities with which to fuddle the good old public.

We have heard a lot lately about two men sharing a bed in a French hotel and the usual speculation as to what may have happened in it.* You only have to go a little way back to discover that travellers often had to share a bed whether they chose to or not. In the 1750s, Henry Cavendish, the famous scientist, and his brother Frederick journeyed to Paris together. When they arrived in Calais they stopped at an inn and had to sleep in a room where someone was already in bed. It was a corpse laid out for burial. (The Cavendish family were famed for silence until a timely injection of Cecil blood in the last generation set them talking more than most.) Lord Brougham wrote of Henry, 'He probably uttered fewer words in the course of his life than any man who lived to fourscore years and ten, not excepting the monks of La Trappe.' Nothing was said by the laconic pair till they were well on the road next morning. Eventually Frederick said, 'Brother, did you see?' 'Yes, I did, brother,' Henry answered. Just think what would happen now. First the hotel manager would be sent for and given a dressing-down, as he often is by spoilt travellers who don't like finding a dead person in their room. Then the rich headlines would follow: 'Duke's nephews practise necrophilia in French hotel'. And there is the question of incest . . .

* David Ashby, MP for Leicestershire NW 1983–97, had shared a hotel bed with a male friend whilst on holiday, as an economy measure. Both denied any homosexual relationship.

The other day I was on my way to London airport, ridiculously early for the plane as usual. I stopped to fortify myself for the journey by looking round Chiswick House. It never disappoints or fails to inspire and fill the observer with wonder. It was a horrible day and the only other people were a party of Americans, the most knowledgeable acting as guide. One asked, 'Which is the portrait of Pope?' The woman said, 'There he is. You can always tell Alexander Pope. He's kinda skinny.'

Journalists and even ordinary people have a strange new habit of leaving out the Christian name when writing about women. It immediately turns the subject into a different person. I cannot recognise my sisters Nancy and Diana as Mitford and Mosley, or another sister when she becomes Treuhaft (though she is sometimes Mitford too, and then confusion reigns). And something unnatural happens to that most feminine of human beings, the American Ambassador to France, when she is referred to so baldly as Harriman. I think it started a few years ago with criminals. Somehow it is all right for Hindley and other murderesses as they hardly deserve a Christian name anyway, but it is extremely muddling when applied to normal women. I don't mind about Thatcher, Bottomley and Beckett. Having chosen the dotty career of politics, which turns them into Aunt Sallys from the day they were elected, they can stand up for themselves. Must we now drop the Aunt? If so, Sally is no good alone and anyway we're back to a Christian name. What a conundrum. I can't see why the reporters do it. It surely isn't to save space – just look at the acres of paper they have to cover with something: acres which become hectares on Sundays. Perhaps it is to do with them not liking the idea of women being proper women. The female journalists are very quaint and contrary, so we can expect something outlandish from them. I suppose it doesn't matter much, but when Hillary is in the news and she turns into Clinton, it does make one blink a bit.

Can we do away with: women who want to join men's clubs, *Cupressus Leylandii*, bits of paper that fall out of magazines and, lately, bits of paper which fall out of those bits of paper, people who say (and write) 'talking with' when they mean 'to', flowers in fireplaces, magpies, writing paper with the address at the bottom or, worse, the American trick of putting the address on the back of the envelope which you throw away and then have to retrieve, female weather forecasters, drivers who slow down to go over cattle grids, hotel coat-hangers, Canada geese, 'partners', liquid soap machines where the thing you press to get the stuff out is invisible, sparrow-hawks, audience participation, punning newspaper headlines and locked gates? And can we bring back: scythes, sharps and middlings, Invalid Bovril, brogues, mourning, silence, house-wives, telegrams, spring cleaning, snow in January instead of at lambing time, nurses in uniform, muffins, the 1662 Prayer Book, pinafores for little boys, fish shops, Bud Flanagan, Ethel Merman and Elvis Presley?

The television and the radio delight in feeding a morbid inter-est in illness and accidents with an ever-increasing number of programmes showing frightful things happening to people. Green-clad surgeons getting their heads and hands together over some bit of body, stretchers bringing a harvest of victims of horrifying accidents, and a difficult birth or two vie with each other to delight us. Turning on the radio, hoping for a cheery tune, I heard, 'Yes, blood blisters on the roof of the mouth can be very unpleasant.' I should jolly well think they could, but blood blisters are the least of the horrors on offer. If you happen to be even vaguely well you feel guilty because you aren't suffering like these unfortunates. Switch the thing off, you say. Well, of course, that's right. But lots of people must enjoy such ghoulish entertainment or it wouldn't be broadcast.

I notice the heavy (literally) newspapers have their individual ways with obituaries. *The Times* usually writes at length about a black American jazz musician who may, or may not, have played in a band with Fats Waller (of blessed memory). They sometimes throw in a grey-faced scientist from Eastern Europe who knew all about some abstruse speciality, a closed book to lesser mortals.

The *Daily Telegraph* describes the deeds of war heroes, illustrated with photos of these handsome men when in their twenties, smart as paint in uniform, with straight partings in their thick hair. The descriptions of their gallantry in winning DSOs, MCs and DFCs with a bar or two, read like thrillers and make one marvel that they survived into their eighties.

The *Guardian* recalls many a dreary politician and their boring, worthy lives, and sometimes one of the judges who make headlines by a surprising judgement or the classic questions only judges dare ask, like what is a Land Rover.

The *Independent* goes steadily about its business and can be relied on for accuracy and funniness, usually lacking in others. Few can resist a fashionable dig at the deceased. The smallest peccadillo is dragged up and enlarged upon in an otherwise blameless life devoted to public service.

The tabloids shout out about everyone, however obscure, in show business or sport. They reserve space to report some particularly grisly kind of death met by these unfortunate people. Perhaps they don't count as an obituary, but are just the usual reporting of the daily horror stories.

The specialist magazines are the most rewarding. The *Poultry World* and the Goat Society's *Monthly Journal* sometimes produce a winner but my favourite appeared in *Horse & Hound* in the days when fox hunting was perfectly all right.

It began: 'So Beatrice has galloped over and taken the last fence into the great unknown', and went on to describe the life of an indomitable country woman wedded to field sports, that special breed which only exists in these islands. It ended: 'Gallop on blithe spirit, and may you find your heaven in a good grass country.'

I hope she did and I hope there is still no plough in heaven.

There is something mysterious about bread. I don't mean pale, floppy loaves steamed to death by 'bakers', but the home-made sort, mixed, kneaded and cooked by human hand in a real oven.

Bread is uncertain, in that the same recipe followed by different people produces very different versions of the 'staff of life'. Perhaps it is something to do with the yeast, alive and almost kicking. Perhaps this magic agent reacts to the mood of the breadmaker or the oven. Whatever the reason the variations are very much part of the charm.

Children who have never tried home-made bread are apt to fall upon it and devour slice after slice, ending with a deeply satisfied sigh and 'I can't eat another thing. I'm full'.

Fancy recipes with different tastes, from herbs and bananas to tomatoes and olives, are easy to surprise people with, but are no good for everyday. For the best treat, you should wait till August to beg some wheat straight off the combine, put it through the coffee grinder and see if the resulting bread is not a revelation.

To be in the swim you must change your name. Steel has turned into Corus, which makes you think vaguely of singing, but I bet the steelworkers don't feel much like singing just now; Woolworth suddenly became Kingfisher, a flash of blue on a quiet river and not exactly the image of the old sixpenny high-street stores. Now the post office is to be called something so odd – not a real name but a concoction of letters, like the name of a film star's baby – that I've already forgotten what it is. I suppose stamps and postmen will go the same way. The Royal Commission on Historical Manuscripts is to drop the Royal (of course) and twist itself round till it becomes the Historical Manuscripts Commission. I wonder if that is sharp enough for 2001. Why not call it the Pony Club or the Delphinium Commission? Then it might make an impact. They say that the V & A is threatening to follow this extraordinary fashion because it used to get confused with the clothes shop C & A. I can hardly believe this. If true, what will Victoria & Albert turn into? Maskelyne & Devant? No, that is out of date. Morecambe & Wise more likely. And I'm longing to know what the National Gallery will choose, and Waterloo station, the Royal Observatory, Madame Tussaud's and the rest of the institutions we were brought up with. I fervently hope that John Lewis and Peter Jones won't turn into the Two Ronnies. I love all four too much to contemplate it. Chatsworth has been lumbered with the same name for 450 years, which is far too long. It is time for a change. Suggestions on a postcard, please.

There are some rare treats to come. Elvis is back with a bang and can be seen in all the big cities in a tour beginning in Newcastle. This incredible show is a deeply moving experience – I know because it came to this country last year. There he is on a vast screen in a vast arena, thousands of fans gazing at his beautiful face and inspired by his extraordinary voice. As if this wasn't enough, his real old band surrounds the screen, playing live – the inimitable pianist, the guitarist, the wild drummer and the rest. The Sweet Inspirations, the singers who accompanied him, take clothes a few sizes bigger than in the olden days, but they still make everyone feel happy. It is the man himself who dominates, as he always did, and the adoring fans drink it in, knowing every word and every gesture, unable to sit still in their seats till the whole arena erupts in clapping and shouting to celebrate the greatest entertainer ever to walk on a stage. ELVIS LIVES. He is often seen in supermarkets. I wish he would call at our London Farm Shop in Elizabeth Street.

Last week I had lunch with three friends, two of whom live abroad and come to London about once a year. The talk ranged over all kinds of subjects and it is refreshing to discover how untouched they are by the pounding of the media. They have never heard of Jeffrey Archer ('Is he one of the Archers?'); think a micro-wave is something to do with hairdressing; mix up Laura Ashley with sex-change April of that ilk; and ask if Cecil Parkinson is a photographer (vague memories of Norman and Beaton no doubt). Hoping for even more surprising gaps in their general knowledge test, my London-dwelling friend and I cast another fly, but this time with no success. They have heard of Mr Blair.

I wonder if it is computers which think up such strange names and addresses for the customers of the firms for which they work. Or is it specially dotty secretaries whose minds are on other things while they write? I should love to know. Some are wildly imaginative and endow the customer with a different character, or even another nationality, from the steady old English people they really are. One mail order company thinks I am called 'Mr/Ms Hess Of', the subject of an undiscovered poem by Edward Lear perhaps, or a German ex-royalty. (They have kindly sent me an 'Exceptional Customer Award suitable for framing and displaying in the Hess Of Home'.) A friend is the Viscountess Mrrrrrrrrr. She finds it difficult to pronounce and thinks it sounds as if she is getting into a cold bath. Another friend, who is an architect, has become Mr Jebb Ariba, which suggests he was born in Ghana or Nigeria. Liberty's (no upstart mail order company here, but an old-established firm who you might think would get it right) sent a proper letter on beautiful paper. Below the date is written 'Duchess D.E.V., Chatsworth, Chatsworth, Chatsworth, Bakewell, Derbyshire.' It begins 'Dear Sir' and goes on to describe a dress of 'Tana lawn in a floral print of particularly feminine style and two colourways'. It doesn't seem to have occurred to them that a Sir might prefer trousers. And I know Chatsworth is big but it really isn't necessary to repeat it three times as it is quite easy to find if mentioned just once. I look forward with interest to more and better names and addresses on the brightly coloured pamphlets which announce that you've won £25,000. Look closer and you find that, alas, you are the only person on the list who has not. Odd.

I know the Turner Prize is stale buns now, as it happened months ago, but I missed it at the time and have since become fascinated by how it is decided. Someone at the Tate kindly sent the bits of paper about it, written in a special language which is not easy to understand. The photos of the prize-winning works of art don't help much either. It seems that the prize is given to a 'British artist under fifty for an outstanding exhibition or other presentation of their work in the twelve months preceding 30 June'. It is awarded by a jury consisting of four, or sometimes five, good men and true, and a foreman (sorry, chairman). The jurors have a wonderful opportunity to find the artist guilty and sentence him to a term of no work and generally keeping quiet for however many years his art deserves. Amazingly, instead of doing this they give him £20,000. I'm all for people giving each other £20,000 as often as possible, but the reason in this case seems so very strange. According to the press release, last year's winner is said to 'play an interesting game with the relationship between art and reality' and has a 'refined sensibility in the handling of materials which range from hardboard and crushed steel to asphalt'. Very nice. In one of his exhibits, according to the foreword of the brochure, 'lurks the gap left by a shifted saucepan lid'. Good. A runner-up showed a glass case called 'A Thousand Years'. Inside was a box of house flies, a piece of rotting meat (I think) and what looks like an electric fly-killer. As the proprietor of a butcher's shop, I am pleased to see the meat, but – oh well. Another runner-up says, 'I access people's worst fears.' A third competitor uses dogs' messes. Dogs' messes *are* my worst fears and too often accessed in this house. There will be lots of fine artist's material when I get a new puppy, so I hope he'll come and give me a hand to our mutual advantage. And so it goes on – but why drag poor old Turner into it? Channel 4 gives the money for the prize. I like Jon Snow, his ties and his news, but I think I shall have to give him up for a bit.

Could some clever reader tell me what a quantum leap is and where I can see one performed? Who the chattering classes are and where I can listen to them? And what a learning curve is and how I can climb on to one?

CHATSWORTH

THIRTY YEARS' PROGRESS

Clearing out a drawer last week I found the minutes of a meeting held on 6 July 1965. Those present were Tim Burrows (then Currey & Co.'s Secretary to the Trustees), Hugo Read (then Chatsworth agent), Dennis Fisher (then Comptroller) and myself.

The familiar worries of expenditure exceeding income on house and garden were discussed and various large jobs needing to be done were listed.

'Mr Fisher and Mr Read mentioned the following which would probably require attention in the next four years: –
• Greenhouses – repairs and renewal of heating system.
• Connection of the house to the new main drain.
• Renewal of roof over north side of house sometime in the next twenty years.'

Apart from these, and the possible redecoration of the library, they 'could not foresee any major expense for which they would have to call in outside contractors, but emergencies might arise and they thought it would be prudent to allow between £7,000 and £10,000 a year for major items which their own staff could not cope with'. I wonder what we four would have thought had we known then the number of 'special jobs' which have cropped up every year and have been successfully completed since 1965?

The minutes continued – 'Mr Burrows enquired if there was any possibility of increasing the takings from the public. It was agreed that the provision of a café or other catering facilities (which would bring in more money) would not only spoil the present character of the place but would also very likely cause more trouble than it was worth by encouraging people to leave much litter about the gardens.'

At that time the only refreshment provided for our visitors was the cold tap in the wall by the Lodge which now carries a notice 'Water for Dogs'.

It was much the same with the shops. The idea was it was unfair, and greedy, to expect people to part with more money than the entrance fee (then 5/- for adults and 3/6 for children for house and garden). It only dawned on me slowly that people actually wanted to take something away to remind them of their visit and that they were hungry and thirsty as well. Now a lot of people come on purpose to eat and to shop.

Thanks to those who look after the restaurant and the shops, they are generally thought to be the best of their kind. The reason I am bold enough to say this is because of the number of people who ask to come and see how both these thriving departments are run. Not only are we all very proud of them, but they are two highly successful businesses providing what accountants call 'a significant contribution' to the house and the estate.

We have come a long way in thirty years. Perhaps we ought to become consultants!

MEMORIES OF CHATSWORTH IN 1950

Andrew and I, Emma aged seven and Sto six, lived in Edensor House with an extraordinary number of domestic staff, squeezed into what are now flats, and a frightening butler who would tell anyone who would listen that he had known better places. If we had more than three people to stay they lodged at Moor View (a cottage at the top of the village) and were soon known as the Suicide Squad. There were horses in the Edensor House stables and the Estate Office was in the upstairs rooms.

There were no cattle grids in the park – hence the wires still above the garden walls at Edensor to prevent the deer helping themselves to flowers and vegetables. Deer, cattle and sheep regularly wandered out of the park at Edensor and Calton Lees, but they didn't get far because there were always people about on foot or bicycle to herd them back in. Everyone walked or cycled. There were two cars in Edensor – the vicar's and ours.

Meanwhile, Chatsworth was looked after by the Comptroller. Ilona and Elizabeth Solymossy, Hungarian sisters, arrived there in 1948. The Hungarian sisters, trained as a teacher and a chemist, came to England as refugees in 1938 and worked as cook and housemaid to my sister-in-law Kathleen Hartington (née Kennedy) in her house in Smith Square, London, after she was widowed. Kathleen died in a plane crash in May 1948 and in August that year my mother-in-law persuaded them to come to Chatsworth to organise the mammoth task of cleaning the dirty old house in readiness for re-opening to the public in 1949. They, and their Eastern European staff (no English people would do such work at that time), were well settled here by 1950. They lived in the Bachelor Passage and the Cavendish Passage.

After they had been here a few years one was less likely to open a drawer and discover, as I once did, a miniature of Duchess Georgiana, a Women's Institute programme of 1932, a bracelet given by Pauline Borghese to the Bachelor Duke to hide a crack in the marble arm of a statue of Venus and a crystal wireless set.

It was then that I began to realise the extraordinary devotion to the house which had been shown by the comptroller Mr Shimwell and his men since the family left in 1939. To the surprise of our advisors later in the 1950s, there was no dry rot, thanks to the vigilance of those years.

I remember five or six joiners, greatly charming and always ready for a chat. What they did all day I don't know, but the clocks chimed as one on the hour, an eerie sound in the huge empty rooms. Mr Maltby was the Head House Carpenter, a most loveable character who had 'put the house away' in eleven days in September 1939 to make it ready for the school which was being evacuated to Chatsworth, and so he was an encyclopaedia of knowledge as to where furniture and all the rest was heaped and whence it came – he remembered where it was placed before the dormitories and classrooms took over in 1939.

The Solymossys used to tie up their heads in dusters, like Beatrix Potter's Miss Moppet, and attack a room at a time, their whole staff working together till it was clean and then on to the next one. There was a fog of dust everywhere and by afternoon their faces were unrecognisable. They worked very hard, but the rooms remained sadly shabby. There was rationing not only of food and petrol, but everything was hedged about with regulations. You had to get a permit to spend £150, the maximum allowed in a year for repairs and redecoration irrespective of the size of house, so there was no chance of making it look better.

My father-in-law lived alternately at Churchdale and at Compton Place in Eastbourne and spent the weeks in London, and my mother-in-law always went with him. After Andrew's elder brother, Billy Hartington, was killed in 1944 I never remember him entering the house at Chatsworth. From time to time he came to the garden, but that was all.

It was a sad place, cold, dark, empty and dirty. Even so, there was something compelling in the atmosphere and it was always an excitement to explore the shuttered rooms, but the spirit of the place had gone and only an incurable optimist could guess it would ever return.

On 26 November 1950 my father-in-law died suddenly while at his favourite occupation of chopping wood in the garden at Compton Place. Andrew was in Australia at the time. He came home to the sadness of losing his father and to worries over the death duties that affected the lives of so many connected to Chatsworth as well as the immediate family. 1950 was not a cheerful year for this place.

THE OLDEN DAYS BROUGHT UP TO DATE . . . AND NOW

My sisters and I were brought up close to the land. We knew it from the sharp end – trying to augment our meagre pocket money by keeping hens and goats and selling their produce to our long-suffering mother. She had a real chicken farm whose slender profit paid our governess. Only the soft-shelled and cracked eggs came into the kitchen and Nancy used to say the only chickens we had to eat were the ones that died. Not quite true, but – oh, what would the Health Police make of that? I expect there is a law against children keeping chickens now, but those were the days of freedom before the office wallahs spent happy hours thinking of ways to stop us doing anything we fancy.

A rule invented in the early 1930s was the tuberculin testing of cows. My mother had a herd of Guernseys that produced superb milk, cream and butter for the house as well as for sale. She had a deep mistrust of anything scientific, including doctors. When she was told that three cows had reacted to the test she hurried off to the cowshed. As always in such cases, they were the best-looking animals in the herd. 'What, get rid of those beautiful creatures? Certainly not. The children can have the milk.' And have it we did, with no ill-effects.

Forty years passed and in the 1970s the Environment was invented. At Chatsworth, we began to get letters from teachers who had brought their pupils round the house and wanted to take them on to the surrounding land to learn how it is used. Reading their questions and comments brought home to me that what I knew so intimately when I was young is a closed book to most children now.

Ignorance has escalated as 'family farms', with their mixed livestock, have all but disappeared. Animals and birds are shut away in buildings and all people see as they dash along the roads are some Friesian cows, a few sheep and unknown crops, fenced off in fields where humans are not welcome.

In 1973 we decided to set up the Farmyard at Chatsworth, to explain to the children that food is produced by farmers who also look after the land and that the two functions are inextricably mixed.

The milking demonstration is the highlight of the day. The audience remains riveted to the spot, fascinated, shocked and delighted by this twice-daily ritual. One little boy from the middle of Sheffield said to me: 'It's the most disgusting thing I've ever seen in me life. I'll never drink milk again.'

This reaction is not unusual, but you never know what is going to capture their imagination. A friend who farms in the Home Counties had a party of London children down for the day. He spent hours explaining the theory and practice of dairy farming and finally asked what had interested them most. After much nudging and giggling, one of them said: 'Watching the cows go to the toilet.'

What happens to the milk from the very much tuberculin and brucellosis-accredited cows in our Farmyard? You are not allowed even to give away this dangerous stuff because it has only been cooled, not pasteurised, sterilised, homogenised or any other 'ised'. If the children had so much as a taste we should be closed down pronto.

Amazingly, there are not (yet) any regulations forbidding calves to drink their natural food, so when they have had their share we, brave as lions, use the rest in the house. What my mother called unmurdered milk is quite different from the bought stuff, which has been through so many different processes it has lost its savour. Our homemade butter and thick cream is a daily delight and we all seem quite well on it.

It is not only children who are far removed from country matters. Some teachers who visit the Farmyard are surprised to hear that a cow has to have a calf before she gives milk; they don't connect these two facts of life.

Nor is ignorance of the natural cycle confined to town dwellers. A well-known fund-raiser for rainforests (grown-up) lives deep in the West Country and often passed the garden of a friend of mine who grows dahlias. After the first frost of October, she telephoned my friend in a rage: 'Why have you poisoned the dahlias? They are all dead and horrible and brown. How could you do such a thing?' (The rainforest lady can never have read Mr Jorrocks's joyful autumn cry, 'Blister my kidneys, the dahlias are dead!' But then I don't suppose she approves of fox hunting.) Irritated beyond words, my friend answered: 'Yes, and I'm going out now to do the same to all the oaks and beeches round here.'

My husband is an excellent fellow in every way, but he is not a countryman. The grass in the churchyard is an annual problem as it is in most villages. I suggested putting sheep in. Most suitable, I thought, Lamb of God, Sheep of my Hand, the very thing. 'We can't do that. Everyone will be furious.' 'Why? Isn't it a simple and practical thing to do?' But he was adamant and another untidy summer passed. When pressed for the real reason, he said: 'Can't you see, it's out of the question – the sheep would lift their legs on the gravestones.'

Our Farmyard is popular (100,000 visitors a year) but it has its critics. A woman brought a party of children who are junior members of an animal welfare organisation. She wrote to tell me they enjoyed the day but there was a serious objection because the children were conducting a survey on how the animals are treated as an attraction for the public.

They liked the free-range chickens – until the children started their picnic and then they were exasperated by the close attentions of the chickens and suggested that they should be penned after all. They concluded that the trout in their big tanks were bored and that 'the cluster of people round the rabbit pen put the animals in a predator/prey situation'. I really don't know how to amuse bored trout and cannot cope with human predators, so I broke the rule of a lifetime and did not answer her letter.

Once a year, on Schools' Countryside Day, we expand beyond the Farmyard to cover the whole estate. On Wednesday, 2,500 Derbyshire schoolchildren aged nine to eleven, and their teachers, spent the day in the park and saw the outdoor departments of the estate – farming, forestry and game – demonstrating their work.

Both teachers and children hear from the men whose lives are spent practising the mysteries of looking after the land and its products. Those of us brought up with them take all this for granted, but the vast majority have little idea of the seasonal toil which is an endless game of animal, vegetable and mineral.

Enormous tractors trundle over from our arable farm and bring potatoes, sheaves of wheat, barley, oats, linseed and oilseed rape. Except in the case of potatoes, few people know the difference between these crops, nor do they know their uses. When the wheat is pointed out it is vaguely connected with bread, but the rest are a complete mystery.

The gamekeepers' plot is the most popular. The children are fascinated by the pheasant and partridge chicks, mallard ducklings, ferrets, traps (including some old traps, now illegal) and guns. They see clay pigeons shot. Some of the teachers have a try and some of the children say they would like to shoot the teachers. There is pandemonium over bagging the spent cartridge cases.

At the forestry demonstration, Paul, a young forester born and bred at Chatsworth, and Phil, explain how woods are planted, weeded, pruned, thinned and eventually felled and that the cycle is then repeated. Because trees take longer to mature than a human lifetime, it seems difficult to understand that this country's only self-generating raw building material is a crop and has to be 'managed'.

Trees produce the most extreme reactions. Paul told me: 'On seeing the saws, several children remarked: "Do you enjoy killing trees? Don't you feel guilty? Why don't you blow them up with dynamite; surely that would be quicker? Do you only cut down trees to make money?"'

A head teacher asked: 'Couldn't you let the trees die naturally before you cut them down?' Watching the mechanical tree harvester: 'Don't you use axes any more?' Paul concluded that neither teachers nor children understood forestry. 'They see it as legalised vandalism. Their idea that we only destroy is based on media coverage of rainforests. A few teachers thought we were pulling the wool over the children's eyes but others were keen to know more.'

In desperation the young foresters pointed to the huge panorama all round with groups of trees young and old and Capability Brown's plantations bordering the park and asked: 'Do you like what you see?' They answered: 'Yes.' 'Well, that is what we do – we keep it looking like that.'

Those privileged to own land must explain to people who very naturally wish to use it for recreation what it costs in money and people to keep it looking attractive enough for them to want to ride, walk, run and sit on it. The beauty of the country was largely man-made in the days of cheap labour. Now that we are struggling to maintain the fine balance between man and nature, it would be helpful if walkers and other users understood the price of keeping hedges, stone walls, gates, farm and forest roads, streams and woods in order. In spite of the ever-thickening fog of bureaucracy the landowner still has the joy of ownership – but he also has all the responsibility and those who use the land have none.

The Farmyard, and now Schools' Day, have had an effect on the Chatsworth men who meet the teachers and children. It has been brought home to them that their jobs are not understood by the majority of visitors. Wallers, keepers, drainers, foresters, sawyers, butchers in the Farm Shop, shepherds, tractor drivers and stock-men – all would like to spend some hours explaining their age-old skills brought sharply up to date. But how can they be spared from their jobs? Who is to pay for their time?

Who is to tell visitors that these are the people who make Chatsworth and its surroundings what it is? Chatsworth and similar places could be huge outdoor classrooms, but all any of us can do without encouragement from on high amounts to a drop in the ocean.

We are told that 67 people are leaving agriculture and associated industries every day. Could not some of these, not academics but the real people, return to their roots to teach?

Perhaps it isn't worthwhile. I can see the day coming when gang mowers will cut the grass fields, the arable land will be left to its own thistly devices, paths through the woods will become impenetrable jungles for which ramblers will have to be armed with machetes. And then who would be killing the trees? We can drink French milk, eat Argentinian beef, import flour from America and timber from the Baltic. It would save a lot of work.

But I will grow a lettuce by the front door, just to prove I can.

Who are tourists? What are they? You, me, friends, relations, most of the people we know and millions we don't. Why do we tour? What makes people come to Chatsworth?

It is no new phenomenon. The house has been open for people to see round ever since it was built. In the late eighteenth century the table was laid on 'Open Days' for anyone who wanted dinner.

In 1849, the railway reached Rowsley, three miles away, and brought 80,000 people to go round the house and garden that summer. The Duke gave instructions that the waterworks be played 'for everyone, without exception'.

Huge crowds visited Chatsworth at the turn of the century on Bank Holiday weekends. The tour of the house and garden was free until 1908 and after that the fee – one shilling for adults and sixpence for children – was given to the local hospitals. It was not until 1947 that the revenue from the visitors went towards the upkeep of the place.

I have listened and talked to the people who have come here for nearly fifty years. The points of interest have changed, but the place has not – there is no fun fair and no entertainment except the house and its contents. The same goes for the garden. Perhaps that is why only the genuinely interested come. Vandalism and litter are not problems.

Forty years ago a regular remark from women seeing the cast-iron fireplaces in the state rooms was 'look at all that black leading'. Few women under the age of seventy know what black leading is now.

They are still astonished by the size of the house. A girl who complained about the price of a ticket, saying she didn't like paying so much to see a few old-fashioned rooms, reached the end of the tour and said: 'I'm knackered. Bring me a chair.'

Attitudes towards places such as Chatsworth have changed completely in the last fifty years. After the war there was a strong feeling against privately owned big houses and estates.

In spite of this people came, if only to criticise. The government's penal taxation laws were gleefully underlined by local government officials who did their best to make things difficult.

A typical instance was the vociferous lobby, instigated by the socialist MP for West Derbyshire and chairman of Derbyshire county council, to bring the A6 through the park a few yards from the house – an idea which would be unthinkable now.

The public has led the change in attitudes – conservation and preservation are all the rage and you are suddenly a hero for keeping the roof on; the cries of 'pull it down' from the 1950s and 1960s are long forgotten.

In 1976 the Duke of Bedford wrote a very funny letter to *The Times* about Woburn. He concluded that 'the average person comes to historic houses because he has bought a car and needs to drive somewhere in it. The number that come for real enlightenment are so few that it is distressing.'

Twenty years on people want to see works of art. Television programmes such as the *Antiques Roadshow*, have sharpened interest in the objects displayed. And when a Jane Austen novel is adapted for television, the briefest glimpse of someone's front door makes it an object of pilgrimage and crowds flock to see the hallowed spot.

A house lived in by the descendants of the family who built it is thought to be more interesting than one belonging to a government department or other organisation, however well presented. There is a keen curiosity about the incumbents.

American visitors find it impossible to believe that anyone

actually lives in this Derbyshire Disneyland. Children ask: 'Have they got satellite telly? Do they wear crowns? Was the duchess a girl groom?'

They are shocked by Laguerre's naked figures on the painted ceilings and think them out of place in such a posh house.

I am often asked if we mind the lack of privacy during the summer months. On the contrary, I should mind if no one came. Chatsworth needs people to bring it to life.

We are lucky in that the place is so big there is space for all. It is so well built that when the state rooms are full of visitors you can sit in our part of the house below unaware there is anyone about. When it re-opens every spring it is intensely pleasing to be able to show people the results of our winter's work.

Some visitors make surprising statements. There is a portrait of me by Lucian Freud, painted when I was thirty-four. It is said to be not exactly flattering. A woman was overheard saying in a gloomy voice: 'That's the dowager duchess.' Then, even gloomier: 'It was taken the year she died.'

A man, looking at Sargent's picture of the Acheson Sisters in their exquisite long white dresses of the Belle Epoque, said to his wife: 'Those are the Mitford girls. It is extraordinary to think two of them are still alive.' It certainly is. It was painted in 1901.

And I didn't know whether to be pleased or sorry when someone said to a warden: 'I saw the duchess in the garden. She looked quite normal, really.'

The view from here is beautiful. Looking out of my window over the garden and the river to the park and the woods is a pleasure I never cease to enjoy. There are no telegraph poles, no concrete edges to the road, no double yellow lines or anything else vexatious to the eye. The people who come to walk here, like Lowry figures, give scale to the landscape. They lean on the parapet of the bridge gazing at the view from the opposite angle.

Morning and evening the park is empty of people, and the sheep and deer become its undisturbed tenants. On stormy days these ruminants are like weather vanes, telling you the direction of the wind as they choose to lie down in the lee of this hill or that. On the first hot day of the year the ewes crowd together under a tree for shade like old women at a meeting, and you know that spring has truly come.

Talking of sheep, the other day I needed a simple technical guide to the native breeds (over fifty of them). I rang up my friend, the secretary of the National Sheep Association, to ask if he had an idiot's pamphlet on the subject. 'Yes,' he said, 'we produced one for the Food and Farming Exhibition in Hyde Park in 1989.' A gripping read it turned out to be.

The meaning of the words in the glossary stumped even language experts among my friends like Paddy Leigh Fermor and Jim Lees-Milne. One sheep disease has regional names of intriguing diversity: sturdy, bleb, turnstick, paterish, goggles, dunt and pendro are all gid. I looked up gid. No luck, it isn't there. You, Dear Reader, are expected to know exactly what gid is, and I'm quite sure that you do.

In church at Edensor, while the glorious language of the 1662 Prayer Book with its messages of mystery and imagination fills the air, I find my mind wandering back to the Oxfordshire churches of my childhood, first at Asthall and then at Swinbrook, where the same language was spoken in different surroundings.

Both St Mary's Swinbrook and St Peter's Edensor have seventeenth-century memorials which are worth going a long way to see. At Swinbrook, they commemorate two generations of the Fettiplace family, who owned the surrounding land till the male line died out in the nineteenth century. The subjects, who are weighed down by stone armour and lie stiffly on their sides, are of about the same date and as arrestingly beautiful as the memorial to Bess of Hardwick's* Cavendish sons in Edensor church.

The feel, smell and taste of the oak pews at Swinbrook (I suppose that all children lick pews under cover of praying for their guinea pigs) are not the same as those at Edensor. They were put in by my father, who paid for them with the money he won by backing a long-priced Grand National winner owned by a cousin. He wanted a horse's head carved on the end of each one, but the Bishop would not allow such frivolity, which was hypocritical of him, as I am sure he knew the source of my father's bounty perfectly well.

Sixty-six years ago, my sister Diana, aged fourteen, played the organ at Asthall. She thought any tune would do for the voluntary as long as it was played slowly enough. 'Tea For Two' was repeated again and again, unrecognised (or so she says) while waiting for the moment when the Venite was sung to more predictable music. We don't get those surprises at

Edensor because we have a proper organist. The sermons are preached in the parson's own voice, not a put-on holy one. They are the best I have ever heard.

Now Christmas is upon us again. Everyone is a year older and there will be some new actors in the nativity play, which is given by the Pilsley schoolchildren in the Painted Hall at Chatsworth (the audience has out-grown the chapel). The furious faces of some of the older boys, with their dishcloth head-dresses and dressing-gown cords all over the place, reflect the expressions of the descendants of the figures they are supposed to represent and whose photographs we see daily in the press.

* Elizabeth Countess of Shrewsbury (*c.* 1527–1608). Married as second husband Sir William Cavendish who purchased the estate of Chatsworth. Widowed in four marriages, she inherited her successive husbands' estates and indulged her passion for building, including a house on the site of the present Chatsworth, and Hardwick Hall.

Thousands of people come to walk in the park at Chatsworth all the year round. There is no way of telling how many, because it is free. Most people enjoy it, or presumably they wouldn't come, but every now and again a letter of criticism arrives.

Last week a woman wrote to say she was 'disgusted by the animal faeces on the grass, every few feet' and that she and her grandchildren couldn't play ball games in case of stepping on them. Oh dear. I suppose she wants us to buy a giant Hoover to attach to the JCB and sweep 1,000 acres of well-stocked ground before breakfast in case she gets her new shoes dirty. Sorry, Madam, but you had better go and find some municipally mown grass where your unhappy grandchildren can play their clinically clean games without the fear of stepping on the unspeakable. What a frightful grandmother you must be.

There is nothing like a spot of flattery to cheer one up, especially when it comes in an unexpected and roundabout way.

Roy Hattersley is a regular visitor to these parts. When writing a piece for the *Guardian*, he described his dream house, which he discovered when walking in the backwaters of Baslow, a mile or so by footpath from Chatsworth. He felt he could live in it happily ever after. Good.

The house is in a private road. The Deputy Leader of the Labour Party, taking no notice of the resident of a cottage opposite who challenged him with the classic, 'Can I help you?', meaning, 'What are you doing in this private road?', gazed lovingly at it through its shrubbery. The straightforward, unfussy square building of local lion-coloured stone is roofed with stout stone tiles, and, he said, fits the landscape as naturally as if it had been hewn from the living rock. (It was.) He wondered if it was put up for 'some minor Cavendish functionary or the assistant engineer in a new-fangled Victorian water company'. He thought it had the self-confident respectability of a nineteenth-century vicarage, and he liked the fact that it is all of a piece.

Its simple shape was decided upon after looking at a number of drawings of one-sided, over-glazed houses with all the other strange variations which make a building look as if it has had a stroke. When presented with a drawing of a house like this one, planners are apt to say this is all right, but what we should like to see is a Good Modern Building. Anyway, I am very glad Mr Hattersley likes this house. So do I. We built it in 1972.

CAMELLIAS

At Chatsworth you can find examples of most styles and dates of gardening represented somewhere in its 105 acres. Our situation on the edge of the Pennines, 500 feet above sea level, and the resulting harsh climate, dictate that only the hardiest plants succeed out of doors. For this reason, the glasshouses are of vital importance. Nowadays they are best known for the Muscat of Alexandria grapes in the autumn and camellias in the early spring.

The spring here is often disappointing. Even in April there can be frost and snow so it is then that the frost-free 'cold' houses full of camellias come into their own; their brilliant colours and perfect form, untouched by weather, are an ever cheering sight. When you go through the glass door and get out of the wind you find yourself in another world; 'the eternal calm of the greenhouse'.

Camellias have been grown here for over 150 years. Joseph Paxton, gardener, engineer and builder, was appointed Head Gardener at Chatsworth in 1826 when he was only twenty-three. He was an innovator and passed on his enthusiasm for all things new to his employer and friend the 6th 'Bachelor' Duke of Devonshire. The Duke describes himself as having been 'bit by gardening' and was easily persuaded to finance expeditions to the east and to America to bring back plants, many hitherto unknown in this country, to furnish his greenhouses. Among his favourites were camellias.

The stars of the collection are a pair of C. *reticulata* 'Captain Rawes' variety – called after the East India Company captain who brought them back from China. They were planted in the 1840s in the central and highest part of Paxton's Conservative Wall (so called because it conserves heat), a glass case which runs 331 feet up the hillside. At a height of 3 feet the trunks are 2ft 5in in circumference, and the camellias reached the 26-feet-high glass roof many years ago. Who knows how tall they would be had the roof grown with them. Between them is the pure white double C. *japonica* 'Alba Plena'.

In early spring the huge semi-double rose pink flowers of these camellias, with their waxy petals and gold stamens, look so exotic you wonder if they are real. People stop and stare and I have often heard them say, 'They must be plastic.' In a good year the wall seems to be solid rose pink, so close are the flowers.

Andrew and I were married in London in April 1941. The air raids were very bad during the week before our wedding and the windows of my father's house, where the reception was to be held, were blown out. The rooms looked bleak, but my mother nailed up folded wallpaper as mock curtains and my mother-in-law sent a mass of these astonishing blooms which, thankfully, saved the day in drab wartime London.

Thanks to the people who look after them, Chatsworth has had many successes at the RHS Camellia Show in London. Competition is getting hotter every year, but Ian Webster, who is in charge of the greenhouses, wins his share and more of first prizes. A regular winner is the blood red 'Mathotiana Rubra', a variety which is difficult to strike from cuttings, so we see our small tree as producing rather rare flowers. I have known this plant for fifty years and it never fails to perform in

March. There are a bewildering number of varieties now. New ones are listed every year, but I still like the old ones best. The simple white flower of 'Alba Simplex' is the essence of purity. I love the old-fashioned pink and white striped japonicas and the precise way the petals of the formal doubles are arranged, like flowers in a Victorian bouquet. Andrew's favourites are 'Jupiter', a single japonica of intense red, and 'Mrs D. W. Davies', blush pink with waxy flowers six inches across. The aptly named rose-form doubles could easily be mistaken for the striped Rosa mundi – till you remember the time of year. The earliest to flower is *C. sasanqua*. It is a welcome sight in November and has the advantage of being slightly scented. A succession of camellias are the only decoration we have on the dining table from December to April, but such is their beauty and variety that you could never tire of them. They are arranged on a silver plate so you look down into the flowers. We use a round table when we are alone, but if there is a party we put several plates of flowers down the length of the bigger table. They make a brilliant effect, with the pink and red tones picking up the colours in the curtains and carpet of the dining room. Ian Webster arranges them in a one-inch layer of oasis in the bottom of the plate, adding just enough water to soak it. He covers the oasis with camellia leaves then cuts the flowers with just enough stalk to go into the oasis so the blooms rest on the leaves. (Be careful when handling the flowers, by the way, as they bruise very easily.) Small trees in tubs also come indoors but for short periods only as they're not keen on the dry atmosphere in the house.

JEAN-PIERRE BÉRAUD
10.viii.1956 – 13.x.1996

Last year on one of those rare October days which take you back to summer and make it impossible to believe in the coming winter, Jean-Pierre Béraud was killed in an accident. He was forty.

His death had a chilling effect on Chatsworth. People went about their work in a daze. For a long time we could not believe that so vital a man had gone forever. One cannot imagine what this tragedy meant to Diane, their boys, his French family and his loyal staff.

Jean-Pierre made an unforgettable impression on everyone he met. The proof of the loss that was felt was the number of letters I had from my family, friends, acquaintances and strangers. The Prince of Wales, the Lord Lieutenant, the High Sheriff, the Chief Executives of companies who had dined in the Carriage House, heads of local government, distinguished chefs and people I have never met wrote to me as if I had lost a member of my family.

The story of how a young man from the suburbs of Paris came to England and made his name and his home at Chatsworth is an unlikely one.

My daughter, Sophy, and others, were disappointed with our food. She said, 'Why don't you ask Aunt Diana [Mosley] to find someone in Paris who might like it here and who can really cook?' At that time my sister had a flat over a famous restaurant, Chez Pauline in the Rue Villedo. She asked the *patron* if he knew a young cook who would consider the job. No, he did not. A week later he told her a boy called Jean-Pierre wanted to go to England – but he had already left. My sister got his home address near Paris and strangely enough his parents lived not far away from her.

Then Jerry comes into the story. Jerry Lehane is an old family friend, who has been butler/driver with the Mosleys for over forty years. He guessed the Bérauds would have no telephone and took a note from my sister to their flat in Palaiseau. Madame Béraud gave him the address of a hotel in Portman Square where Jean-Pierre had found work. My sister and Jerry were to go to London the next day. Jerry wrote: 'Lady Mosley and I went along to the hotel one afternoon to see if I could find him. They said he was on duty but after some persuasion they went and got him. He met Lady Mosley outside the hotel in the car and it was arranged that when he finished his duties I would return and pick him up and take him to Chesterfield Street to meet you. The rest I am sure you know. Going up to Chatsworth must have seemed a million miles for Alan [Shimwell, my long-time driver] and Jean-Pierre – not being able to have a conversation.

'The next time I saw him was at Chatsworth where he had laid out a wonderful tea tray in his room and I could see from the happiness in his face that he had fallen in love with Chatsworth: *Shasworth* as he used to pronounce it, with his French accent and his lisp. He talked and talked about *Shasworth* and the Duchess and Duke. I only wish I had had a tape recorder that day. After that meeting we became good friends. He told me something which I always remember. He said he was having difficulty with somebody and he was longing to discuss it with the Duchess. He compared it to if you wanted to see God – you had to get St Peter's approval. So he said one day he had decided why go to St Peter when he could go straight to God!

'The last time I saw him was at Mrs Jackson's* funeral. We had a chat and he was still delighted with how Chatsworth was developing. He said he would talk about it again, but . . .'

When Jerry brought Jean-Pierre to Chesterfield Street for the interview one of my sons-in-law came to translate because, to my shame, I can't speak French. I learnt that he had worked in some of the best restaurants in Paris since he was thirteen years old. He was now twenty-two. I asked him if he could make *sauce Béarnaise*. He gave me a pitying look and I realised I had made a gaffe.

In spite of this unpromising start, he agreed to come to Chatsworth for three months. I think he would have clutched at any straw to escape from the hotel kitchen where there was not one Englishman — and he had come to London to learn English.

From the day he arrived we were reminded what good food is. I had to act 'cabbage' and everything else till he learnt enough English for us to communicate the essential to each other.

His ambition was to go to America and seek his fortune. We talked about it and, through my sister-in-law, I found what seemed to be a suitable job for him. He left Chatsworth and we missed him. Soon after he had started work in New York and the Bahamas, the Queen and Prince Philip were coming to stay. I rang up his employer and said, if I pay his fare, can Jean-Pierre come back and cook for them? It was arranged. The food was perfect and all went well.

On the Monday morning following, Jean-Pierre came to see me. 'I'm not going back to America,' he said. 'Oh you MUST, it is Mr X's busy season and he's depending on you.' 'I want to stay here,' he repeated. After some argument he did go back, but not for long. The reason was simple — he had fallen in love with Diane.

Life with Jean-Pierre wasn't all plain sailing. In the early days he used to burst into my room saying why couldn't he have this and that AT ONCE, why was everything done so slowly here . . . Derrick Penrose remembers not dissimilar occasions – but Jean-Pierre's temperament and his passion for getting things done made it impossible for him to be calm and wait, it must be NOW. We used to laugh about it afterwards.

He saved the Farm Shop from closure when it was making losses, setting up the kitchen which turned it to profit, laying the foundation of what it has grown into today. His energy was by no means expended by cooking for two old people and their occasional guests. So, long before he became manager there, he made all kinds of things for the Farm Shop and kept exact accounts of every ounce of flour and every minute of his time. One winter he made 3,000lbs of marmalade by hand to be sold and then stormed into my room saying he would never cut up another orange. (Mind you, I hadn't asked him to do it.)

When we took the Devonshire Arms Hotel at Bolton Abbey in hand, Jean-Pierre was chef there for some months. There were no proper pots and pans. He didn't wait for a budget from the directors, but dashed to Leeds and bought a *batterie de cuisine* on my personal account. Then he took over the catering for the visitors to Chatsworth – first in the inconvenient west and north bits of the stables. Later Bob Getty and he designed new kitchens and made the Carriage House into what I believe is acknowledged to be the best restaurant attached to a house which is open to the public.

Bakewell Rotary Club made him a member – a rare honour for a foreigner.

He saw a demand for cooking lessons and, ever thorough, he attended courses at Prue Leith's in London and the famed Manoir aux Quat' Saisons near Oxford to see how it was done.

His lessons were soon booked up and his pupils returned again and again. Filming for a television company was to have started in January . . .

So often I used to say 'What ARE we going to do?' about whatever was concerning me and the answer was always the same: 'DON'T WORRY' (to rhyme with 'lorry').

As well as looking after our kitchen and the Carriage House (which soon made a mighty contribution to estate overheads), he had thriving businesses of his own in Matlock, Bakewell and at Carsington Reservoir. He was on the crest of a wave.

After the disaster, among the marvellous letters I received was this from Peter Day – 'Cookery is an art but not so much a fine art or an applied art as a performing art, like dancing, acting or singing. It is of the moment and then gone, and has to be spot on.'

I was struck by this, even awe-struck, in Jean-Pierre's case when the staff and their families were invited to see the big table in the Great Dining Room with all its silver and special decorations ready for the great dinner for the Society of Dilettanti, to which Andrew was host. There amid all the wide-eyed admirers strolling round the table were Jean-Pierre and his family – only a minute or two before he had to go down to the kitchen to *cook* this mighty meal in prospect! I think I vaguely thought everything would somehow have been prepared days in advance. But I realised then with a shock how much Jean-Pierre's work (or art) was like going on stage for a great performance and giving his audience an evening of pleasure, a transport of delight – something to get right on the night, every night.

In his case his whole life and character were like this, immediate and direct, all passion with no side, front or anything else to come between him and others. Everyone who knew him knew that storms were followed instantly by sunshine. Jean-Pierre could not have been more at one with the lively art of which he was master, and memories of him will never be other than vivid.

Another letter which put the thoughts of all of us into words was from Simon Seligman – 'I know that you have lost a kindred spirit, a brilliant, creative and original man. He was like a blazing comet in my life, even in the few years I knew him, so I can imagine some of the loss you must be feeling.'

Jean-Pierre was one of the most remarkable men I have ever met. He was a true friend to Chatsworth and to me.

* Pamela Jackson, née Mitford, sister of Deborah Devonshire.

HOT SOUP says the notice on the road outside the Post Office in Edensor, the village within the walls of Chatsworth Park. This notice covers the rough lane from Bakewell which brings walkers past the cottages, built from a Victorian pattern book, to the public road which runs through the 1,000-acre park.

Hot soup and teas in the winter, ice cream and teas in the summer are a major part of Nigel Johnson's business as a sub-postmaster in a small village. Now, like to Eleanor Rigby's grave, nobody comes.

The Post Office is part of a suddenly forgotten landscape, put voluntarily out of bounds to the thousands of people who come here from Sheffield, Chesterfield, Nottingham and further afield to walk in all weathers at all times of the year and to the thousands more who come from all over the world to see the house and garden. Not since 1967 have I looked out of my window to see no one on the bridge, the focal point of the park, the place where people stand in the afternoon sun to stare at the golden windows which light up the west front of Chatsworth. The bridge is halfway between the north and south entrances to the unfenced acres of grass where children and dogs are welcome, people can run and shout and play games or picnic by their pram under a tree. This is how it has been during the sixty years I have known the place and now, suddenly, it is empty, like an early morning photograph before anyone is about.

I hardly dare write it, but there is no outbreak of foot-and-mouth disease in the immediate neighbourhood, yet this place is changed out of recognition.

Our house and garden should have been opened to visitors

on Wednesday. There has been the usual rush to get everything ready, the place looks immaculate, clean and shining, a new exhibition of twentieth-century works of art has been set up, restoration of sculptures and redecorations are there to be seen, the shops are full of new and exciting things, the restaurant ovens are waiting to be heated up. But the doors are shut.

The seasonal staff, 166 of them, have been put off, 15 people in the gift shops, 70 catering staff, 66 ticket sellers, car parkers and wardens. The Farm Shop in Pilsley is open because it is not in the park, but is as quiet as it would be in a January snowstorm and 15 assistants have had to go. The free car park in Calton Lees is bound by one of those unclimbable wire builders' fences, almost an insult to the thousands of people who usually use it.

Statistics stare us in the face, but the difficulties affecting the people who are made redundant are as different as the individuals themselves. They depend on the employment generated by the half million visitors who come here over the seven months from now, yet these people are miles away from the farmers whose stock is lost and spirits are crushed. All the same, the lives of these Chatsworth employees have been cruelly disrupted.

How long will it last? How long will people stick to the rules? WHAT ARE THE RULES? No one seems to know. Mixed messages fly through the air. One minister tells us not to go into the country. Another suggests tourists should go to the north-west, presumably to see and smell 80,000 rotting carcasses. What a way to run a country.

People have been exemplary in respecting the notices asking them not to come to the park, but on a fine weekend when the birds are singing the longing to be out of doors and to let the children loose on the grass may soon be too strong a temptation for our neighbouring city dwellers wanting fresh air and freedom; till now these precious commodities have been available here in endless quantity.

Chatsworth house, garden, park and woods and the further landscape are as one, the cattle and sheep grazing out of doors are as much a part of the place as the Rembrandts are indoors: they support one another to make the whole.

Farming here goes in harmony with nature and the huge numbers of visitors. If the sheep and the deer go – which God forbid – an integral part of the place will go with them. It is the spectre of such a disaster which the people who look after this place are living with in a kind of limbo. And it is repeated all over the country.

Our 4,500 ewes have started lambing: there is usually a cheerful atmosphere in the caravan by the lambing sheds where the veterinary students and other seasonal helpers snatch a quick cup of tea between lambing a ewe in trouble, penning the newborn lambs with their mothers to avoid 'mis-mothering', filling the hay racks and water bowls. The necessary precautions are meticulously carried out. It goes without saying the lambing staff must arrive and leave the buildings spotlessly clean and they have to allow five days between lambing here and going to the next job or back to college. They have their own special car park in the yard with disinfectant and scrubbing places. Everything is done as efficiently as ever by our magnificent staff, but even Radio 2 is turned off.

Some lambing shepherds traditionally start in the south of the country, where lambs are born earlier in the year, and work their way north to the lowlands of Scotland a couple of months later. This year there will be no ewes in these areas for them to tend.

Most of the 'cade' lambs – the weakest of triplets or those born to a ewe which has died – are mothered on to a ewe with a single lamb and enough milk for two. But the surplus are sold on to people who come from here, there and everywhere who bring them up on the bottle. There can be none of that this year – no strangers are allowed near. The cades will be 'tapped on the back of the head' and that will be the end of them.

In our so-called civilised society we have become used to being more or less in control in everyday life, whether it be in farming, shop-keeping or opening a house to the public. Now there is fear of the unknown, like a medieval plague.

Politicians come and go on the television between the harrowing scenes of human and animal misery, making things worse with their endless words and wishful thinking and apparent inability to make or implement decisions. Their shiny cars, neat suits and hateful hairstyles are a world apart from the muddy Land Rovers, layers of sweaters and waterproofs and broken faces of the Cumbrian farmers.

An astonishing fact is that none of the recommendations of the Northumberland report written after the 1967 outbreak have been carried out or apparently even considered. It seems incredible when you realise those like Lord Plumb, with a lifetime's experience of farming and farming politics, worked for nine months on the Committee of Inquiry after that outbreak. He and his colleagues came to conclusions full of common sense, even down to the details like the fact that there should be a sufficient number of captive bolt pistols so that pistols could be set aside for cooling without holding up the slaughter.

I very much doubt if Mr Brown has ever held a gun with a hot barrel, but practical countrymen like those who wrote this report know exactly the sort of problems continual shooting would create.

I wonder if he knows that meat is still imported here from countries where foot-and-mouth is endemic? I wonder if he knows anything?

This same Mr Brown, who is meant to be in charge of agriculture in this country, has not been to the north-west since the epidemic began. Can you imagine the politicians of old ducking their responsibilities in such a cowardly fashion?

To top up this catalogue of disaster, we are told there will be 'an election' or two elections on 3 May. Everyone I have talked to here agrees it is positively obscene even to consider such a thing while this national emergency is with us.

Here, there is an eerie atmosphere and near-silence. Only the Prime Minister goes on talking.

BOOKS AND COMPANY

STRANDED!

I cannot imagine why I was asked to contribute to this series where you have to choose and describe ten books for company on the Trans-Siberian Railway. I have read very few books and I have minded finishing them so much that I have often vowed not to start another. Coming to the end of some gripping story or reaching the inevitable death of the subject of a biography is like losing a friend whom you have begun to depend upon night and day in a secret liaison with the author. It is no good saying you can read it again. It is never the same the second time.

I imagine that looking out of the train window hoping to spot a bear or a sable might pall after you have trundled by the first million birch trees. Russian and Asian birds would be meaningless to one who only likes blackbirds and thrushes, and I imagine the agricultural scenes, fascinating to start with, would be as repetitive as the birches.

So I must think about ten tiresome books and the reasons for choosing and lugging them up the steep steps of the train. (I hope it still looks like the train in the opening scene of the film *Anna Karenina*.)

Books of reference do not have the same trouble with the ending because you don't read them straight through, so they can't get the hold on you that the other kind do. And when you are old you forget what you have looked up (and why) and you happily do it all over again. *The Oxford Book of Quotations* will do very well and I can go on being surprised by the number of everyday sayings from Shakespeare and the Bible. Of course it has the unfortunate side of whetting the appetite for more, but it will keep me happily occupied for many hours. I am at home with our copy, blue cloth cover with dark rings where sloppy wine glasses have been put to rest. So that is book number one.

The second book is short, only 1,237 words (a lesson to the writers of thousand-*page* biographies of dreary politicians which litter the visitors' bedrooms at Chatsworth), small, neat and light enough to make up for the bulk of my first choice. The print is excellent and the illustrations are second to none. As a shopkeeper I revere it as the best book on retailing ever written.

It is *Ginger and Pickles* by Beatrix Potter. Ginger, the yellow tom cat, and Pickles, the terrier, kept a village shop which stocked most things required by their customers. The shop was patronised by the locals, rabbits, rats, mice, frogs and tortoises which lived around Sawrey in the Lake District at the turn of the century. The mice were rather frightened of Ginger and the rats were frightened of Pickles. Ginger made Pickles serve the mice because they made his mouth water and he could hardly bear to see them going out with their little parcels. Pickles felt the same about the rats. But they realised that to eat their customers would be bad for business. The rats shopped extravagantly and Samuel Whiskers ran up a bill as long as his tail.

In spite of being nervous of the proprietors, all these creatures crowded into the shop and bought a great deal of whatever took their fancy, especially toffee. But Ginger and Pickles made the age-old mistake of giving unlimited credit.

Nobody paid and there was nothing in the till. They could not afford to buy food for themselves and had to eat their own goods – biscuits and dried haddock – after the shop was shut.

The ever-present village policeman (oh where is he now?) terrified Pickles because there was no money to buy himself a dog licence. Tabitha Twitchit ran the other shop in the village and insisted on cash down. In spite of stocking less attractive goods she prospered.

Things at *Ginger and Pickles* went from bad to worse. Eventually they went bankrupt, shut up shop and retired. Nobody cared. Tabitha Twitchit, now a one cat monopoly, put everything up ½d. Pickles became a gamekeeper and Ginger, surrounded by the latest in traps and snares, grew stout in a rabbit warren. Thus they got their own back on their debtors. The watercolour of Pickles in his new job carrying a gun, his long-nosed face peering round a wall, in pursuit of the rabbits who had found the counter to be just the right height stays in the memory, as does the illustration of him serving a hedgehog (Mrs Tiggy-Winkle the washer woman, no less) with a bar of soap, entering it in a note book, bowing and saying 'With pleasure, madam'.

After a while a dormouse and his daughter began to sell peppermints and candles. When John Dormouse was complained to about candles which drooped in hot weather he stayed in bed and said nothing but 'very snug', which, the author tells us, is no way to run a retail business. The moral is don't sell faulty goods and never give tick.

My third book is Patrick Leigh Fermor's *Between the Woods and the Water*. I am sorry to say I have not read it, but I look at it every day as it has been on the table by my bed since it was published. It comes under the dangerous category because I know that if I am rash enough to start it I will miss it terribly when it is finished. My journey will be the ideal opportunity to try his journey and if I keep it till last and am still floundering about with the others when I arrive at the other end of the world I can go on looking at it like I have for years.

Next comes *The Best of Beachcomber* by J. B. Morton. The world has turned upside down since the column in the *Daily Express* delighted us and now the characters, so outrageous then, are all over the place in real life. Narkover and the headmaster, Dr Smart Allick, are quite tame as public schools go. Captain de Courcey Foulenough's bid for a seat in Parliament makes me mourn Screaming Lord Sutch, whose slogan of 'Vote Loony You Know It Makes Sense' was reminiscent of the Captain's policy for Democracy and Duty Free Lard.

The Captain was elected for South Mince and Tiddlehampton in spite of disgraceful scenes at his meetings in the headquarters of the Mince Steam Laundry Playing Fields Association. His opponent, the lovely Miss Boubou Flaring, stood as an Independent Liberal or an Independent Progressive Liberal – she could not decide which. Foulenough dismayed his supporters by changing his platform to Independent Progressive Liberal and saying 'a split vote is just as much fun as any other sort of vote'. He stood for 'work for all, friendship with every nation, national reconstruction, national revival, higher wages, higher exports, higher imports, lower taxation, rearmament, peace, co-operation, co-ordination, and no closing hours'. This seems strangely familiar in 1999.

The next headline announced: 'Foulenough in'.

No sooner had he taken his seat in the House of Commons than the mace was missing, which was only to be expected from one educated at Narkover under the third generation of Smart Allicks. 'Speculation ran, or rather waddled, rife as to the motives of the theft. The name of Foulenough is being freely mentioned, and it is assumed that he walked off with the symbol of British umtarara in a fit of absent-mindedness. Nobody can believe that he intended a deliberate insult to the majesty of the House, et tout le bataclan du tralala.'

The entertainment offered by the Filthistan Trio is a bit near the knuckle now. The three Persians, who played see-saw in the hall at the Ritz by placing a plank across the belly of the fattest, most likely own that hotel of sacred name by now, although they returned to Filthistan long ago.

You may remember the twelve red-bearded dwarfs. They plagued Mr Justice Cocklecarrot by their inane answers to his questions in the case brought by Mrs Renton against Mrs Tasker, who habitually pushed all the dwarfs into Mrs Renton's hall. As we are no longer allowed to call a dwarf a dwarf and no doubt we will soon be stopped from describing a beard as red for fear of insulting its owner, it is refreshing to read the transcript of this famous case. The political incorrectness of Beachcomber is pure joy today.

The fifth book is *The Curse of the Wise Woman* by Lord Dunsany. It should be required reading for all politicians who wish to understand Ireland and the Irish. Although it is seventy years since it was published, and the events described took place a hundred years ago, little has changed. The infinite contradictions, the unseen but deeply felt currents of conflicting thought so apparent to the lovers of that country are brought before the reader with a terrifying impact in the first few pages.

Mountain and bog are described by one whose childhood was spent drinking in the very essence of Ireland. The author was as one with both in his understanding of that mysterious, haunted land. His description of a hunt makes me thankful that whatever Mr Blair may decree in England he has no power to stop fox hunting in Ireland. He should read it. If he has any imagination he would be caught up with, and then overwhelmed by, the thrill of it, the sight and sound of a pack of hounds in full cry over the empty January land that was the west of Ireland at the turn of the century.

The narrator was a schoolboy at Eton, spending the Christmas holidays in his faraway home. He describes Mrs Marlin, the Wise Woman, her power as a seer, her cabin on the edge of the bog, her son who was the author's ally and knew from his mother when the geese would come and where to find snipe on shooting expeditions over the treacherous shining bog, all written with the comprehension that only an Irishman has of his fellow countrymen.

Mrs Marlin saw the destruction of her world coming with the machines of the Peat Development Company, which arrived to cut the turf. Her curses terrified the operators and all were the victims of the larger power of nature when the bog itself moved and engulfed the lot of them.

Number six is a book I could not be without. *The Oxford Book of English Verse* – not the smart, thick, heavy new edition but Arthur Quiller-Couch's 1900 anthology reprinted in 1920 on feather-light India paper. The inscription '*Unity Mitford from Uncle G. 8 August 1925*' is inside the cover – my sister's eleventh birthday.

One of the requirements of our home education was to learn a poem by heart each term. As our governesses often left and a new one came, the easiest way to do this was to choose the poem learnt the term before. Several times I got away with this simple ruse. The poem I loved was 'The Lament of the Irish Emigrant' by Selina Dufferin. The first lines 'I'm sitting on the stile Mary, Where we sat side by side, On a bright May morning long ago, When first you were my bride' still bring tears to the eyes. No new edition includes these sentimental, tragic verses dedicated to a victim of the famine leaving his home, his dead wife and baby for the New World.

This leaves me with four more books to bundle into the hold-all. I confess I am stumped. I might take Thomas Hardy's *The Woodlanders*, but I think it would make me unbearably homesick, so these six much-loved volumes will do. I must go back to looking out of the window or copy my friend who has done that journey and find a pack of cards for a spot of Patience to pass the time till the samovar comes round again.

BEST GARDENING BOOKS

There are enough books on gardening to fill miles of shelves and they proliferate at an alarming rate. In the October issue of *The Garden* there is a list of 706 NEW titles on subjects as diverse as *Vascular Plants of Minnesota* to *Cites Cactaceae Check List* via *Fern Names and Their Meanings* and *A Key to Egyptian Grasses*. Add them to those already in print and you will be totally fuddled and have years of reading ahead.

To choose a favourite from such a bewildering variety is almost impossible. I imagine that the *Desert Island Discs* rule, where you are not allowed the Bible or Shakespeare, applies. That eliminates the loved reference books: the RHS *Dictionary*, Bean, Hillier's *Manual*, even Graham Thomas's sixteen volumes of distilled wisdom. Having sadly put these aside I find I like the old books best. Like old cookery books, they are quite different from those published now. They were ordinary book shape, the text was printed on thick, almost blotting, paper. There were no photographs, or a few hopelessly bad ones in black and white with a glimpse of forgotten elms beyond the garden wall. They are a pure pleasure to read.

In the last few years we have been bombarded by the new style of gardening books. They have grown in size as well as numbers. They are too heavy to hold, so shiny they make you blink and the photographers (they are mostly photographs) can't have a decent night's rest in May and early June as they dash from Cornwall to Sutherland while the fashionable flowers are out. Striped tulips, striped roses, alchemilla, crambe and allium must be caught in their prime. The wielder of the camera pauses just long enough to add the Kiftsgate rose with its mates Bobbie James and Wedding Day breaking down apple trees in the old orchard.

All very wonderful but I would like to see these gardens in August when the photographers have gone away.

With some famous exceptions I don't want such books myself, but I am thankful that they exist because very soon they are reduced to half price and sell like hot cakes in the shop at Chatsworth.

So, back to the old friends. I love *Potpourri From a Surrey Garden* by Mrs C. W. Earle, first published in 1897. It is sprinkled with reassuring turn-of-the-century advice on bringing up children, food and health as well as sensible words on gardening.

In the days when they lived in the same vicarage for decades reverend gentlemen produced some lovely books on flowers. Try *In a Gloucestershire Garden* by the Reverend Henry N. Ellacombe, *A Prospect of Flowers* by the Reverend Andrew Young, and latterly the Reverend Keble Martin's best-seller *The Concise British Flora*, a worthy successor to those two blessed volumes of my childhood by Bentham & Hooker.

These aren't gardening books, you'll say, because they are about wild flowers. But tell me of a garden today which dares not have an ever-growing plot of corncockles, poppies, pink campion and clover?

E. A. Bowles and his crocus, V. Sackville-West, that mistress of English who set a gardening fashion sixty years ago which is still going at full steam ahead – the list of loved ones grows. But just wait till you open *The Anatomy of Dessert* by Edward Bunyard, 1929. Let him describe the minute difference between varieties of peaches, the very week at which they are at the zenith of deliciousness, the way a melon should be handled and the smell of a perfect fig.

In doing so he conjures up the dream garden, its greenhouses, hot beds, heated walls, fruit cage, nuttery and of course the sublime head gardener, who produces these marvels to the minute for the delight of the owner and his guests.

There is no question of anything so vulgar as selling the delectable produce to people who might not appreciate their finer points. Mr Bunyard could not have left home for so much as a day between May and October or he would have missed the prime moment of one or other of his fruits.

Sometimes he is lyrical. In the chapter on pears he writes: 'Happy those who were present when Doyenne de Comice first gave up its luscious juice to man. Here at last was the ideal realised, that perfect combination of flavour, aroma and texture of which man had long dreamed.' And so he describes all the fruits grown in this country, denigrating or eulogising according to his taste.

A more matter-of-fact help for amateurs and professionals alike is *The Small Garden* by Brigadier C. E. Lucas Phillips. How I wish I had met this man whose handsome face is on the last page of my paperback of 1962, now nicely browning at the edges.

He is at his best when describing the downside of his subject. Pest No. 1, he says, is the jobbing gardener. If he had lived till now I wonder if he would have said it is the strimmer?

The chapter called 'The Enemy in Detail' and the treatment thereof is so funny and so well written it carries you along like a thriller. What other gardening writer would describe cuckoo spit thus: 'Inside a mass of frothy spittle is a curious soft creature which, on disturbance, will attempt to escape by weak hops.' The Brigadier tells you all you need to know. Seek no further and send the rest of your books to the jumble.

Now for THE favourite – about a kitchen garden, which I prefer to lawns and flower beds.

It is *The Tale of Peter Rabbit* by Beatrix Potter. Held in the palm of the hand, the luxury of wasted space on the pages, the razor-sharp narrative, the warning by the hero's mother not to go into the neighbouring garden because his father was put in a pie there by the gardener's wife, makes you long to see what the place was like. You must read several pages before you arrive there while anticipation mounts. How much better than being begged to visit with opening hours and price of admission attached. I'm sure Mr McGregor would never have allowed people in and would have attacked the British public with his rake or any other weapon close at hand.

Beatrix Potter is not only my favourite author, she is my favourite artist. The illustrations have the magic quality of leaving a lot to the imagination. You are only allowed a corner of the cucumber frame, a couple of pots of chrysanths (no flowers on them luckily), some meagre cabbages, a gooseberry bush, a little pond, one robin and three sparrows. But you can picture the whole through the Westmoreland mist.

The gooseberries, whose net impedes the escaping rabbit, are not Leveller or any such shiny and tasteless invention. They are red and hairy, Bunyard's 'ambulant fruit', good enough to please the master himself.

The two classic edgings to the vegetable beds are beautifully drawn, stone for a stone country and box, which looks right everywhere.

I confess that nostalgia plays a part in my love for this book. Mr McGregor's dibber, a wooden wheelbarrow, a real besom, real flower pots and a proper tin watering can are balm to the eyes of this old-age pensioner. A proper gate too, made on the place and not bought from a garden centre.

Peter feasts on lettuces, French beans and radishes till he feels sick. He goes in search of parsley to settle his stomach and comes across a pond. He can't (but we can) enjoy its construction of this Lake District stone, no concrete to be seen, and the water lilies and flag iris which grow in it. The trouble is a white cat studying the goldfish whose tail 'twitches as if it were alive'. She is as much of a threat to a rabbit as Mr McGregor himself. The relief when our hero just manages to escape after so many hazards is enormous.

But it is the image of that northern garden which has stayed in my mind's eye all my life and it is without doubt my favourite.

FOURTEEN FRIENDS
by James Lees-Milne

James Lees-Milne was looking for a title for his latest book. We were discussing it and one of my granddaughters asked what it was about. Fourteen friends, I said, all dead. Without hesitation she said 'Stale Mates'. An excellent title, I thought, before I read it. Dead the mates may be, but stale they are not. Brought to life as the author knew them, they are described in his inimitable way. He remembers an absurd or sad detail which stays in the mind and nails some facet of the personality of his subject to a T.

I was interested to know about the hardships of John Fowler's early life, of which I knew nothing. I often wondered who his face reminded me of and J L-M has it with Tenniel's Duchess in *Alice in Wonderland*. Latterly, he tells us, courage was necessary on the part of the client to ask John to work on a house. Courage was needed to be his servitor. I carried his patterns for him when we were doing up a house belonging to the National Trust. He sent me scurrying up and down the Long Gallery at Sudbury, drawing curtains to get a certain light, undrawing them, pinning bits of stuff here and there and moving furniture at his command. It was no good crying for mercy. He would have given a pitying look at such frailty when, already mortally ill, his whole being was focused on the job in hand. But when we got home in the evening his barked out orders were forgotten and we laughed till bedtime. J L-M's portrait of John describes him perfectly and is one of the best in the book.

Kathleen Kennet* discovered that J L–M was asked by *The Times* to write her obituary. She bombarded him with letters full of details about her achievements, even pursuing him by post to Italy to keep him up to the mark lest he should leave out a plum or two. It would have been easier if she had written her own obituary, like distinguished people write their entries in *Who's Who*. I am quite glad that KK is one of the mates I did not know. Yet J L–M loved her.

Vita Sackville-West is another matter. She was the inventor of a style of gardening which is still mimicked all over the world, a poet and an original, but seeing her craggy face and shapeless form in the photograph we know so well it is impossible to believe that she inspired such passion as is described. But we must believe it, because no one was immune. Men and women alike fell under her spell. Her husband referred to her affairs as her 'muddles'. So muddled am I by the variety of her conquests that I long for explanations. Why did she have to 'masquerade as a wounded Tommy in the streets of London' to delight Violet Trefusis? At a charity concert where Vita recited, Lady Crewe, the organiser, announced that 'she would pass the Queen round to the left like port'. J L–M 'remained a faithful fan' and exhorts us to do likewise. I just wish I had met this heady mixture of Clark Gable and Marlene Dietrich with 'eyes of glowing coal' and an exceptionally beautiful voice.

The description of Henry Yorke/Green† makes me wonder why J L–M took so much trouble over him and wonder even more how people could have enjoyed his dreary novels, the quotes from which are dispiriting in the extreme. He states that Henry had 'very beautiful manners'. This sentence might have been left out had he been a fellow guest when the Yorkes stayed with us in Ireland many years ago. Henry sat in a heap for a week and did not speak except to say, when gazing out of the window at the rain, how much he hated the country. His wife was indeed saintly to look after this morose man until he died.

Two who were changed out of all recognition as time slipped away were James Pope-Hennessy[‡] and Everard Radcliffe. The former was beautiful, funny and clever with intuitive charm and was an inspired writer. His friendship with J L-M had its ups and downs, and some of the downs must have been hard to forgive, but 'his merriment was infectious, his charm insidious'. On a National Trust jaunt to Suffolk he says to the author: 'Being with you is like being with myself, only nicer.' No wonder Jim rejoiced in such company. Alas, drugs, drink, and 'mad larking' turned Jamesey into a near-demon who met a grisly end. J L-M's last glimpse of his beloved companion of better times, from the top of a bus in Trafalgar Square, makes the blood run cold.

Radcliffe inherited Rudding Park near Harrogate. He was as much in love with the place as Vita had been with Knole and devoted his life to the well-being of its estate and to adding works of art to embellish the house and garden. When money troubles caught up with his extravagances he played a pro-tracted game of cat and mouse with the National Trust over his inheritance. On the point of signing, and without a word to the Trust, Everard put the place on the market and decamped to Switzerland, leaving the love of his life to become the inevitable conference centre. His story is nearly as sad as poor Jamesey's.

Fourteen Friends is compulsive reading. The author's gener-osity of spirit shines through the descriptions of the disparate characters we come to know. He notes the faults as well as the virtues of his mates, but he does not criticise, and loves them in spite of all. Lucky people.

* Kathleen Kennet, sculptor. Married (1) Captain R. E. Scott of the
Antarctic (2) 1st Lord Kennet.
† Henry Yorke, novelist under the pseudonym Henry Green.
‡ James Pope-Hennessy, biographer. Murdered 1974.

A MINGLED MEASURE
by James Lees-Milne

Everyone who enjoyed the other 'Kubla Khan' diaries will fasten with joy onto this volume which covers the years 1953–71. J L-M was no longer working full time for the National Trust, so there are no more hilarious descriptions of meetings with owners of houses considered for handing over. But it is a wonderful picture of the life of this observant man who describes places, artists, writers, neighbours, friends and relations and allows us into some of his own thoughts.

Forty years on, some people seem as extinct as dodos – Eddie Marsh, for instance, who criticised so sharply a manuscript of J L-M's that it made the author miserable for days; a rag-and-bone man uttering his cries in Thurloe Square and Hilaire Belloc setting himself on fire by his candle while staying with a friend. J L-M arrived at Nice airport at 3.40 a.m. and walked the six miles to Alvilde's (his wife since 1951) house in Roquebrune. The installation of electric light at Westwood Manor in Wiltshire is noted and deplored. These are memories of a long lost world.

The L-Ms lived at Roquebrune for ten years, she passport and tax-bound, he going to and from his flat in Thurloe Square. They hob-nobbed with the locals, from Prince Rainier to the curé's cousin (her mother kept a tame hen whose tail feathers trimmed the frame of her photo – the hen's I mean, not the mother's), the Graham Sutherlands, the local goatherd and annual visitors to the coast including Winston and Clementine Churchill. There lived a witch in the village and Somerset Maugham down the road. When a mistral blew up, spreading sparks which caused a disastrous fire over their garden of little ledges up the steep hillside to the very walls of their house, I didn't mind as much as I should have done.

In 1964 the L-Ms moved to Alderley Grange in Gloucestershire. 'The perfect mid-Georgian house', wrote Candida Lycett-Green. 'Inside a grand and generous staircase rose from a pale stone-flagged hall patterned with black stone diamonds.' Here Alvilde's twin accomplishments of cooking and gardening were appreciated by all who had the luck to taste or see the results of her work. In spite of frequent visits to London for the opera (where they always seemed to land in the Royal Box), plays, exhibitions and some committees of the National Trust which still bound him to that organisation, one feels that the diarist was really at home in that magic part of the country.

He walked in the woods with his whippets and in spite of saying he always looked at his feet he noticed everything. The more he noticed and loved what he saw the more gloomy he became over what was happening to England. He often found himself among friends who bewailed the state of the country, politically and aesthetically. His favourite places were threat-ened by motorways or drowning in a reservoir – even a new cowshed filled him with gloom. Watching the 1972 TUC Congress on the television convinced him that 'communism must come to this country within twenty-five years'. I do hope he is comforted by the fact that there are only three years to go and it somehow doesn't seem likely. The same year Denys Sutton 'thinks an immediate revolution possible and an author-itarian government absolutely essential. George Weidenfeld said exactly the same thing a week ago.' Well, well.

Later that month 'Caroline Somerset took the Weidenfelds

round Badminton and Lady W. said to C., "Did it take a long time to find such a beautiful house?"' I expect that was several Lady Weidenfelds ago.

A friend who had been to Chequers told J L–M that Mr Heath, unable to bear sleeping in the room which had been Mr Wilson's, chose another. That is the most human thing I have ever heard about Mr Heath.

'Went last night to the Handley-Read collection of Victoriana at the Diploma Gallery. The hideousness and stuffiness of the furniture and ornaments beyond belief – sheer lodging house, and no wonder both Handley-Reads committed suicide last year.'

I've never heard of the Handley-Reads or their horrid collection, but the aesthete in J L–M was not surprised by their grisly end after one glance at what the poor things had accumulated.

People who have grown up since the years of the war and immediately after can have little idea of what this country owes to J L–M. He rescued, almost single-handedly, scores of delectable buildings, each one unique. It was before the word 'heritage' was chucked around to justify keeping everything from a badger sett to a banjo. No one bothered then. Pull them down, leave them to rot, these buildings will never be needed again, was the attitude of those in command. Had it not been for his dogged persistence against all the odds, including public opinion, local government opinion and up, up to the Cabinet itself, none of whom had the slightest interest in things of beauty and legislated accordingly, the poor old heritage would have been a great deal poorer. J L–M is far too modest to underline any of his achievements, but he is lauded by everyone who remembers them.

In my ignorance I could have done with some guidance here and there. Who was Father Illtud Evans, whose death saddened (only momentarily, I admit) J L–M? Why did Monica

Baldwin want help? I long to know more about Bertie Towers, who bought ancestors to go with a manor house and of whom 'Alec Clifton Taylor had little opinion'.

There are a number of spelling mistakes, wrong dates and asterisks the second time a person is mentioned and some places don't appear in the index – unworthy of the house of John Murray and surely not the fault of the writer. Never mind. I read it with intense pleasure because *A Mingled Measure* brings J L-M into the room, and who could be a better companion on an autumn evening?

DEAR MARY
by Mary Killen

What trouble people get themselves in, what mix-ups and muddles, and not only in 'social life' where the chilling word etiquette still appears to rule. (I thought it had gone with the war: wrong as usual.) Every hour of every day the most worrying things seem to happen.

Many of them arise from the inhibited British being unable to face unpleasantness head on. It would be much easier to say to an offender 'you smell' or 'please stop eating in such a disgusting way', but we have been brought up not to do that. Instead we ask Mary Killen and she knows just how to smooth the way, whatever the problem.

I have great sympathy with some of her correspondents – the unlucky SM of Wiltshire, for instance, who sat next to the Foreign Secretary at dinner, didn't recognise him, asked what he did, failed to hear the word Foreign and spent the rest of dinner discussing shorthand typing. Too late to ask for advice, I am afraid.

ES of W11 has joined a health club in Notting Hill and lives in terror of seeing Antonia Fraser bare. You must buy the book to see the inspired answer to this one.

Since beloved David Cecil died I am no longer troubled by the problem of CS of Islington who asks, 'What is the correct way of removing spittle which someone has accidentally spat onto one's face while talking enthusiastically?' So I didn't bother to read the answer.

I pity poor AM of Fonthill whose wife is addicted to telephoning faraway friends before the cheap time. If my father had caught me doing that, his reaction would have been to hand out the short, sharp shock treatment which a Home Secretary advocated for certain offences a few years ago. I don't suppose nice Mary would ever suggest anything so drastic, but I heartily recommend it to AM.

LG of Ludgershall asks how to stop her weekend guests stealing books. I'm afraid that is a dreadfully difficult question, especially as they always bag the most readable. Mary's solution, copied from the late Lord Moyne, tells LG to have a supply of stiff cards and make the borrower write his name, address and date of borrowing and put it in the space in the shelf where the book was. A good plan, but not as threatening as that of my sister when she was married to the same Lord Moyne. Their bookplates read, 'This book was stolen from Bryan and Diana Guinness.'

The perennial agony of forgetting names is the subject of two letters. DL of SW1 suffers from it, and as he/she works in publishing and I presume has to attend such ghoulish entertainments as book launches, he/she will be delighted with Mary's clever solution. But what struck me about his/her letter was not the problem but the fact that he/she states, 'Flattery and ego-stroking are integral parts of my job.' How I should love to meet this individual, surely the rarest of birds in that profession where bosses and employees all seem to lack the most basic good manners (always excepting the late Jock Murray).

The best thing about being old is having grown out of minding most of the social pitfalls described in these letters. In years gone by I was as vulnerable as the next person and one frightful evening stands out. I found myself sitting at dinner next to M. Pompidou, then President of France. He spoke no English, I no French. Our host sat opposite us across a narrow table, greatly amused by our predicament. We sat there crumbling bread and trying to smile at each other. Dear Mary, where were you that evening?

I ONCE MET

edited by Richard Ingrams

The *Oldie's* *I Once Met* is a game of Consequences full of unexpected twists and turns. If only the famous had known they were being met by someone who was going to describe the encounter years later they would surely have behaved differently.

One exception, I guess, is Field-Marshal Lord Montgomery of Alamein, who would still have barked out a ticking-off to the unlucky boy from Westminster Abbey Choir School in which he was interested. In 1953 he more or less ordered the boys to take photographs of him and his page standing in a nearby doorway dressed to the nines for the Coronation. David Ransom was one of them. The next day the *Daily Mail* carried a photograph of the scene. In the foreground stood young David bent over his box Brownie camera. Alas, one of his socks had collapsed round an ankle. Such sloppiness was too much for the old soldier and the next day the poor fellow was summoned to the headmaster's study to face Monty himself, who reprimanded him in military fashion.

Many meetings with famous actors and actresses are described. In my experience such encounters are nearly always disappointing. It is better to watch them plying their trade than to meet them face to face. Selwyn Powell saw a brilliantly funny performance by Harpo Marx in a variety show at the Palace Theatre. He followed him back to the Savoy to photograph him for *Picture Post* – but not one word does Mr Powell remember of what the great comedian said. (Now I come to think of it, wasn't Harpo the one who couldn't speak?)

When A. N. Wilson was twelve he called on L. S. Lowry to seek advice on painting. The house in Salford was coal-black outside and chaotic inside. The artist, 'his white hair *en brosse* like a polar bear's', told the boy he preferred the Sunderland seaside because he couldn't paint trees. Twelve-year-old boys don't know when to leave, so after hours of his unplanned company Lowry said he would see A. N. back to Manchester and delivered him to his mother who was having tea at Marshall & Snelgrove. In this case it would have been interesting for the roles to be reversed so we could know what L. S. thought of A. N., who didn't dare go back for the portfolio of paintings he had left behind.

Oscar Hammerstein cured Donald Sutherland's stomach ulcers by a prescription of a soluble capsule and a packet of Dreft washing powder taken daily 'for a while'.

John Mortimer met Robert Graves on a sofa (I told you it was Consequences). Graves said to Mortimer, 'Jesus Christ, of course, lived to the age of eighty, when he went to China and discovered spaghetti.' Jo Grimond, also on the sofa, asked, 'In which gospel do we read that Jesus Christ went to China and discovered spaghetti?' 'It's not in a gospel. It's a well-known fact of history,' answered the poet.

Vincent Brome, an ardent admirer, interviewed the dying H. G. Wells. Wells let loose a diatribe against God, the monarchy, Parliament and Bernard Shaw. Women, whom Brome imagined Wells had been rather fond of, were a necessary encumbrance to the life of a man. Humanity itself was dismissed as 'a parcel of sweeps'. Brome left, disillusioned.

The Last Squire of Erddig was a natural for the series. When Mr and Mrs Michael Strachan went to see the house newly opened to the public, they found the Squire struggling with a clockwork spit from which hung a stuffed pheasant. He asked where they were from. 'Scotland,' they said. 'So you know David Baird?' They did. On the strength of this unlikely exchange the Strachans suggested taking him out for dinner. A series of disasters with boarded-up restaurants followed, ending with the hospitable Squire asking them to stay the night in his nearby cottage. His last guest had been a tinker: 'splendid fellow, but needed a bath'. So did the purple sheets in the spare room, and the Strachans were thoroughly flea-bitten.

Sir Alec Guinness, Fangio, Lord Wavell, Matisse, Graham Greene, Hitler, Sir Jack Hobbs, Richard Widmark and Sir Matt Busby all come out of it rather well. Philip Larkin, Ronnie Kray and E. M. Forster don't. Neither does Randolph Churchill.

More Cartoons, also edited by Richard Ingrams, and *The Oldie Dictionary of Our Time*, edited by Mike Barfield, were included for review with *I Once Met*. Alas, I don't understand either of them, in spite of trying quite hard. But I do understand and can thoroughly recommend *I Once Met*.

THE NATIONAL TRUST MANUAL OF HOUSEKEEPING

by Sheila Stainton and Hermione Sandwith

Not since Mrs Beeton's *Household Management* of 1861 and its many updated editions has such a complete guide to house-keeping (or house-*maiding* rather, as surely house*keeping* includes food and the kitchen) been available to those who have charge of what are now called historic houses. Through this absorbing book the housemaid herself is turned into the next best thing to a museum curator.

After forty-one years at the job I am shaken by the number of things which can go wrong. I am conscious of sins of omission which spell disaster. The mysteries of how, or, more importantly, how not, to treat the objects in your care are explained in fine detail and we learn the latest methods of conservation and the professional care of all manner of things. The way to clean rooms from cellars to attics, and the infinite variety of their contents from model ships to ancient textiles, big game trophies to marble floors, are described. The methods set out are by perfectionists for perfectionists. No short cuts, no sweeping the dust under the carpet. The dire consequences of slacking are a purple warning to all who care for 'things'.

The book is aimed at houses which are 'put to bed', i.e. dustsheeted from top to bottom, for the winter. Houses which are lived in often have their busiest time round Christmas so some of the rules do not apply to them.

The houses were built, decorated and furnished at the behest of their owners to be lived in. The owners had families which meant children, dogs, canaries, white mice and other pests which discomfited the starched housekeepers of yesteryear. Yet the houses survived with a surprising number of artefacts intact. The deeper you get into the book the more amazed you are that there is anything left at all and the guiltier you feel about actually using a room or its furniture.

Hide and seek, sardines, kick the can, catapults, roller skating down passages, billiard fives and other pastimes of successive generations of children belonging to the house would drive the authors of this book mad. What would they make of the 6th Duke of Devonshire ('The Bachelor Duke', 1790–1858) writing of his childhood at Hardwick Hall: 'I turned the recess [of the dining room], in which the billiard table now stands, into a kind of menagerie: a fishing net nailed up under the curtain confined the rabbits, hedgehogs, squirrels, guinea-pigs and white mice that were the joy of my life from eight to twelve years old. The smell caused by these quadrupeds and their vegetable diet was overpowering; but I would have been very surprised had any objection been made to their residence here.'

The gallant housemaids worked away through the rough and tumble of family life, turning huge mattresses daily, and carrying hot water to distant bedrooms. They served a long and stern apprenticeship which taught them much of what we learn from this book.

The hazards of keeping the simplest things in order appear to be overwhelming. If it is too difficult consult an expert.

We know that light is the enemy (Granny used to say that moonlight was even more destructive than sunlight) and blinds must be kept down. We must beware of 'dust and airborne pollution, fluctuation of temperature and humidity, attack by moth and worm'. If the rooms get too dry my instinct is to open the windows – but in flies the carpet beetle. Having made a meal of the spireas in the garden he turns his attention to the Axminsters. Birds also fly in so you must put a net over the windows. In this house, they choose the best pictures on which to make messes. Thinking of messes, I looked up 'dog' in the index for advice on the inevitable where they are concerned, but could only find 'dog-eared'.

And what about the infamous bacon beetle? I bet you didn't know that this little epicure, denied the food after which he is named because there is no breakfast in National Trust houses, likes nothing better than to gorge himself on a globule of fat from the belly of your best stuffed fish.

If the rooms are too damp surely the answer is to light the fire. But if you have steel grates you must engage a metal conservator to put them right in the morning. That would be expensive at Chatsworth as he would be a daily visitor in the winter.

Outdoor shoes are banned. Dust-proof mats do their job perfectly, but the way your shoes stick to them gives you the terrifying sensation of being unable to run away from a pursuer in a bad dream.

Disease is rife among inanimate objects. There is a bronze disease and a pewter disease, mother-of-pearl gets Byne's disease, and ink attacks the paper on which it is written. Minerals are not always healthy. The diseased stones at Chatsworth so enthralled my sister Nancy that she described their malady in one of her books, *The Pursuit of Love*.

We have come a long way since Granny went round Hardwick with a little mallet banging the furniture to give concussion to the woodworm.

I greatly admire the National Trust for setting such standards. I know they carry them out because I have seen them at it. It is going to be a job to live up to them. After reading this book I am going to try to be acid-free myself, to eschew the company of exuberant children and animals, and generally look to my housekeeping.

There is a mine of information here and the list of suppliers of equipment and materials and their addresses is an invaluable work of reference in itself. I shall look after my copy with proper care.

HOW TO RUN A STATELY HOME
by John, Duke of Bedford and George Mikes

All Russells are clever and original, and the 13th Duke of Bedford is no exception. His lovely little book, *How to Run a Stately Home*, has been re-published in paperback fourteen years after it first appeared. It will give immense pleasure to all in the trade and to the millions of people who support it.

Let us remind ourselves why the Duke threw himself into the stately business with such gusto, shocking his peers who disapproved of the publicity he sought and so readily found.

In 1953 his father died unexpectedly, and he found himself the owner of Woburn: house, works of art, garden, park, farms, woods, and the rest that attaches itself to such a place; and there was a bill for the regulation £5,000,000 death duties. Lesser men would have taken the advice of the family solicitor, sold up and fled to Monte Carlo: not the Duke of Bedford. Immediately he began to feel the irresistible pull of the Territorial Imperative.

Reading a book on monkeys he realised why he was determined to hang on to it. 'It all started with the monkeys who each insisted on having his own special private place up in the trees of the primordial forests. We humans have inherited this healthy and natural instinct from our ancestors: we must each have our own place. This territorial imperative is, basically and ultimately, the impulse that makes me go on fighting. I want my own place. This place happens to be it and I am determined to keep it. I am the owner . . . of a magnificent Stately Home; I am also the monkey on the tree.' He set about making Woburn the most famous and visited house in England, and in no time he succeeded.

The Duke had owned the place for eight years when he wrote the book and much experience had been gained. By then he felt qualified to tell the others how to do it, and in the nicest possible way he has done so. It is remarkable how his fiercest critics have come to heel.

His advice to ditherers who could not decide whether to open their houses was 'go ahead', and they all have. *But first build your lavatories.* They all have. A friend of mine who is a distinguished architect tells me that his most usual commission by far is for lavatories. The Duke goes on to the tea room, the complement of lavatories (or have I put the cart before the horse as it were?). These two are the prime necessity for a successful Stately. Then comes the essential shop.

After you have given thought and energy, as well as having spent a great deal of money, on this holy trinity, you must pay attention to the hangers-on: the house, garden and park. However, having got the first three right the latter will fall into place beautifully.

Why do people come? the Duke asks himself. Because they have got a car and they must drive it somewhere. They can spend a day in the English equivalent of Disneyland, a world of make-believe, of Rembrandts and Sèvres, state rooms and tapestries which have nothing to do with reality. No one can imagine putting a baby to bed or knitting in front of the fire in such rooms and so they are transported to the unfamiliar plane of someone else's rarefied life. In an hour or two the visitor can be back in the womb-like security of his own car. He has seen wonderful things; he is glad to have seen them but the last thing he wants is the responsibility of owning them.

That may be true, but what brought the crowds to Woburn

was the benign and friendly presence of the Duke himself, exuding his fondness for the human race, always on hand to chat, to sign and to sell. He was Exhibit A in wonderful surroundings.

After fourteen years the language seems a little old-fashioned. Stately Homes have become Historic Houses. Their owners are no longer people like the Duke of Bedford but trustees who, for some unknown reason, always come from London. Lavatories were Toilets for years, now they are Facilities and are apt to sprout bossy notices like Now Wash Your Hands. Tea is still tea as far as I know, but the part of the estate which is open is a Unit, a Scene or a Complex. Souvenirs are Gifts now, except on Sundays when they must revert to being Souvenirs to satisfy the Alice in Wonderland trading laws.

The word 'heritage' only appears once in this book and then in its proper context. Environment, conservation, vandals and leisure are not mentioned at all. Good.

And so we learn How To Do It. Having done it, the Duke left the Stately scene as he had arrived. Grandson of the Flying Duchess, son of the Duke whose best friend was a spider, he is much missed as the undisputed innovator in the little world of Houses and Castles Open To The Public.

I suppose our friends are as honest as the next lot, but it is odd how books disappear. Not the fat and heavy biographies of politicians in two volumes which no one could read in bed (or out of it), but the attractive ones you pick up over a weekend and don't have time to finish. They vanish like summer snow and although I sometimes search every room in our huge house I never find the missing loved one. So I have resorted to selfishness, gathering irreplaceable volumes in my room where it is unlikely that anyone would bag one, even from the pile on the floor. Perhaps my unstealables would not appeal to everyone. *Fowls and Geese and How to Keep Them* (1935, 1/6d and worth every penny); *Book* by Lady Clodagh Anson and *Another Book* by the same author – classic descriptions of Anglo-Irish life before the Great War; nice, thin 1930s Betjemans, *Continual Dew* and *Mount Zion*; the real *Oxford Book of English Verse* on India paper, the poems chosen by that professor whose name is a mixture of duvet and sofa, Sir Arthur Quiller-Couch; *What Shall We Have Today?* by X. Marcel Boulestin (what did X. stand for?), and *The Life of Ronald Knox* given to me by good, kind Evelyn Waugh, who knew I can hardly read, so mercifully the pages have no words on them. They are all blank. A book which would disappear by next Monday if left in a visitor's room is *A Late Beginner*, Priscilla Napier's autobiography. Brought up in Egypt and seeing pyramids against the sunset from her nursery window, she asked, 'What are they, Nanny?' 'Tombs, dear. Where's your other sock?' You can't do better than that and I do not want to lose it. The works of George Ewart Evans are next to *The Secret Orchard of Roger Ackerley* by Diana Petre, *White Mischief*, *The Prince, the Showgirl and Me*, *The Day of Reckoning*,

Rio Grande's Last Race and books with pages covered in print, dash it, by E. Waugh, P. Leigh Fermor and J. Lees-Milne. Most precious is *The Last Train to Memphis: The Rise of Elvis Presley*. If that goes I give up.

PATRICK LEIGH FERMOR* AT EIGHTY-FIVE

Paddy Leigh Fermor eighty-five? Not possible! Yet I am told he was born in 1915 and that it is his birthday today. Hardly a grey hair, upright, trudging for miles up and down dale or swimming for hours according to whether he is in England or Greece, he is adored by my youngest grandchild as well as his own generation; an ageless, timeless hero to us all.

I first saw him nearly fifty years ago at a fancy dress party in London. He was a Roman gladiator armed with a net and trident and his get-up suited him very well. I had heard of him, of course. Everyone had. By 1956 the story of his exploits in occupied Crete had been made into the film *Ill Met By Moonlight* with Dirk Bogarde as Paddy. It is still shown on telly from time to time.

It was in 1942 and '43, living so closely to them in shared danger, that he became deeply devoted to the Cretans and the bond between him and his old comrades is as strong as ever.

Paddy and his great friend Xan Fielding† had lived in the Cretan mountains disguised as shepherds (I wouldn't put him in charge of my sheep, but never mind) for eighteen months, in constant danger of being caught by the enemy, before the spectacular coup in 1944 when he and Billy Moss, an officer in the Coldstream Guards, kidnapped the German commander, General Kreipe, which earned him the DSO. Their prize was bundled into the back of the German official car while Billy Moss drove them through a town in the black-out, Paddy sitting on the front seat wearing the general's cap in case anyone should glance at the occupants.

After a four-hour climb on foot to the comparative safety of a remote cave in the mountains, they spent eighteen days together going from one hiding place to another and sharing the only blanket during the freezing nights. When the sun rose on the first morning and lit up the snow on the summit of Mount Ida, the general gazed at the scene and quoted a verse of an ode by Horace. His captor completed the next six stanzas. Such a duet under such circumstances must be unique in the history of war.

When he was sixteen and a half he was sacked from King's School Canterbury for holding hands with the greengrocer's daughter, sitting on a crate of veg. What to do next? A military crammer was tried but didn't seem to suit, so he mooned around London making friends who lasted a lifetime. At the age of eighteen ('and three quarters' he says for accuracy) he yearned to go to Greece. He could not afford the fare so he walked there. What a lesson to young people now who write to strangers asking for money to enable them to travel. Years later his walk inspired *A Time of Gifts* and *Between the Woods and the Water*, perhaps the two most acclaimed of all his books, winners of endless literary prizes and translated into more languages than probably even Paddy knows. His love of Greece prompted him and Joan to build their glorious house on the sea at Kardamyli, living in a tent and working with the masons till it grew into the idyllic place where they live now.

He is one of those rare birds who is exactly the same with whoever he is talking to. Children recognise him as a kindred spirit. With his formidable scholarship and prodigious memory he is just as able to spout Edward Lear or 'There was an old Woman as I've heard tell, who went to market her eggs for to sell' as Marvell or Shakespeare via Noël Coward for grown-ups.

I have got stacks of letters from him. They usually begin 'In Tearing Haste' or 'In Unbelievable Haste' and the writing jolly well shows it. This one is dated 1956, when I evidently had omitted to ask him to give a hand at my funeral: 'Your lovely letter was marred by this business about pall bearers. You tell me all about enlisting John and Xan with never a hint of asking me, when I am exactly the right height, own a dark suit and a measured tread and would really look sad.' Forty-four years on, this is a bit near the knuckle.

He wrote me a hilarious account of a disastrous visit to Somerset 'not Willy to me, alas' Maugham at the Villa Mauresque. He was taken there by Ann Fleming. All went well the first day, but soon he got deep in the mire by imitating someone who stammered. As this was an affliction of Maugham's and one about which he was extremely sensitive, it was too much for his host 'who offered a limp handshake and said "Well" (I won't indicate the stutter, too late, alas!) "I'll say goodnight and goodbye too, as I'll still be in bed when you leave."' Worse was to come. 'I had a new case with a zip and when I zipped it up the beautiful Irish linen sheet with WSM embroidered on it caught and was torn with a rending noise from top to bottom. There was nothing for it but to do a bunk.' He was cheered to learn 'that Cyril [Connolly] had once been made to leave the Villa Mauresque for picking and eating the last avocado on the single tree'.

These sort of letters make me look forward to the post.

Try and get him to sing his translations in Italian of 'John Peel' and 'Widdecombe Fair' – John Peel's hounds, Ruby, Ranter, Ringwood and True, turn into Rubin, Vantardo, Rondo Bosco Campinelli and Fidele,

Tom Pierce, Tom Pierce, lend me your grey mare
All along, down along, out along lea

becomes

Tommaso Pierce, Tommaso Pierce, prestami tua grigia
  giumenta
Tutti lungo, fuori lungo, giù lungo prato

and Cobley's gang are

. . . Gugliemo Brewer, Giacopo Stewer, Pietro Gurney,
Pietro Davey, Daniele Whiddon and Enrico 'awke
Ed il vecchio zio Tommaso Cobley e tutti quanti, etc.

– and 'It's a Long Way to Tipperary' in Hindustani. Or the longest palindrome 'Live dirt up a side track carted is a putrid evil' delivered, for some unknown reason, in the broadest Gloucestershire accent. Just the entertainment for a winter's night.

Andrew regards him as a latter-day Byron and thinks it fitting that Byron and Paddy share the same publisher. Handsome, funny, energetic and original, he is a brilliant, shining star – how lucky my family and I are to have had such a friend for so long. Happy birthday, Paddy!

* Patrick Leigh Fermor (1915–2011). Writer, traveller, war hero and polymath.
† Xan Fielding (1918–91). Heroic wartime secret agent and author.

BEING PAINTED
by Annigoni and Lucian Freud

We had seen some portraits which Annigoni had done and Andrew decided to commission him to paint me. I had to go to his studio in London every day for a month. We couldn't talk to each other since he spoke little English, and I no Italian. The telephone often rang and I would answer it for him; it was usually a girlfriend.

There was no discussion about how I would pose; he was the Master and he would decide. He almost always painted an imaginary landscape in the background with a fisherman, which was a sort of signature. I got the distinct impression that painting me was just a chore for him; he was not enjoying it much.

Lucian Freud's picture of me, painted four or five years later, was a different matter. Lucian is an old friend and a charming, generous man (at least to his friends). I think I was the third member of our family that he painted. I went to his studio for three hours every morning when I was in London, over several months. I can still remember the strong smell of paint in his studio. He works very slowly, often starting from one eye. Sometimes, when I arrived, he would say, 'I had a wonderful night. I removed everything I did yesterday.' (He often works at night.) People say I look sad or bored in the painting. I defy anyone not to look a bit wooden after sitting for so long.

There were interruptions, with bailiffs calling. Lucian is a huge gambler, and his fortunes seemed to change all the time. Sometimes, because he had pawned his car, I lent him mine, and once when I arrived for a sitting he held out my car keys and said, 'This is all that's left' – the car had been stolen.

I'm not sure that I can judge the success of pictures of myself. I think my head is a little too big in the Annigoni, and perhaps his is more of a pretty picture; whereas Lucian captures the essence of people. He doesn't like anyone to see a painting before it is finished. Eventually we were allowed to look. When Andrew arrived at the studio, someone else was already there. Andrew looked long at the picture until the other man asked, 'Who is that?' 'It's my wife.' 'Well, thank God it's not mine.'

ROAD FROM THE ISLES

In the 1930s my parents bought a small island off the coast of Mull. Called Inchkenneth, it lies about a mile out to sea from the tiny village of Gribun: to the west there is no land till you reach America. It is a romantic and beautiful place and in fine weather has a serenity only found in such places which are difficult of access and empty of human beings.

The weather was all important; there was much tapping of the glass and listening to every BBC forecast, as the narrow channel between the island and Mull became very rough with little warning, and we were often cut off for days at a time. For this reason the island had to be self-supporting in the necessities of life, and could produce some luxuries as well. There was a walled kitchen garden which had been there when Dr Johnson stayed on the island in his tour of the Hebrides in the eighteenth century. Oats, hay and potatoes were grown on the small enclosed field and we had lobster pots and trawled for mackerel, and at spring tides there were even oysters and mussels for the picking. We kept chickens and ducks, so there was no shortage of eggs. Sheep and bullocks completed the farm stock and grazed the unenclosed hill.

There were three house cows. To have a continual supply of milk was the aim, of course, but the problem of calving at a certain date, never easy, was made acute by the fact that each cow had to swim to Gribun to visit the bull. Cows can swim well when they have to. There was a large sloping rock which the cow was led across, and the tide had to be just right so that with a mighty heave she was pushed into the water without too much fuss. The boat at once set off, towing the cow by a rope around her horns. All too often it started to blow a gale when this vital journey was to take place – and so another three weeks would go by until we could try again.

The result of such curiously vague mating arrangements was that one summer, when the house was full of visitors and children, all the cows were dry and there was nothing but tinned milk, which no one liked. So my mother decided to buy a goat. She found a British Saanen of uncertain ancestry and gave it to me. She was called Narny and a more charming animal you could not imagine: everyone liked her from the beginning. She was free to go where she liked, and she used to jump on to the retaining wall of a steep bank by the kitchen door to be milked – fresher milk there never was.

My mother soon added more goats to the farm stock and had some beautiful British Saanens, large and quiet, and wonderful milk producers. It was an ideal place for them as they had the run of the island, a mile long, and were able to graze on ledges and places where even the sheep did not dare go. They had bells round their necks, and the whole effect was beautiful when they were grazing on the stretches of grass and salty herbs which ran down to the sea.

I was on Inchkenneth when war was declared in September 1939 and had to go back to Oxfordshire. Naturally I could not leave my goat behind so, together with a whippet and a Labrador, we set out on a journey which, at that time, took twenty-four hours.

We left the island at 6.30 a.m. in the dark. At low tide there was a long walk over seaweed-covered rocks, and it was impossible to reach the boat without stepping into a pool or slipping over. Wet, and often grazed as well, there was another hazardous walk over the rocks on the coast of Mull to the tin hut where the car was kept. Sometimes that car was agonisingly stubborn about starting. There was no other means of transport, and it was eleven miles across Mull to Salen where the mail boat called only once a day to go to Oban, so one could be stuck for twenty-four hours if the car did not co-operate. The goat travelled in the rickety old luggage trailer covered by a tarpaulin against the driving rain.

The mail boat was well equipped for such passengers as my animals. At that time it was the only transport for all farm stock as well as humans; one could safely give anything from a bull to a book of stamps to the staff, and either would be miraculously delivered to the right person at the other end.

The boat took three hours to get to Oban, with two stops on the way, through some of the most beautiful scenery in Scotland. There was a long day to pass in Oban, as the London train did not leave till the evening. After a few weeks on the island it was always exciting to see shops again, and the goat and the dogs dutifully followed round. A greengrocer and a butcher provided their meals for the day.

It was dark again when the time came to go to the station at the other end of the harbour. Goat in the guard's van, dogs in the carriage, we settled down to one of those endless war-time journeys with a dim light and crowded train.

In the middle of the night we arrived at Stirling, where we had to change and wait for an hour for the London train. I milked the goat in the First Class Waiting Room, which I should not have done as I only had a third class ticket. Luckily, no one noticed. The dogs were delighted with their unexpected midnight drink of new milk, and, relieved and refreshed, we boarded the London train.

There was a long queue for taxis at Euston, and I was rather apprehensive that when my turn came the driver might not be too willing to take on such a curious assortment of passengers;

but luckily he turned out to be one of those cheerful Cockneys who are not put out by anything, and the four of us arrived at my sister Nancy's house in perfect order – just 9d extra on the clock. She lived in Blomfield Road and had quite a big garden, so Narny feasted on Nancy's roses. Enough pruning was done in two hours to last for a long time – as all goat and garden owners will understand.

Paddington Station was within walking distance, but the hurrying London crowds did not notice the dishevelled party of girl, goat and dogs.

Narny lived for a long time, produced twins every year and an enormous amount of milk, but I shall always remember her for her perfect behaviour on the journey from the Hebrides to her new home at Kingham in Oxfordshire.

CHILDHOOD

My childhood seems to belong to another world. Some thought our upbringing strange, even then, but we didn't – children just accept what they find.

I was born in 1920, in my parents' house in London, the youngest of a family of seven, six girls and one boy. My eldest sister, Nancy Mitford, was sixteen when I was born – then came Pam, Diana, Tom, Unity and Jessica.

My mother's dearest wish was to have a big family of boys and every time another girl was born there was bitter disappointment.

Nancy used to tell me with glee of the gloom that descended on the house when they heard of my birth.

Until I was six we lived in an Elizabethan manor house called Asthall in the beautiful Cotswold valley of the Windrush and a few years ago, when the house was for sale, the agent took my husband and me to see round it. I had only been in it once since we left to live at Swinbrook, seventy-two years before. It was a strange feeling to see the empty rooms and to remember how many people had lived there from 1919 to 1926 – seven of us children, Nanny, a nursery maid, a governess for the older ones, Mabel and her helper in the pantry, Annie the head housemaid and two young girls under her, cook and a kitchen maid, an odd man, Mr Dyer – and my father and mother. In this company our lives were secure and regular as clockwork. We had parents who were always there, and an adored Nanny who came when Diana was three months old and stayed for forty years.

'The barn', converted by my father and separate from the main house, was a haven for Nancy, Pam, Tom and Diana. They had the run of my grandfather's excellent library – Nancy and Diana always said it gave them their interest in literature. Music was my brother's passion and his piano was in this big room.

Our nursery looked out over the churchyard and we younger ones were forbidden to watch funerals, which of course made them more fascinating, and we always did. Jessica and I once fell into a newly dug grave, to the delight of Nancy who pronounced that we should have bad luck for the rest of our lives.

Our animals were as important to us as were the humans in the house – mice, guinea pigs, a piebald rat belonging to Unity, poultry and goats. The big animals of farm and stables, the garden which seemed so huge to a small child, the village beyond the churchyard, the Post Office where acid drops were 1½d a quarter in a twist of paper weighed on the same brass weighing scale as the letters – that was our world. We knew no other.

In the summer we bathed in the river and in winter we skated on the flooded frozen fields between Widford and Burford.

Nancy wrote a lot about our childhood, of course, in *The Pursuit of Love* and *Love in a Cold Climate* which, to her amazement, became best-sellers, and people still ask me, 'Was your father really like Uncle Matthew in the books?'

He was, in lots of ways. He could get terrifyingly angry and we were certainly in awe of him, but at the same time he was wonderfully funny and the source of all the jokes in the family. He and Nancy together were better than anything I've ever seen on the stage.

The fact that one couldn't always judge his mood made things exciting and we all played the game of Tom Tiddler's Ground to see how far we dared go before he turned and bellowed at us.

He hunted my older sisters with his bloodhounds, which surprised the neighbours. He was punctual to the second. If he expected someone at one o'clock, he would start looking at his watch at six minutes to and with a furious face say, 'In seven minutes the damn feller will be late.'

In London he did all his shopping at the Army & Navy Stores and used to be there well before the doors opened at nine. When my mother asked why he had to arrive so early, he said if he left it any later, he was impeded by 'inconveniently shaped' women.

My father was no good at business and always seemed to be on the losing side of whatever he went into. He was one of the first in the Great Gold Rush in Canada in the 1920s but the acres he staked out were the only ones for miles where there was no gold.

Because of this land and other similar ventures, plus the depression of the Thirties, we lived in smaller and smaller houses and I was thankful when I grew up that there was no longer room for parties of young people to come and stay, as I observed from the safety of the nursery how terrifying it could be for the unsuspecting young men-friends of my sisters.

My father did not exactly make them feel at home. If there was a pause in the conversation at meals, he used to shout down the table to my mother, 'Have these people no homes of their own?'

One friend was banished into the snow because he bent

down to pick something up for my father and a comb fell out of his pocket. A man, carrying a comb ... He was the nineteen-year-old James Lees-Milne, the distinguished writer who remained friends with us all to the end of his life, in spite of this strange treatment.

My parents hated social life and we seldom saw anyone but the family, local uncles, aunts and cousins, and each other. I never remember them going out to meals and hardly ever having anyone to our house until my sisters grew up. I suppose my mother was taken up with everyday life and so many children, but my father used to go to London to attend the House of Lords where he was Chairman of the Drains Committee. He came back with rich tales of his fellow peers, who were even odder than they are now. At home, he saw to the farms and woods and the multifarious jobs to do with an estate.

Being the youngest, and sometimes the favourite of my father, I soon learnt that tears nearly always succeeded in getting me what I wanted and getting the others into trouble for teasing me.

In other ways though, being the youngest wasn't so good. I never had any new clothes, always the wretched cut-down things of the sisters. Pocket money was less, just because of being younger. My sister Unity, called Bobo, had far more than even her age warranted, because my mother said she *liked* money more than the rest of us. This led to a shouted chorus which was used about everything. IT IS UNFAIR, Bobo's got a rat and lots of money and I haven't got anything.

IT IS UNFAIR was the great cry. But as everything in life is unfair, perhaps the sooner it is realised the better.

My mother had unusual views on health. We were brought up on the Jewish laws about the subject – no doubt very wise in the climate of Israel before refrigerators, but hardly necessary in Oxfordshire. We could only have meat which 'divided the hoof and chewed the cud' and fish which had 'tails and fins', therefore no pig meat and no shellfish was allowed.

My father, of course, had what he liked and we used to long for the sausages which he had for breakfast and the cold ham covered in burnt sugar which appeared on shooting days. Once in a while, Mabel used to risk all and let us finish what came out of the dining room, and we danced round the pantry with a delicious end of congealing sausage.

My mother didn't believe in doctors. Her theory was that if everything was left alone the Good Body would right itself. If we were very ill, a masseuse used to appear. We were the envy of our friends in that we not only weren't forced, but we were not allowed medicines or, the panacea of all childish ills, Syrup of Figs or, worse still, castor oil.

She wasn't in the least interested in whether or not we had been to the lavatory. She knew it would happen sooner or later and if it was later, well, never mind. The Good Body would work in the end.

And we were never made to eat food we didn't want. This was rare in those days and I am always thankful for it. I think it is a refined cruelty to force children to eat what they don't like or to finish something they don't want.

Our own curious ideas of food were usually given in to, if rather unwillingly. Bobo lived on little else but mashed potatoes for two years, and I had a passion for bread sauce which I had with every meal, and Bovril spread on bread and butter. My mother tried to put me off this by saying it was made of old horses' hooves. I suppose it was the equivalent of children nowadays only liking chips and ice cream.

When Jessica had acute appendicitis my mother conceded that her appendix must come out. The operation was done on the nursery table. No one thought it in the least bit odd, having it done at home. We were all a bit jealous of the fuss made of her and there was a great deal of 'It is unfair' when the appendix was given to her in a jar full of that stuff that preserves such things.

My mother was before her time in many of her theories. We always had bread made at home out of wholemeal flour. But we longed for, and continually asked for, Shop Bread, though we hardly ever got it.

She and my uncles regularly wrote to the papers on what they called Murdered Food – refined white sugar, white flour from which the wheat germ had been removed, and so much else which is fashionable now, seventy years on. They were considered to be eccentric then.

An instance of her contempt for the scientific was when tuberculin testing for cows came in when I was about eleven. We had Guernsey cows and the butter, milk and cream they produced were wonderfully good. Three cows reacted to the test. My mother was told. 'Which are they?' she asked. As always in such cases they were the three best-looking in the herd. 'What, get rid of those lovely animals? Certainly not! The children can have their milk.'

And have it we did, with no ill effects of any kind, which served to underline her distrust of scientists and doctors.

We didn't go to school. My father didn't approve of education for girls. My brother, yes, he went through the conventional programme without question, but the girls, no. He didn't mind us learning to read and write, perhaps because my mother taught us till we were seven, but the idea of anything more annoyed him very much indeed.

My mother didn't agree. She hadn't any money of her own, so she started a chicken farm. Only the cracked and soft-shelled eggs came into the house and my sisters said that the only chickens we had to eat were those which had died. From the small but regular profit, my mother paid for a governess – so, to the schoolroom we had to go. I don't know if there were Schools Inspectors in those days. If so, would they have got past my father?

I am sorry to say that there was not just one governess, but a succession of the unfortunate women. We were perfectly foul to them and made their lives intolerable, so naturally they left. My sisters had been through a fair few of them before I came on the scene. And we may have been awful to them, but some of them were pretty peculiar too.

Miss Pratt only liked playing cards, so we played Racing Demon from 9 till 10.30, half an hour break, then again till lunch. We became very good indeed at it.

Miss Dell encouraged us in the difficult art of shoplifting – well, stealing really.

None of us ever went in for an exam of any kind. We were spared the torment that children suffer now and I certainly would not have passed any of them.

My best friend during all these years was our old groom, Hooper. Every moment that I was not forced to be doing something else was spent in or around the stables. We understood each other completely, which I suppose was just as well, as he had a terrific temper (which I discovered years after was due to some terrible experiences and shell shock, suffered in the Great War).

I believe people now would think my parents were taking a bit of a risk, allowing a child of ten or so to spend so much time with such an erratic fellow. When Bobo did something which annoyed him, he'd say, 'I'll take yer in that wood and DO for yer.'

But he never did.

To me, he was the human end of the horses and ponies I so adored, and the stables were my heaven, as were the woods and the little roads, many of them still untarred, of the few miles round about, which in the days before horse boxes were our boundary.

We went to church of course. My father used to take the collection and tortured us by stopping twice at my aunt and giving her a nudge the second time. She would frown at him and slap his hand, which started us on the peculiar agony of church giggles.

My sisters were all very strong characters and totally different from each other, yet like all families, we still have a strong link which has survived grown-up differences of politics. We were an awful family for nicknames, and all seven children had constantly changing names for one another.

Nancy was a tease on the grand scale, and because she was so much older and so much cleverer we younger ones used to believe her. Nothing was ever dull when she was around.

We were once set a question by my mother of how we would budget if we were to live away from home on a set amount of money – £300 a year, I think it was. We all broke it down most carefully, so much for rent, so much for rates, heat, light, food and clothes. Nancy finished ages before the rest of us. She had just put down – Flowers £299, Everything Else £1.

Her success as a writer was born first of all from her wonderfully accurate observations of my father and our family life, and when she graduated from novels to historical books, their success was due to sheer hard work. Totally uneducated, she applied herself with complete dedication to her subject and set it down as only she could.

The next sister, Pam, was as different from Nancy as you could imagine. Immersed in country life, her animals, her garden and above all her kitchen – she was a wonderful cook – she was the Martha of the family.

My brother Tom was the third child, adored by both parents and all sisters, hardly known to me, as he always seemed to be away at school. Lawyer, musician and soldier, he was killed in Burma at the very end of the war. My parents never recovered from this tragedy.

Diana came fourth, the cleverest of the family and beautiful to look at at all ages.

Then Unity, funny and loyal and brave, bigger than life-size in every way. She died when she was thirty-four.

Jessica was the sixth, the curly-haired favourite of Nanny, and my beloved companion and ally against the others when persecuted. She lived in America and fought fiercely for the cause of the under-dog. Like Nancy, she has a certain reputation as a writer. When she was little, she dreamed of a completely different life to that in which she was brought up. Pocket money and Christmas windfalls from uncles all went into her Running Away Fund. Her sights were set on a bed-sitting room in the East End of London.

A most determined character, she did indeed run away, in 1936, and when we discovered she had gone to fight for the Communists in Spain, all Nanny said was, 'But she didn't take any clothes to fight in.'

Nanny was a wonder, really a saint. I never saw her cross or heard her say an unkind word to anyone, and highly tried she must have been. At the same time she didn't mete out any praise, and sat on any signs of vanity which my sisters might have been forgiven for having.

'Oh Nanny, I can't go to the party in this AWFUL dress.'

'It's all right, darling, no one's going to look at *you*.'

This dictum was carried a bit far when Diana, eighteen years old and staggeringly beautiful in her wedding dress, said, 'Oh Nanny, this hook and eye doesn't work. It will look awful.'

'It's all right, darling, who's going to look at *you*?'

The only holidays we ever had (it was the days before everyone had to go away for holidays) were with Nanny's sister, whose husband had a hardware shop in the main street of Hastings. The wonderful smell of paraffin and polish, the beautiful brushes hanging down from the ceiling, and the freezing cold grey sea, with a ginger biscuit as reward for going in, was lovely in its way, but as we couldn't take ponies, goats, rats, mice, guinea pigs and dogs, it seemed a waste of a fortnight to me.

I look back on my childhood as a very happy time. It is unfashionable to do so, I know, but the idea of school, so longed for by my sisters, was anathema to me. Spared that horror, I suppose I was conventionally and boringly happy, and thought our upbringing was like everyone else's.

But, on looking back, I don't think it was.

HOME TO ROOST
and Other Peckings

To my great-grandchildren
born and as yet unborn

INTRODUCTION
by Alan Bennett

I knew the minute the call came from Derbyshire that there would be no escape. I had been here before: it was Miss Shepherd all over again.

This might seem unkind, the resemblance between a smelly, deranged and filthily raincoated vagrant and Chatsworth's fragrant chatelaine emeritus not immediately obvious. But they are the same, both strong-willed single-minded women wanting something out of me: Miss Shepherd a haven for her van, the Dowager Duchess a foreword for her book. 'Can I bend you to my will?' sister Nancy used to say. Quite.

Note that I have a difficulty calling her Debo (though nobody else does). My acquaintance with duchesses, dowager or otherwise, is scant and feeling it a bit soon after only one meeting to be on first-name terms I settled for Ms Debo while she in her turn called me Mr Alan. I suppose it's a kind of nickname and she is well used to that, the Mitfords having so many nicknames for each other one wonders how they could keep track. Her said sister, Nancy, called her 9, a reference to her supposed mental age; the myth of her own stupidity one that has clung to her all her life and which she still expects us to believe.

Famously unlettered, Ms Debo claims to be like her father who only ever read one book (*White Fang*) and found it so dangerously good he never wanted to read another. And though I feel much the same about opera I don't believe it of Her Grace.

Still it's ironical that having written a story about Someone who discovers the delights of reading I now find I am writing a foreword in praise of Someone Else who never has.

Among the handful of books the author does admit to having read I am delighted to find Priscilla Napier's *A Late Beginner*, a favourite of mine and full of the lost lore and language of nannies. Seeing this recommended, I thought I'd tell her to read Mary Clive's *Day of Reckoning* only to turn the page and find that she already had.

Debo's book ticks so many of my boxes that I'd better start with a mistake (what critics call 'an egregious error') so as not to seem sycophantic. The book begins with a lengthy list of the 11th Duke's offices, appointments and other distinctions ranging from the presidency of Chesterfield and Darley Dale brass bands to being runner-up as White's Club 'Shit of the Year'. However, the list omits (entirely understandably to my mind) the duke's brief sojourn as a governor of Giggleswick School (I think he may have owned the land on which the school is built but that's by the way). This governorship may be a piece of information his relict wishes to suppress as indeed he only attended one governors' meeting, afterwards appearing on the platform in (among other things) yellow socks. Now it happened that the previous day a youth in the sixth form suspected of Bohemian tendencies had been bawled out by his housemaster, the proof of his decadence (and a possible portent of future effeminacy) a pair of yellow socks found in his locker. Following the duke's appearance on the platform, whatever penalties had been imposed were briskly rescinded so there was one boy at least who had cause to bless the name of Cavendish.

Not having read many books has its drawbacks, though it might appal Debo to know that she thereby fulfils one of W. H. Auden's requirements for a budding writer, namely knowing a few books inside out. He would also approve of her fondness for lists and she of his fascination with lead mining and the geology of Derbyshire.

It's a county she revels in. Saddled with her irrepressible Mitford voice she enjoys Derbyshire for its dialect, instancing 'starved' which in Derbyshire means cold. This usage is not confined to Derbyshire, as my mother, who was originally from Halifax, was fond of it. She took it further and applied it to the weather, which she'd describe as 'starvaceous'. 'Mash the tea' is another Derbyshire expression that's shared with Leeds, and it's a handy one too. 'Make the tea' is pretty general and might mean 'Pour it out'. 'Mash the tea' is more precise, meaning 'Put the tea in the pot'. So 'The tea's mashed' means it's just waiting to be poured.

This is a lady who will have seen plenty of teas in her time, teas on terraces, teas in tents, teas with farmers, teas with tenants. She's someone who knows about gooseberries and can discriminate between parsnips. She's on first name terms with her hens, up to the minute on sheep, and pigs, I'm sure, eat out of her hand (which incidentally requires nerve).

To my surprise she's quite charitable about flower arranging, a hobby in my experience that's prone to turn its votaries into hell-hags. 'If you think squash is a competitive activity,' says one of my characters, 'try flower arrangement.'

Though I don't know why I should think it's just flower arrangement: rhubarb growing may be equally cut-throat and I'm sure there's no love lost over leeks and marrows. This is a world Debo has seen much more of than me, having trailed round more than her share of village fêtes and local shows with their ancient categories: 'Three tarts on a plate', 'An edible necklace', or (a favourite, this) 'A garden on a tray', the pond invariably represented by a bit of silver paper.

But there are worlds elsewhere and, surprisingly, one of the most interesting pieces is an essay on tiaras which is not a topic to which I've ever given much thought: I didn't even know that diamonds could be dirty. It's a lovely essay, the kind of vignette you might well have found in the old *New Yorker*.

Debo remembers once having to don the family diamonds, tiara, necklace, stomacher and all, in order to play the lead in the local WI's *The Oldest Miss World in the World* ('My hobbies are hens and world peace'). One just wonders whether she told the insurers.

Both of us having been despatched round provincial book-shops, we share memories of that shaming humiliation of the writer's life, the book-signing.

Writer (pen poised): To whom shall I put it?

Reader (brightly smiling): Me!

Bolder and more pedantic than I've ever dared to be, Debo baulks at signing a book 'To Granny' when it's not her granny, a detail I never let trouble me at all. But I agree with her that anyone who skips a dedication and just wants a signature almost deserves a kiss besides.

Faced with a queue, the staff of the bookshop can get quite bossy ('Her Grace will not be signing bus-tickets'). I'm so anxious to be liked I'm happy to sign bus-tickets and even betting slips if it helps. On one occasion a young man, not having bought the book or anything else, turned round and told me to sign the back of his neck. Which I did. When he next washed I don't like to think.

Deborah Devonshire is not someone to whom one can say, 'Joking apart . . .' Joking never is apart: with her it's of the essence, even at the most serious and indeed saddest moments. At the heart of this collection are three pieces of a different order and all remarkable: diaries of the inauguration of President Kennedy in 1961, of his funeral two years later and an account of the 'Treasure Houses of Britain' exhibition in Washington in 1985.

JFK was a family friend not because famous people know other famous people but through his sister Kathleen (Kick) Kennedy's marriage to Andrew Devonshire's brother, Billy, who was shortly afterwards killed in Belgium. A few years later

Kathleen herself died in a plane crash and is buried at Edensor on the edge of Chatsworth Park. Jack Kennedy was therefore a friend of the family in good times and bad and this brought an invitation to his inauguration as president in January 1961. Reluctant to go (the call of the moors) DD kept a diary of the proceedings, which in their cheerful chaos seem more like India than any English ceremonial.

At one point the newly elected president calls her over to stand beside him while the parade goes by . . . the president having a cup of coffee and a biscuit in gaps between contingents of the three-hour procession. At one point one of the marching troops breaks ranks to take a snap of the president on the podium. Trooping the Colour it certainly wasn't.

What's winning is the fun she gets out of it, and a component of the fun she gets out of life is that she seems to have no sense of entitlement. Standing next to the newly inaugurated JFK she thinks of it as an enormous treat and when later he climbs over seven rows of chairs just to have a word, though frozen to the marrow she is in total heaven.

That she is a natural diarist is plain from the oddities that catch her eye, the piece ending as she drifts off to sleep in the British Embassy while outside in the bedroom corridor her husband whispers to the ambassador Sir Harold Caccia the secrets Prime Minister Macmillan had entrusted him to bring over.

Her account of Kennedy's funeral, that terrible Thanksgiving of 1963, is so heartfelt it is difficult to read. Afterwards she is sympathising with the ambassador David Ormsby Gore and his wife. 'It will be very difficult working with the new administration – no intimacy, no shared memories and no jokes.' And the jokes aren't the least of it so that her account of even this wretched weekend manages to end on one. Fog having diverted the funeral party to Manchester, this means a night at Chatsworth where she recalls the (very thin) Prime Minister, Alec Douglas-Home, wondering if perhaps he crept into bed and lay very still she wouldn't have to change the sheets for Princess Margaret who was coming the next day.

I've never thought of Alec Douglas-Home as much of a joker but that's the thing about this lady. She brings it out in people. Good for her.

ALAN BENNETT

I MARRIED

I married:

The twice mayor of Buxton
A Knight of the Garter
The chairman of the Lawn Tennis Association
A parliamentary under-secretary of state
A minister of state in the Commonwealth Relations
    Office
A freeman of the Borough of Eastbourne
A holder of the Military Cross
The chairman of the British Empire Cancer
    Campaign for twenty-five years
The patron-in-chief of the Polite Society
An Old Etonian
A Knight of the Order of St John, Derbyshire
A steward of the Jockey Club
A peer of the realm
A Major in the Coldstream Guards
The patron of twenty-seven livings in the Church
    of England dioceses of Derby, Bradford, Ely,
    Southwell, Chichester, Sheffield and Lincoln
A member of the Horserace Totalisator
    Board
The Vice Lord-Lieutenant of Derbyshire

The prime warden of the Worshipful Company of
    Fishmongers
The author of a book on a famous racehorse
A member of the Garden Society, Society of
    Dilettanti, Grillion's, The Fox Club and The
    Other Club
A graduate of Trinity College, Cambridge
A vice-president of the London Library
The president of the Royal Hospital and Home for
    Incurables, Putney
A soundly beaten Conservative parliamentary
    candidate for Chesterfield in the 1945 and 1950
    general elections
The president of the Devonshire Club, Eastbourne
The president of Derbyshire County Scout Council
The president of the Thoroughbred Breeders'
    Association
A member of the Western European Union,
    Council of Europe
The president of the Royal Commonwealth Society
    (who was sacked after an excellent speech on
    Rhodesia)
The president of the Building Societies Association
A member of the Roxburghe Club
An honorary doctor of law at the University of
    Manchester
A Privy Counsellor
The author of an autobiography
An honorary doctor of law at Memorial University
    of Newfoundland
The president of the Matlock and Eastbourne
    branches of Mencap
A vice-president of the All England Lawn Tennis
    and Croquet Club

A member of Brooks's, White's, the Beefsteak and
    the Turf Club
An honorary doctor of law at the University of
    Salford
The president of the National Deaf Children's
    Society
The first peer to join the Social Democratic Party,
    which he left to sit on the crossbenches in the
    House of Lords (and was then abolished)
The Master of the Worshipful Company of Farriers
The runner-up in White's Club 'Shit of the Year',
    Private Eye, 1974
The president of the Royal National Institute for
    the Blind
The chancellor of the University of Manchester
The major shareholder in Heywood Hill Bookshop
    and founder-donor of the Heywood Hill Literary
    Prize
A president of the Bakewell Agricultural and
    Horticultural Society
The president of the Conservative Friends of Israel
The president of Derbyshire County Cricket Club
An honorary doctor of law at the University of
    Liverpool
A front bench spokesman in the House of Lords on
    transport
The president of the National Council for One
    Parent Families
The patron of the Barnardo's Year of the Volunteer,
    1986
The president of the Longshaw Sheepdog Trials
The president of the Federation of West Derbyshire
    Mental Health Support Groups
The proprietor and chairman of Pratt's Club

An honorary Colonel of Manchester and Salford
    Universities' Officer Training Corps
The president of the African Medical and Research
    Foundation (which runs the Flying Doctor
    Service)
An honorary member of the French Jockey Club
The president of Chesterfield Football Club
The president of Eastbourne College
A trustee of the National Gallery
The chairman of the Chatsworth Estates Company
The president of Chesterfield and Darley Dale Brass
    Bands
A man after whom a variety of sweet pea was
    named
The patron of the Midland Cairn Terrier Club

I have changed my name three times but I have only been
married once.

*Deborah Mitford (1920–) married, in 1941, Lord Andrew Cavendish
(1920–2004). In 1944, on the death of his elder brother, Andrew inherited
the courtesy title of Marquess of Hartington. After his father's death in
1950, he became the 11th Duke of Devonshire. In spite of being a government spokesman on transport, he never held a driving licence; he was
never the owner of a Cairn terrier and was piqued at being voted only
runner-up for the White's Club award (Lord Lambton was the winner).
This list of his offices and distinctions is by no means exhaustive.*

THE LAND AGENTS' DINNER

Anyone who chooses land agency as a profession has to know everything about everything, from drains to fine arts, from roads to Rembrandts. He must be able to talk in their own terms to lawyers and loonies, gamekeepers and golfers, ploughmen and planners, prime ministers and policemen. Land agents can do just that and a thousand other things besides; they are the people who cheerfully face the problems that will affect the future spirit and appearance of the country and the villages to which we are all devoted.

They and their wives have to be ready to face any emergency. The great-aunt of a friend of mine was married to the Sandringham agent during the reign of King Edward VII. Queen Alexandra used to wander into the houses round about, taking with her whatever guests she had staying. One day, the agent's wife was, as usual, bent double in her garden when the maid came rushing out shouting, 'Come quickly. Come quickly. There are THREE QUEENS in the hall and I don't know what to do with them.'

At Chatsworth we have been very lucky in the marvellous people who have ruled in the estate office. Until my father-in-law died, there were seven agents spread around the country from Carlisle to Eastbourne. His mother, Evelyn Duchess of Devonshire, carried on a running fight with all of them. She loved interfering almost as much as I do. The unlucky Hugo

Read, who looked after Hardwick Hall where she lived, was the recipient of many a sharp note, usually on her favourite subjects of woodworm, dry rot and drains. She stayed on at Hardwick after 1957 when the government took it for death duties and transferred it to the National Trust. In her eighties, she became a prime exhibit herself, always joining the visitors for tea. On the subject of the tearoom, Hugo received the following note from her: 'Mrs Norton still makes her horrid little pink tarts, but they seem to have been enjoyed by two Nottingham businessmen.'

Her husband, Victor, the 9th Duke of Devonshire, was a real countryman. He loved cricket and when he saw to his distress that, in spite of a large intake of likely lads in the way of sub-agents and pupils, the Chatsworth cricket team was not doing too well, he got annoyed with Mr Hartopp, the agent. In desperation, the latter put an advert in several local papers which read: 'Wanted. Plumber for estate maintenance work. Must be a good wicket-keeper.'

The duke's head agent, Sir Roland Burke, was also honorary director of the Royal Show and for many years it was more or less run from the Chatsworth estate office. Burke served his apprenticeship at the Royal, starting in the lowly role of assistant steward in the Poultry Tent and ending up kneeling on the straw in the showground to be knighted by the King. When my father-in-law succeeded, one of the first things he decided to do was to get rid of Roland Burke. He couldn't bear him. But the difficulty was how to do it. My father-in-law was a very kind man and rather shy. He spent ages composing a speech for the awful interview. He decided to hang it on economy and made up a long rigmarole about how the estate could no longer afford the luxury of a head agent. Burke arrived and the duke began, 'Regretfully it is necessary to make some cuts and economies . . .' but before he could get any further, Roland interrupted and said, 'I have been thinking along the same lines and realise that economies have to be made. Therefore, I am quite prepared to sacrifice my third groom.'

Those of us who live and work in the country must all be acquainted with autocratic and authoritative gamekeepers – a race apart, who are accustomed to special privileges because of their special position. At Chatsworth there reigned for forty-five years the ultimate in the profession – one John Maclauchlan. He lived in a house with a Paxtonian tower, had his own chauffeur and called the Duke of Portland 'His Other Grace'. He and the old Duke of Devonshire used to tool round the country in the back of a huge brown Rolls-Royce (not that the duke ever referred to it as such but would order the 'Stink Hog' to be brought round). It was driven by Mr Burdekin, the duke's chauffeur, whose instructions were never to exceed 25 miles per hour. On the rare occasions when he went a little faster, Victor would bang on the glass partition with his stick and shout, 'Burdekin, Burdekin, what do you think you are, a crazy cow with a tin tied on its tail?'

Maclauchlan had the ear of the duke and always got his own way. He heartily despised Sir Roland Burke and the other agents. Once when King George V was shooting at Chatsworth, the King turned round before the start of the best drive to see a group of eight or nine men standing, as he thought, uncomfortably close. 'Who are those men?' he asked Maclauchlan. 'Oh, take no notice of them, Your Majesty. They are just a posse of agents. Shoot them if you like.' When Andrew and I first went to live in the village of Edensor, next to Chatsworth, Mr Maclauchlan sent for me (there was no suggestion of his coming to our house). I arrived, of course, at the right time, was shown into the parlour by his daughter and the great man entered. 'Lady Hartington,' he said, 'I have sent for you to tell you that you can go wherever you like.'

I often think Victor Duke and my father would have made wonderful keepers. Victor would have been a tremendously conscientious and steady beat keeper, and my father would have been a terrifying head keeper with his entrenching tool at the ready. Poachers would have been what the newspapers describe as 'at risk' in his domain. Both men understood the ways of birds and beasts but neither was what my father called 'literary coves'. My father would not have wasted time reading – a trait I have inherited from him and one which made my sister Nancy call me '9', as she said that was my mental age. She used to address envelopes to me as '9 Duchess of Devonshire' and introduced me to her smart French friends as 'my 9-year-old sister' when I was well over forty.

My father's attitude to reading was most sensible. He only ever read one book and that was *White Fang*. He loved it so much he never read another because nothing could ever be as good. 'Dangerous good book,' he used to say, 'no point in trying any more.' I remember an unfortunate woman coming to lunch with my parents. The reason I remember is because no one outside the family was ever asked, so it was a very special occasion. The poor soul was ugly, something my father didn't allow – the sort of woman he called 'a meaningless piece of meat'. It was the time when everyone was talking about Elinor Glyn and her work. Casting round for a subject to break the silence, I heard our guest say, 'Lord Redesdale, have you read *Three Weeks*?' My father glared at her. 'I haven't read a book for *three years*,' he replied (an exaggeration as it had been twenty since he had read *White Fang*).

How surprised my grandfather-in-law and my father would be at the change in standards of housing in the country now. They didn't live to see bathrooms, let alone the double garage, central heating and downstairs lavatory which are now the order of the day. The two men were like a very ancient friend of mine who invited me to shoot in Gloucestershire recently. We were walking through a wood, miles from anywhere, when we came upon a ruined cottage – just a chimney stack, a couple of steps and a heap of stones. My friend looked lovingly at it and said, 'It's the most extraordinary thing, you know, you can't get a feller to live in a place like that any more.'

They would have understood Mr Hey, our beloved friend who looked after Bolton Abbey for many years and who in old age grew to look exactly like the grouse he loved. Mr Hey was, to say the least, careful with money. He was once telling me about a tenant who was getting restive about the length of time it was taking to put a bathroom into his house. 'We really must do something for him,' I said. 'Well, I've given him a shower.' '*Have* you, Mr Hey?' 'Yes, I've taken a slate off the roof.' He used to send the most fearsome bills after our annual stay at Bolton Abbey, every conceivable item written into them, almost including the air we breathed. The last line was always the same: 'Mousetraps − 9d.' I could never understand why we couldn't reuse the ones from last year. But that's agents for you, they have to balance their books somehow.

January 1983

THE SMALL GARDEN
by C. E. Lucas Phillips

Of the vast number of books on gardening – fat, shiny and heavy with photographs – that fill our shelves this has long been my favourite. First published in 1952, it met a post-war enthusiasm for beautifying your plot. This reprint is good news indeed.

The author was a handsome Brigadier, decorated for distinguished service in both world wars. He was also an inspired writer, an original who holds the attention of the reader with his instructions on even the duller aspects of gardening. He tells us he is an amateur writing for amateurs. Too modest, but it is an encouragement to beginners and succeeds in making us want to try to get it right.

It is nothing if not thorough. The basics are explained, the step-by-step stages that lead to the pleasure of growing whatever you fancy, for anyone who knows one end of a hoe from the other. There is a glossary and a cultural calendar (it is a comfort to see 'cultural' used in this context and not coupled with 'heritage', describing some outrageous kind of art). Lucas Phillips tackles the vexed problem of plant names in the same robust way as the other difficulties met in learning how to deal with the vegetable kingdom. Many of his instructions are positively poetic: compost, its components and how to mix them, the value of liquid manure of a 'deep tawny hue' (but when it comes to adding 'a trifle of soot' you may have to admit defeat should your house be without coal fires). Other unlikely subjects are so well described they carry you along with intense pleasure.

There is much to go into before you dig. Fifty pages go by before he puts spade, fork and hoe to the earth. There are some surprises in the chapter on tools ('The Gardener's Armoury'): 'the dibber should be handled with care . . . in unskilled hands it is a menace to the infant plant.' I never looked on the good old dibber as a menace but his reason for the warning is logical.

The seasons and the work they bring are explained in simple language you cannot forget. Digging and manuring in the autumn allows the frosts to break up newly dug clods, working on particles of soil moisture as it does on water pipes, bursting and crumbling heavy soil into a fine tilth with great efficiency. The comparison to domestic burst pipes brings this process of nature home to every British householder. Early-spring east winds, with their 'harrowing breath', bring you to the coming of summer and the author begs you not to disturb the roots of established plants when keeping the ground clear of invaders, but a little light hoeing 'to slaughter the weeds' is in order.

I know of no other gardening book that engages our interest in subjects dull as ditch water and vaguely unpleasant as well, apt to be skipped in search of something more attractive. You have to read on for fear of missing some descriptive gem and you remember what he says because of how he says it. His language gets better and better. Cuckoo-spit: 'Inside a mass of frothy spittle is a curious soft creature which, on disturbance, will attempt to escape by weak hops.' You can't beat it.

He is at his most lyrical describing the plants he loves. The lesser known species anemones, for instance, 'have a chaste and porcelain beauty', fragile and virginal. *Eremurus* are 'elegant ladies of hyacinthine appearance of 6 ft stature and more. Expensive . . . Beware slugs.' The best he can say of the easily grown Valerian is 'Beloved by Winston Churchill'. He does not spare us his dislikes and warns that after flowering in 'barbaric splendour' in late spring, the Oriental poppy is a 'grizzly mess'. You can't have one without the other. *Salvia splendens* is a 'pillar-box red bedding plant which startles the optic nerve in August'. Cecil Beaton had the same anti-scarlet prejudice and called this salvia and its colour-mates 'retina irritants'.

The pages on roses produce their own loving descriptions. How Lucas Phillips would have enjoyed the modern tribe of new/old roses which answer all needs with their scent, vigour and complicated beauty. Looking to a brighter future, he barks out orders to amputate newly planted ramblers to within 15 inches of the ground, thus preventing any flowers in their first year, and makes sure we obey by adding that this is 'a cardinal injunction not to be funked'.

Much of the Brigadier's writing is delightfully dated. Many bright little plants are 'gay' and in my battered old paperback he recommends a dependable insecticide, DDT – edited out of this edition now it is illegal. Slugs, bugs and bacteria are likened to Fifth Columnists. The new generations of gardeners may wonder at the meaning of that. Weeds are classed in three degrees of abomination, the worst being the tap-rooted varieties, 'underground creeping horrors'. Couch grass and ground elder are 'vegetative serpents, brutes which laugh at the hoe as love laughs at the locksmith'.

The chapter on the kitchen garden takes us steadily along, with all the favourites and their needs clearly described. It is embellished with simple line-drawings (we have already seen a little masterpiece entitled 'How Not to Water'); one page ends with 'a gallery of oddments', which show their age as today they are no longer odd but fashionable – kohlrabi, celeriac and salsify.

Having profited by the Lucas Phillips wisdom and followed his ways in making a new garden – or improving an old one – to our (and his) liking, we arrive at the last chapters, where he excels himself. 'Know Your Enemy', something the old soldier studied in his military career and applies forcibly to the deceptive calm of the garden, is his title for the introduction to this section. Who could forget the picture conjured up by scab and canker 'going hand in hand'? It cries out for a drawing by Edward Lear of these brotherly pests advancing on your apple trees. He quotes Erasmus Darwin in 1790, 'Crack follows crack, to laws elastic just / And the frail fabric shivers into dust.'

We are jolted into full attention by the originality and often hilarious descriptions of 'Friend and Foe' and, best of all, 'The Enemy in Detail'. Who else but our now beloved author would describe the larva of the ladybird (a friend) as 'agile, torpedo-shaped, resembling a minute crocodile'? You have got to learn the difference between the 'brisk' centipede (friend) and a millipede (foe). The latter has 'innumerable very small legs and, when worried, gives off an obnoxious smell from his stink glands'. The idea of a 'worried' millipede is something I have never considered but I will now – assuming I can tell it apart from its fewer legged rival, the friendly centipede – and I will do my best to give the former a nervous breakdown. I am afraid the children's dear old tortoise is entirely an enemy.

The worst garden pest by a long way is Man ('ignorant and lazy'), led in his assault on nature by the Jobbing Gardener. (Fifty years on, would the worst pest be the strimmer?) Birds are in a special category and have become 'a serious problem . . . pestiferous to fruit'. RSPB please note.

Dip into this book and you will find yourself digging. Dig and you will be rewarded.

2006

THE ORGAN RECITAL

When two or three old people are gathered together in the name of lunch, you can be sure of the subject of conversation to start the ball rolling. Illnesses of all shapes and sizes are the thing and the Organ Recital* begins. Heads, bodies and legs are dissected; noses, throats and ears, skin and bones, arteries, liver and lights, and (Blair's favourites) hearts and minds. Once you start on minds you are in for a basinful. Of the two it is better to stick to hearts and whether or not you are allowed to walk upstairs.

Hips and knees lead to bones. Stomachs, teeth and gums, closely allied as it is not much use having one without the others, can lead to a dissertation on dentistry. Impacted wisdom teeth are good but there is a trick called root canal treatment that takes almost as long to describe as the lengthy treatment itself, with your jaws jammed open till the cows come home. There is a strong sense of competition, even as to the waiting time at hospital (length of); tales of woe are capped and re-capped as the Organ Recital progresses.

Various syndromes that I've never heard of are trotted out as a part of everyday life and sympathy is expected from the listener. Doctors come in for praise or criticism. Surgeons are either haloed magicians or bunglers who ought to be struck off. A curious thing is that they are always described as 'my GP' or 'my surgeon', when they are ordinary independent people who don't belong to anyone. Consultants are described as 'you know who

I mean, the big kidney man' or whatever the man's favourite bit of body happens to be.

Look out when it comes to food, which is either very good or very bad for you. Lumped together as 'diet' it is dangerous ground because the dish you are giving someone for lunch will have come in for a pounding before they sit down to it. An extraordinary phenomenon, unknown to our parents, is fads. An invitation, especially to a municipal or university celebration, often has 'Special Dietary Requirements' printed on it, with a space for you to fill in. What you and I never see are the replies, so we don't ever know if the invitees just put 'caviar'.

If a grand person is among the guests, his/her PA will telephone to say, 'I thought you would like to know that X cannot eat . . .' and then follow all the most delicious foods one after another. Next time this happens I plan to say, 'Why can't they just say "no thank you"?' If the guest is very grand indeed and suffers from some strange religion, there is little you can safely offer. Better steer clear as such social life has become full of pitfalls.

You must leave at least ten minutes for the Organ Recital, which leads seamlessly, as they say now (what are these non-existent seams that people go on about?), to Trolley Talk, the romance of the aisles, the thrill of the checkout, the way favourites are repackaged or moved round the supermarket and hidden from the most determined shopper. You will be lucky if you get away with six minutes on this subject. Then you can agree how wonderful it is that we never hear of Blair now and what a pity it was that Mr Cameron ever mentioned grammar schools.

August 2008

* An expression borrowed from the late Lord Annan.

THE FARMERS' CLUB DINNER

Thank you very much for asking me to come here tonight. I do not know how I dared accept but I was blinded by flattery and, as usual in these cases, the invitation came some time ago so I was sure I would be dead by now. The people at this dinner are the cleverest in the world in the profession I admire most in the world, and I ought to have known that if by some strange chance I was still alive, the terror of my role would induce a heart attack. But to propose the toast to Agriculture and the Farmers' Club is a tremendous honour and one I appreciate more than I can say.

The only people who ever ask me to give a talk are the Women's Institutes, usually the ones very near at hand and always in January and February when they think a proper speaker might get stuck in the snow. A few years ago I wouldn't have been bold enough to do even that but I was thrown in at the deep end. I was staying with a friend in Sussex who is secretary of her local WI. The day of the meeting coincided with my visit and a secretary's nightmare happened: the speaker failed. Faced with an expectant audience and nothing doing, she said, 'YOU must talk.' 'I *can't*,' I protested, 'what on earth could I talk about?' 'Tell them about Chatsworth,' she said. 'I *can't* . . .' In the end I did. They were bored to death. In deep Sussex I'm sure they'd never heard of Derbyshire, let alone Chatsworth. But polite as the WI always are, they listened to the end of this awful experience. When we got home I asked my friend what the real talk should have been about. She got the programme down from the mantelpiece and the title was, 'Ramblings of an Old Woman'. So that is what you're getting tonight.

The reason I feel so proud to be here is because the people who work the land are the men I like and admire more than any others – especially the men of the hills and hard weather, men who live for and by their land, their cattle and their sheep, who are not ruled by clocks and train times, who are not parasites living off other people's efforts, or critics (except of course of governments), who are not always looking over their shoulder wondering what other people are thinking of them, but are totally independent and go about their hard and exacting tasks according to the seasons, as their fathers and forefathers did before them. They are the men who do the work and they are the men who command my respect.

Since marrying and moving to Derbyshire during the war, I have been surrounded by such people. Several characters stand out: one was George Hambleton, who died not long ago at a ripe old age. He had walked a Shire stallion and then became a cowman. Little is said or written about the stockmen, horsemen and shepherds whose lives are spent with the animals in their charge. On them depends the welfare of the stock, and therefore the success or failure of their division of the farm. George was one of those men who understood his animals by instinct and was in total sympathy with them. He could see at once if there was anything wrong and was as good as any vet at diagnosis – and as good as any nurse at treating the ailment. Hours mean nothing to such men – cows don't calve to order during weekdays and it would never occur to them to be absent at crucial times. George was quietly critical of some of the young men, fresh from agricultural college, who thought they knew the lot. 'They don't know as much as they think they do,' he once said to me, 'well, *some don't even know what a swingle tree is.*' Such are the people who produce the superb stock for which this country is renowned.

No praise or thanks can be high enough for them and no men expect it less.

Anyone born after George's generation will be puzzled by all the horse expressions in our language – kicking over the traces, working against the collar, taking the bit between the teeth, being trotted out, keeping on a tight rein, put out to grass, can't take his oats – all from a lost world where the horse and its ways were an essential part of life. Gone too are the binders, stooks and ricks, and the threshing days when all the boys in the village enjoyed going ratting. With the changing look of farming, the poets must also change when writing about the country. The first line of Kipling's 'L'Envoi':

> There's a whisper down the field where the year has shot her yield
> And the ricks stand grey to the sun

would have to read:

> There's a whisper down the field where the year has shot her yield
> And the plastic bags shine black to the sun.

Not quite the same thing somehow.

My husband's grandfather, the 9th Duke of Devonshire, loved his farm and his Shires and Shorthorns far more than the extraordinary works of art he lived among. He was no beauty, and was what could be described as 'of bucolic appearance'. The Royal Show, which at that time moved to a different place annually, was one of the highlights of his year. When it was held at Newcastle, the sleeper train from London waited in a siding till it was a reasonable time for its passengers to get up (railways sought to please their customers in those days). Two farmers walking down the platform saw the recumbent figure of the duke, sound asleep in true Cavendish fashion, his pink head on a pillow. 'That's a fine Large White,' said one farmer. 'That's no Large White, that's the Duke of Devonshire,' answered his companion – a Derbyshire man, no doubt, who could tell the difference.

The duke kept diaries which are a joy to read and are an anti-dote to the wordy ways of our masters, the bureaucrats of today. Many entries referred to Shire horses and cows. One describes an equine tragedy in just six words: 'Tremendous thunderstorm. Mother Hubbard dropped dead.' Others read: 'Butterfly cast her calf. Very troublesome.' 'Mrs Drewry's funeral – sad little cere-mony. Much warmer. Shot a few rooks after.' 'Went to see the new church at Flookborough. Thought it rather askew.' But my favourite entry, headed 'London', reads: 'Important meeting in Buxton. Missed train. Rather glad.'

Nowadays, the third Saturday in September is one of the most important days in the year for Chatsworth Farms. It is the day of the sheep sale and, in four hours or so, the harvest of that enterprise is gathered in. I am told it is the biggest one-day sale from a single owner in the country. At daybreak the shepherds start to pen some 6,000 sheep in a field above Edensor. Cattle lorries squeeze up the lane where the notice 'Unfit for Cars' is covered by a fertiliser bag. Children play in tiers of straw-bale seats before the tent begins to fill with men whose Breughel-like faces proclaim their intimacy with the long English winters.

Ian Lawton, the auctioneer, stands in his stall and gives an inimitable performance, like the conductor of an orchestra with a bit of Mr Punch thrown in, stabbing and embracing the air while reciting his exhortations to the expressionless company at breakneck speed. 'Look sharp or they'll walk away. Listen to me now. Keep waving, sir. £37.80 settles it. Square 'em up. There's a lot of service in these. Away they go. A change of tup now and we have Bleu de Maine . . .' At the same time he is able to spot the bidders, invisible to you and me, most of whom have announced they will not be buying today, the lambs are far too dear. Ian keeps up his virtuoso one-man show for three and a half hours without a break, and his gavel, bound in layers of sticking plaster, bangs down ninety times an hour, as the same number of pens, each holding twenty to twenty-five sheep, is funnelled through the sawdust ring. I would give a lot to see him on the rostrum at Christie's. He would make the Bond Street dealers sit up and look sharp or the Rembrandts would walk away: 'Here come the Botticellis, sound in reed and udder, change the tup and you'll get a Van Gogh . . .'

Chatsworth has a Farm Shop, which, although successful, does produce some rather odd complaints. I have had two letters from women who bought a whole lamb for their freezers. Their messages were the same: 'When I drive through the park at Chatsworth, I see the lambs and they have four legs. When I unpacked the lamb I bought from you it had only two legs. What happened to the other two?' Farmers looking for diversification please note – breed a sheep with four legs, forget the shoulders and you'll be made!

This rambling old woman has seen strange changes in the world of agriculture. It seems only yesterday when farmers were heroes, the growers and providers of our food during and after the war. Now we seem to have turned into the enemy, the spoilers of landscapes (which, by the way, farmers invented), poisoners, torturers, perpetrators of all that is wicked. If that wasn't enough, a new language has been foisted on us, impossible for a simpleton like me to understand or keep up with because it is always being added to. Gatts and Caps, Variables and Clawbacks, now Iaccs – all too difficult. The hours of work and frustration caused by hordes of pressure groups, led by well-meaning, single-issue, muddle-headed people who are not countrymen and find it hard to understand the processes of nature, are unbelievable. I'm sure you all know the kind I mean and suffer from them.

Arising out of the enthusiasm of these new rural dwellers, I confidently expect the ones we know will soon be joined by Save the Rat Society, the Protection of Maiden Aunts in the Country Association, Family Planning for Rabbits (this will need a large staff), the Barbed Wire Heritage Group, the Single-Parent Frog Club, the Married Deer Association of Great Britain, the Society for the Rights of Moles and the World Fund for the Promotion of Dry Rot (the Wet Rot Club will be the junior branch). I look forward to hearing from the secretaries of these fruiting bodies, all of whom will be asking for £1 million to get going. I am longing for the findings of a government enquiry into the Fouling of Fields by Farm Stock, and the ensuing legislation which may be difficult to enforce, and new regulations making it illegal for anyone to go out of doors without wearing rubber gloves. But the best of the new societies is a London one. I'm proud to say my sister-in-law is its president. It is called the Society for Neutering Islington's Pussies – SNIP for short.

My family and I spend August at Bolton Abbey, in a magical spot in Yorkshire, where the straight-talking people are economical with words but not with the truth. A man who lives at the end of our lane is wonderfully gloomy. Once, when we had just arrived, he was telling me of the changes in the village during the year. 'So, how's the new postman getting on?' I asked. 'The new postman?' Pause. 'He's made a bad start.' Long pause. 'He's dead.'

I think you'll all be dead if I don't stop, so may I thank you again for a lovely dinner in excellent company and ask you to rise for the toast: 'Agriculture and the Farmers' Club.'

December 1991

DERBYSHIRE

I was brought up on the borders of Oxfordshire and Gloucestershire and have the unassailable affection for that beautiful part of England that everyone who has had a happy childhood feels for their native heath. When I moved to Derbyshire in 1943, Andrew was with his regiment in Italy and I settled into our first proper home in Ashford-in-the-Water with a baby, a pony and cart, two dogs and a pig.

I thought I should never get used to the scale of the Derbyshire landscape, to the size of the hills and valleys, to the hardness of the stone walls, bare of stonecrop and lichen, and to the length of the winters in a climate where May can be as cold as February. I have lived in the county now for nearly forty years and have grown to love the space and the remote places and would not change them for any other.

There is infinite variety in Derbyshire. Some of the most important quarries and related heavy industry in England are just a few miles from high, lonely, limestone hills, criss-crossed by light grey, drystone walls. Thorn and ash trees, bent to the wind, grow along the wall sides, and limestone outcrops show through the thin soil in the sudden rocky clefts of the dales. It is a landscape like no other in England, where you can find globe-flower, Jacob's ladder, water avens, several kinds of orchid and even lily-of-the-valley growing wild. There are old lead mines, windswept villages of stout stone buildings, and incomparable views of a green and grey landscape inhabited by sheep and ubiquitous Friesian cows. The scenery of the dales is made more dramatic near Buxton and Wirksworth by immense quarries, the man-made cliffs outdoing the natural ones, and just as beautiful in their own way – Derbyshire's answer to the white cliffs of Dover.

Another kind of lonely countryside is the moorland around the Derwent Dams, those engineering marvels of man-made lakes surrounded by heathery hills and indigenous woodland. The stone buildings of the dams have a monumental quality and look as permanent as the hills themselves. This is the home ground of the Woodland Whiteface sheep, an ancient breed that was nearly extinct a few years ago until revived interest in rare breeds ensured its survival.

The start of the Pennine Way is at Edale and so popular has this walk become that the paths have grown wider and wider, and the heather and other vegetation is receding under the thousands of feet that pound it every year. Ill-prepared hikers can get a fright when the weather changes without warning, soaking them in rain and enveloping them in mist, with visibility down to the end of your nose. The Way crosses the well-named Bleaklow and Black Ashop Moor, as well as Kinder Scout, 2,088 feet above sea level, where the Mass Trespass of 1932 created famous (and often quoted) publicity for the ramblers, when six of their number were arrested for 'riotous assembly'. Kinder Scout is the highest point of this inhospitable but fascinating country of grouse moors and hill sheep, where shepherds and their collies rule, and where the high road of the Snake Pass is the first to be closed by snow every winter.

If the hills are remarkable, so are the rivers. In 1817, Lord Byron wrote to the Irish poet Thomas Moore, 'Was you ever in Dovedale? I can assure you there are things in Derbyshire as noble as Greece or Switzerland.' Izaak Walton and Charles Cotton spent most of their lives in happy contemplation of the Dove, 'the finest river that I ever saw, and the fullest of fish', wrote Walton. Another crystal-clear trout stream is the Wye, which rises near Buxton and runs through Miller's Dale, Ashford-in-the-Water and Bakewell, underneath Haddon Hall to join the Derwent at Rowsley. The most exciting stretch of the Wye is Monsal Dale, where the tall railway viaduct links the hills. The viaduct is a prime example of the changes in fashion in what is admired and what is denigrated. John Ruskin was infuriated when it was built in 1863 and by what he considered the ruination of the dale, just so that 'every fool in Buxton can be in Bakewell in half an hour and every fool at Bakewell in Buxton'. Now it is revered as a triumph of engineering and for its own regular beauty.

The very names of the villages invite a closer look: Parsley Hay, Chapel-en-le-Frith, Alsop-en-le-Dale, Dove Holes, Peak Forest, Monyash, Foolow, Edensor, Stoney Middleton, Hope, Fenny Bentley, Stanton-in-Peak, Thorpe Cloud, Wigley, Earl Sterndale; and the dales: Chee Dale, Miller's Dale, Deep Dale, Monk's Dale, Demon's Dale, Cressbrook Dale, Lathkill Dale, Crackendale, Beresford Dale and many more.

There are caves, notably Poole's Hole near Buxton and the Great Rutland Cavern under the Heights of Abraham at Matlock Bath, a restored seventeenth-century lead mine in working order. The wealth produced from lead mining was of great importance to the county and the Barmote Courts, where lead-mining disputes were settled, are still held at Wirksworth and other places. Carved tablets showing miners' tools adorn the front of Wirksworth Moot Hall and the big brass dish used as a measure for lead ore since 1513 is preserved here.

The mineral unique to Derbyshire is Blue John, the yellow and blue fluorspar which for centuries has been made into urns, ornaments and even tabletops, as well as smaller objects such as knife handles and jewellery. It is thought to have got its name from the French *bleu jaune*. Blue John pieces are high fashion in antique shops and the prices are as steep as the descent into the

Blue John mines, which you enter under the shadow of Peveril Castle at Castleton. The Peak Cavern (or Devil's Arse) has the largest cave entrance in Britain. In the Speedwell Cavern you travel for half a mile in a boat on the underground canal, and Treak Cliff Cavern is remarkable for its stalactites and stalagmites. Small quantities of Blue John are still extracted.

There is silence and solitude in the uplands of the Peak District, where once the Blue John and lead mines were worked by families as true cottage industries, in contrast with the coal mines around Chesterfield and Clay Cross, and the iron and heavy industries of Staveley, Alfreton and adjacent towns, where the night was lit by flames from the chimneys of the works that carried on their noisy trade twenty-four hours a day. Good arable land runs alongside opencast coal works, reminding us that industry and farming have coexisted in the county since the Romans worked the lead mines.

In 1771, Sir Richard Arkwright set up the first successful water-powered cotton mill in Cromford. Today there is great interest in industrial archaeology and the Arkwright Society has preserved some of the mills for visitors to see. One of the most hauntingly beautiful mills is on the River Wye at Cressbrook, which you come upon unexpectedly in a secluded narrow dale. Another impressive one is at Calver on the Derwent. It was used as Colditz Castle in the 1970s BBC television series and was a realistic model for that grim edifice. The National Tramway Museum at Crich is fascinating, full of memories for grown-ups and of wonder for children.

Derbyshire is physically and psychologically divided into north and south round about Matlock, where the Midlands seem to end and the north begins. This was recognised soon after the war, when local government offices were moved from Derby to the old spa hotel buildings in Matlock, a much more convenient centre from which to administer the long, narrow county. At Matlock accents change and the scenery turns from productive

207

corn land into harsher, higher, grass country. You climb to a height of 1,000 feet before you reach Buxton in the north, where the 5th Duke of Devonshire and Carr of York built the glorious Crescent. Here the average mean temperature in July is 57.5° F – mean indeed! No wonder the inhabitants delighted in the warm mineral springs. Buxton and Matlock were important spas when such treatment was fashionable.

Alas, the baths are no more. I have an abiding memory of a happy afternoon in a peat bath at Buxton, a 'perk' of the mayoress, which I was at the time. It was the colour and consistency of a huge cowpat. I lay in it up to my neck, sweating happily, till ordered out by the attendant who then sprayed me with a jet of clean, cold water to remove the beneficial but clinging brown stuff. I never felt better or smoother-skinned in my life and I rue the passing of the baths.

The denizens of Derbyshire are not as restless as those in the south. Some years ago our local doctor did a survey of the village of Hartington to try to discover more about goitre, or Derbyshire Neck as it is called from the commonness of the disease in this neighbourhood. He found that 90 per cent of the people living in the village were born there, a statistic unlikely to be equalled farther south. Surnames like Wildgoose and Burdekin, which are not uncommon round here, never fail to surprise 'foreigners'. In Derbyshire you don't make tea, you 'mash' it. If someone says he's 'starved', he means he's cold, not hungry. I know several natives who say 'thee' instead of 'you'. My daughter at a Pony Club camp on the outskirts of a remote Peakland village once heard the farmer threaten his erring son, 'Eh John, if thee don't shape theeself I'll belt thee one.' Some swear words have never had the meaning given to them farther south – at any rate, they sound different in a Derbyshire voice. When Andrew stood for Parliament, a friend came to Chesterfield from London to canvass. She asked the driver who met her at the station how Andrew was getting on. 'They like 'im but they say booger 'is party', was the answer. Andrew's candidature was never successful but there is no better way of getting to know a town and its inhabitants than to be a candidate. I have a deep affection for the place and still have many friends there.

The dilapidated Victorian Market Hall in Chesterfield and the shops on Low Pavement nearly succumbed to being put in a giant bunker under the market place, which would of course have been the end of them. Luckily good sense prevailed and they were beautifully restored. The Derbyshire Historic Buildings Trust, with which I was associated for many years, has had much success in saving small, desirable houses from the bulldozer. I hope that many of the stone barns that litter the Peak District may find a new role as night shelters for walkers. They are not the grand cathedral-like barns of the south of England, being often no more than sturdy sheds, but they are an important part of the landscape and many are falling to bits since they are no longer used for agricultural purposes.

The Bronze Age recumbent stones of Arbor Low on a high, bleak site near Youlgreave are worth a visit. I suggested to my sister Pam, who was deaf, that we should go there in the winter when the weekly *Dad's Army* television programme was at its most popular and she replied, 'Oh, Arthur Lowe, I should *so* much like to meet him.' Eyam is famous for its villagers' courageous behaviour. In 1665 a bundle of cloth contaminated by the plague arrived from London. To prevent the infection from spreading, Eyam's parson, the Reverend William Mompesson, persuaded the villagers not to leave. The deadly disease ravaged the small population but it was contained, and Mompesson and the villagers are honoured at an annual outdoor service held in the field where he preached while the disease was at its height.

Much of Derbyshire is Robin Hood country. Inn signs, plantations, a group of rocks near Elton and a big stone outcrop high up in the woods above the old park at Chatsworth carry his name. The legend is that Robin shot an arrow from this stony height, saying he would be buried where it fell. It reached Hathersage, eight miles away as the arrow flies, and although there is no sign of Robin Hood's grave, Little John is indeed buried in the churchyard. His grave was opened in the nineteenth century and a 32-inch-long thigh bone was found, which must have belonged to a man at least seven feet tall.

The immense oaks in the Old Park at Chatsworth are the outliers of Sherwood Forest and some are said to be a thousand years old. The oldest are kept alive by one or two small leafy branches. Their great hulks have rotted and become strange shapes, hollow and full of holes. They support an infinite variety of insect and bird life, and the younger and healthier trees provide big crops of acorns for the deer. We plant twenty or thirty in this part of the park every year and the fallen trees are never removed. Bracken gives the necessary privacy for the calves and fawns of the red and fallow deer.

No one can pretend that Derbyshire is famous for its food, though two delicacies are made in the county: Bakewell Pudding, a strange confection of almond paste, jam and pastry, and excellent Stilton cheese, which is made in a factory at Hartington.

The Peak District National Park was initiated in 1951 to look after some of the finest landscapes and villages. It takes no notice of county boundaries and wanders through parts of Cheshire and Staffordshire, though its main acreage is in Derbyshire. Although only 38,000 people live within the Peak Park, a third of the population of England is reckoned to live within an hour's drive of the Peak District. It is visited by millions of town dwellers from Manchester, Sheffield, Derby, Nottingham, Wolverhampton and Stoke, and the tourist industry is a valuable asset. In the most picturesque parts of the county, the landowners, farmers, smallholders and dwellers are constantly reminded of their heritage by the media, and it is to be hoped that this powerful lobby remembers that the villages will become Disneyland for trippers if they do not also recognise the need for jobs. If the county is to thrive, the limestone quarries, the mines for barites and fluorspar, and allied industries with their furnaces and factories, must go on as they have done for hundreds of years.

Derbyshire has more than its fair share of beautiful country. It also has some remarkable houses open to the public. In the south there is Sudbury Hall, home of the Vernons, which now belongs to the National Trust. Its somewhat forbidding exterior does not prepare you for the beauty of the plasterwork inside, described by Pevsner as 'luxuriant and breathtakingly skilful'. Near Derby are Kedleston Hall, Lord Curzon's Adam palace, and Melbourne Hall, with its splendid formal garden. Not far from Bakewell is Haddon Hall, that most English and romantic of Elizabethan buildings, and east of Chesterfield stands Hardwick Hall, Bess of Hardwick's surviving masterpiece, which never fails to astonish the visitor by the mysterious sweep of the staircase and the vast scale and beauty of the Presence Chamber and Long Gallery.

I leave home less and less often now but every time I return after a spell away, I am struck anew by this county's beauty — something I will never take for granted.

February 1982

LAGOPUS LAGOPUS SCOTICUS
AND ITS LODGERS

A delicacy unique to these islands is grouse. The grand restaurants in London, Paris and New York vie with each other to have the first and best birds on the menu for dinner on 12 August, the opening day of the grouse shooting season. Grouse moors are by their very nature high, wild and remote places. Such privacy is necessary for these elusive birds. No way of 'farming' or artificially rearing them has been devised. Grouse are mysterious even to the keepers who spend their lonely lives with them.

Like people, they are prone to disease. The biggest threat to these winged marvels is *Trichostrongylus tenuis*, or the Trichostrongyle worm, and attacks by these parasitic threadworms can be fatal. If they get the upper hand, the bird population can be wiped out and, instead of healthy broods, the moor is littered with skeletons. Shooting is a culling operation which prevents overpopulation, the cause of this and other diseases.

All ground-nesting birds, their eggs and chicks are at risk of being taken by foxes, weasels, stoats, rats and flying predators, including several species of hawks now protected by law. The weather at hatching time is crucial. A thunderstorm plus hail during the last two weeks of May can be catastrophic to the new chicks. They need warm weather to provide the minute insects on which they feed, until later when their diet consists of the tips of young heather, followed by the seed. The chicks grow at great speed, almost as quickly as broiler chicks turn into supermarket fare. By 12 August, the majority are only about twelve weeks old but even so they can fly like jets and are at their succulent best to eat.

I wonder if the people tucking into their dinners at the Connaught or the Ritz realise how many skilled professionals have made it possible for these birds to reach their tables. Gamekeepers; flankers with flags who guide the birds towards their fate; beaters who walk many miles through high heather and – worst of all – bracken, which on a wet day is no fun; gunsmiths from Spain to South Audley Street; cartridge manufacturers; the makers of Land Rovers and Argo Cats (machines on tracks that can go up the nearly perpendicular hills in Scotland); Mrs Barbour DBE and her coats; dog breeders and trainers; the 'guns' – the eight or so men who stand in the line of butts, on whose shooting prowess 'the bag' depends; pickers-up, the people whose dogs find the birds on the ground after the drive – all combine in a team effort, like an army manoeuvre, before a single bird is shot.

For all sorts of reasons, the uncertainty of the number that will fly over the butts is part of the charm of grouse shooting. Nothing can be guaranteed, least of all the weather. It is a question of First Shoot Your Grouse – not easy in a gale, with rain pelting into your face, hands numb with cold in spite of August on the calendar, or when it's so hot you can't bear to touch the metal on the Land Rover and the dogs drink enough water to float a ship. However, on a perfect day – when there's a breeze and sunny intervals, when the heather is full out and the pollen rising where the dogs hunt for fallen birds, when there's a clear view across the purple heights to the greener ground below – it is an earthly heaven. Or sometimes at Bolton Abbey, it can be raining hard on the tops and you suddenly catch a glimpse of the silver snake of the River Wharfe in its sunlit carved green valley and it is like a vision of the Promised Land.

Grouse fly high, they fly low (like winged rabbits), they

swoop, curve and jink, straight or twisting, singly, in pairs, or in packs of hundreds. They seem to be coming towards you and at the last moment they turn and cross the line three or four butts away. As you watch, disappointed, another bird comes at an impossible angle. You see it too late and a second chance is gone. A strong wind behind the birds increases their speed to a fly past; a wind against them and, hovering in the air almost stationary, they look easy but are as tricky as can be.

Getting the shot birds from the butts on the high ground of the Yorkshire or Perthshire moors to a road and thence to a motorway or an airport is, in itself, a challenge. When everything goes right and the birds arrive in the kitchens, they still have to be plucked, drawn and cooked before anyone who can afford it can eat them. The point of this saga is not just that grouse shooting is the most exciting and the most testing of sports but it also produces a harvest of valuable food.

Should you still be curious about these birds, I must refer you to a book which ought to have a place in every library, *The Grouse in Health and Disease*, Lord Lovat (ed.), 1911. With its accompanying appendix it weighs 7lb 7oz and is profusely illustrated with disgusting pictures of parasites, vastly enlarged ticks and the other lodgers that enjoy living a life of luxury in or on grouse. Perhaps the diners in London and Paris are aware of this but I would love to know if, poised with knife and fork, they have any idea that the expensive luxury they are about to eat can carry up to 10,000 worms, not to mention other parasites. The squeamish will be glad to hear that the worms are happy to live in the gut and so they've gone before the grouse reach the Sèvres plates.

Perhaps it is better not to know but just to enjoy the worms' host with no questions asked, and salute the dedication and skill of the keepers and the rest thanks to whom these epicurean treats have landed on your table.

WRITING A BOOK

Odd things happen when you write a book. The prospective publishers make out a contract – written in double Dutch of course, to confuse – couched in lawyers' language of 'The First Party', 'The Second Party', Marx Brothers' style. And no Sanity Clause. Suddenly the book turns into 'The Work', as in 'hereinafter termed the Work'. That's the first sensible thing they say. *Work* it jolly well is. (Just as *labour* is a brilliant description of having a baby – except that it ought to be called hard labour.)

Anyway, this Work is then the subject of a long rigmarole, beautifully printed on smart paper to make it seem less beastly. But in the middle of some unreadable paragraphs are sentences that strike an ice-cold note. For instance, there is talk about the Resolutions that will be passed if the publishers go into liquidation (which they will if they keep on taking books like mine) and the fate of the Author if he or she fails to deliver the Manuscript by a certain date. (He/she has to look sharp and pay for *everything* forthwith.)

Now I always thought of manuscripts as those immaculately written things on parchment, like Bess of Hardwick's accounts, with swirling, squiggling E's. Not at all, it just means a dreary old typed mess. Rather a relief, I must admit, because if one had to learn to write like Queen Elizabeth I on top of everything else it would be the giddy limit.

Then the publisher mentions something very worrying about what is going to happen to the books that go to the Philippines. Why this remote group of islands has to be singled out as a likely market and how the Filipinos could possibly be interested in the colour of curtains at Chatsworth, I really can't imagine, but I suppose Uncle Harold or someone knows.*

There is only one comforting bit in the whole of this lengthy document. It says, 'The Publishers shall not destroy any stock or sell it off as pulp without first informing the Author of their intention and offering the Author a few copies for personal use.' I think that's jolly nice of them. But what on earth is the author going to do with his few copies? He couldn't want to read them because he's written them. You can't eat them, take a taxi with them or plant them in the garden; you can't wear them or smoke them; they're no good as rat poison; you can't slate a roof with them or even make a decent garden seat. Never mind, it's a kind thought and one must be grateful for that. And so the contract maunders on to its incomprehensible legal conclusions.

The work part of the Work is very difficult to do with the telephone and other aspects of real life going on at home. So I took a room in a hotel by the sea for a few days. *Absolute failure*. The other denizens of the place took pity on an old woman holidaying alone and talked to me all through breakfast, lunch and dinner, both in the residents' lounge and in the darkest corner of the bar. So I took my exercise book to one of those glass-lined bus shelters you find on windswept English beaches, settled happily down, and lo and behold another lone woman came and sat beside me and started telling me about her dog. So I chucked it and went home. I only tell you all this in case you have the fancy to do the same yourselves one day. I think it's better to stick to farming and gardening, Agriculture and Horticulture.

The only thrilling part of all this is being paid for the twaddle you have written. A cheque arrives (the exact sum having been decided upon months ago so you had given up hope) and it looks really pleasing to the eye. But don't bank on it when you've banked it. Look again at the bit of paper and you'll see many a percentage deducted for one reason or another. VAT is mentioned and is horrid. Soon I expect VAT will be payable on VAT and so on, *ad infinitum*, till a minus sign wins the day. The final insult isn't, we have to admit, to do with publishers. It's the tax. And this almost makes the game not worth the candle. But it's all good clean fun. So out with the foolscap and on with a new one.

1982

* Deborah Devonshire's first book, *The House: A Portrait of Chatsworth*, published in 1982 by Macmillan, was commissioned by Harold Macmillan, Andrew Devonshire's uncle by marriage, who became chairman of his family's publishing firm after retiring from politics.

FLORA DOMESTICA: A HISTORY OF FLOWER ARRANGING, 1500–1930
by Mary Rose Blacker

Flower arranging. Oh dear, I thought (having been to so many public functions where flowers are stuck sideways in their holder so the horizontal gladiolus stalks can't reach the water – a worrying style still practised in many a town hall). Never fear. This book is a wonder from start to finish. The author sees the subject with a scholar's eye and recounts the history of indoor fashion in flowers, from the sixteenth century until it reached a zenith of extravagance some hundred years ago.

It is said that cooks are prone to bad temper because their art is destroyed. The transitory nature of flower-arrangers is similar, but luckily for us it has been a subject beloved of artists over centuries and part of the fascination of this book lies in its illustrations. The familiar Dutch pictures of the seventeenth century, when it was cheaper to buy a painting of a tulip by an established artist than obtain a bulb of the precious plant itself, show glorious mixtures of flowers stuffed into containers of all kinds, including the incomparable blue-and-white Delftware brought to England by King William III's Mary. A few generations later, it's back to nature and we are exhorted by Batty Langley, the eighteenth-century Twickenham gardener, to make arrangements in a 'loose manner, so as not to represent a stiff bundle of flowers void of freedom'.

As more exotics arrived in this country, so did the variety of flowers grown in orangeries increase. In 1773, Horace Walpole wrote from his Gothic fantasy, Strawberry Hill, 'My house is a bower of tuberoses.' The Sèvres factory in France and Wedgwood in England produced exquisite vases of all shapes and sizes to hold such wonders. Houses such as Osterley led the way with *garnitures* of up to thirteen pieces lined up on the mantelpiece. The National Trust has a band of volunteers at Osterley who recreate some of the eighteenth-century arrangements using flowers of the period, and that beautiful house is worthy of a visit for this reason alone.

Early nineteenth-century nurserymen, sniffing more business, began hiring out plants for receptions in the great London houses. Teams of gardeners were sent in to set them up and earned praise for their 'happy disposition' of plants at routs and fêtes. Sometimes the lady of the house did the job herself. There is a glorious description of the stout Duchess of Gordon in 1810, up a ladder, dressed in a dimity wrapper, 'knocking in nails to hold a garland of laurel over a picture', doing what 'she can get none of her awkward squad to do for her', before reappearing as hostess in 'the brightest spirits and the brightest diamonds'.

Soon palm trees appeared (at Chatsworth even banana trees). The gardeners and their 'decorators', as the arrangers were called, became increasingly ambitious until they went completely over the top and festooned everything, from chandeliers to plant boxes, in masses of flowers and leaves. 'Fences' of orchids and peonies erected along the tables made it impossible to see your fellow guests. Lady Monkwell, invited to dinner to meet Mr Gladstone, could only hear him for the hedge of peonies in the way. Lady Aberdeen scattered autumn leaves on her tablecloth. (They look like potato crisps but never mind, they were a change from ferns and carnations.) A monstrous innovation was the 'banded dish', a dining-table decoration that consisted of concentric circles of brilliantly coloured flowers arranged on a plate. There is an illustration of it from an American magazine of 1869 and it is the only ugly picture in the book, inexplicably chosen for the dust cover.

Hothouses proliferated in the gardens of big houses. At Waddesdon Manor, which had four acres under glass, a staggering variety of flowers was produced, including forests of Malmaison carnations that are notoriously difficult to grow. I am happy to say that they have appeared again at Waddesdon in profusion – an example of how everything at that house is done in slap-up style. The book is stuffed with anecdotes and reminders of the luxuries of times past. I shall have to go to Lyme Park to see the tobacco plants in the Bright Passage and to Polesden Lacy for a whiff of Mrs Ronnie Greville, that extravagant perfectionist.

My only criticism is of the illustrations of flowers in fireplaces. In our climate, fireplaces are for fires not flowers. The spirits sink on a cold June evening to see a bunch of roses where the welcoming glow ought to be. This is a tiny point in an otherwise perfect book. I hope Mrs Blacker will now tell us what happened to Floral Art from 1930–2000. She must.

July 2000

BOOK SIGNINGS AND LITERARY LUNCHES

Publishers sometimes think it is a Good Idea for an author to do a book signing to give their book a shove. The author is invited to a bookshop where an apparently inexhaustible supply of the wretched things is piled in heaps round Exhibit A, the author.

The staff in the bookshop are kindness itself. They have put a table and chair in the cave of books with familiar covers, so you feel at home. The signing has been advertised and it is a matter of pride to the staff, and terror to the author, to see if anyone turns up. When the appointed moment comes, the author settles in the chair, armed with pen and specs and, with luck, some would-be customers shuffle into view. Even if they have come on purpose to buy the book, they look at several identical volumes as if there might be a difference between one copy and another.

It is strange how few people seem to be buying the book for themselves. He/she picks one up, looks doubtfully at it, turns it round and says, 'It's for my mother, actually.' Younger customers say, 'It's for my grandmother, actually.' 'Oh, good,' says the author, 'that is really nice of you. What shall I write in it?' Long pause, while the buyer considers how the recipient should be addressed, as the author can't very well call someone else's mother/grandmother 'Mummy' or 'Granny'. So the Christian name is chosen. It has to be spelt out, especially if it happens to be Sheila, a trap with a good chance of 'gh' at the end. Luckily, the most usual name is Margaret and, as far as I know, there is no peculiar spelling there. But names get ever more unlikely and you have to listen carefully to the invented ones.

The next customer tells her life story. That's fine as long as there is no one behind her, but it can make the attention wander if you see one or two people who are obviously in a hurry and don't want to hear of far-off school days or a shared Oxfordshire childhood. Then comes a man, rolled umbrella if in Piccadilly, tweed coat and pale trousers if in Burford. 'Three copies? Oh thank you. What shall I put?' 'Just your signature, please.' Quickly done and off he goes. Obviously an excellent fellow, the sort the wireless calls a decision maker. Usually, the messages to be written are pretty ordinary. As yet, I have not had the one a famous author of my acquaintance told me about. A man formed up and asked nervously, 'Could you put "For Marlene – sorry about last night"?'

Bookshop regulars spot the chairs and the pile of identical books and dart in the opposite direction to avoid having to buy out of pity something they don't want. They ask, 'Where are the maps?' or 'Are there any books on beavers?' and make off like lightning.

With luck, the pile has diminished in the hour which has passed. So have the customers. Now you can have a good talk to the shop staff and find out what is really selling while you sign a few copies for stock. The devotion to books of the staff or owner of the shop, as the case may be, shines out and you come away wondering about the charm of the written word.

A literary lunch is another matter. Three authors parade their wares by talking about them after two courses of so-called food for which people have actually paid. Usually there is not much literature on show because the books are 'popular' (or the lunch would be a failure). One of the speaker-authors tells doubtful stories in his allotted ten minutes, to the joy or embarrassment of the audience according to their taste. The other authors look at their watches, mindful of a train to catch. Eventually they all move to the tables where they are to sign and the rubbishy book disappears while the other two, over which the writers have taken real trouble, remain in their original piles, sadly slow to move.

At one of these entertainments I found myself in the company of Jeffrey Archer (before he was famous) and Arthur Marshall, who was indeed famous both for his inimitable radio performances in which he would turn into the school matron and, more important, as a television star. His book roared away. He became a dear friend, the best company ever, and stayed with us at Chatsworth several times. One hot summer day we were walking across the big lawn crowded with people lying in heaps listening to the Sunday band. A woman spotted him: 'Is it?' I heard her say. 'It can't be . . . IT *IS!*' and round they came like bees to honey, for a word, a signed bit of paper, anything to remind them they had actually met the man who made them laugh.

I sometimes read about the other author at that strange Literary Lunch but I have never seen him since.

September 2007

THE TULIP
by *Anna Pavord*

From the dedication to Valerie Finnis, the acknowledged queen of English gardeners, this book is a rare treat. Taking as its subject a single genus of flower, it is written by a scholar and reads like a thriller.

There cannot be anyone who does not love tulips, if only because of the time of year of their flowering. If roses are synonymous with summer, tulips are the tangible evidence of spring. Of course we love them but we may not know that their story is as fascinating as the flowers themselves, with 'a background full of more mysterious dramas, dilemmas, disasters and triumphs than any besotted *aficionado* could reasonably expect'. It certainly is.

The native habitat of the tulip extends from Ankara to Tashkent and it was from Turkey that the first bulbs (or roots as they were called) came to Europe. In 1559, a Swiss botanist described seeing its 'gleaming red petals and its sensuous scent' in a Bavarian garden – the first known report of the flower in western Europe. The traders of the Dutch East India Company introduced it to Holland, where it soon became the object of 'tulipomania', and the madly desired flowers began to change hands for prices far above rubies. The usually stolid Dutch lost their heads over the striped, feathered and flamed flowers, that mysterious 'breaking' of colour which was caused by a virus. It was these flowers that commanded the wildest prices. The mania spread to France. At the height of the madness a man swapped his brewery for a single bulb. The crazy trade reached its zenith in 1637, when the inevitable crash came and trading was banned. Boom and bust is nothing new.

Protestant refugees fleeing religious persecution in Europe in the late sixteenth century took the valuable and easily carried bulbs to use as currency in their adopted countries, including England. They were soon taken up by nurserymen who supplied the owners of the formal gardens fashionable in the seventeenth century. The fancy spread quickly and amateur growers, known as 'florists', joined the tulip train and kept many of the choicest strains going throughout the eighteenth century. Clubs sprang up and tulip shows with attendant feasts were organised. By the 1820s, the rivalry between clubs in the north and the south of England was intense. Inter-club rows of mammoth proportions were commonplace and jealous rivals destroyed each other's tulip beds. At a Lancashire show, the finest entry (according to its owner) was stolen during dinner before it could be judged. Experts differed on standards of judging and views about the form of the blooms; insulting letters to horticultural journals flew to and fro. Judges had to be men of courage. The chapter on 'The Florist's Tulip' is comedy bordering on farce.

Of the many societies formed during the last century, only the Wakefield and North of England Tulip Society remains, where the blooms are shown in beer bottles as of yore. Tulips were the passion of artisans, and workers in the dark satanic mills fulfilled their artistic longings through the beauty of the flowers. The lack of a garden did not stop one engine driver in Derby – he grew his along the railway embankment.

The Tulip is too heavy to read in bed but once you have started there is no question of going to bed so it doesn't matter.

December 1998

UNSTEALABLES

The trouble about book thieves is that they don't see themselves as such. They borrow and forget with no criminal intent. But they pick the best without fail and leave a gap, unnoticed probably for months, and then you want the missing book for a quote, a story – or all of it – and it's gone.

I seldom read for pleasure but every now and then something takes my fancy and I mind so much when I've finished that, like my father, I can't bear the thought of beginning another. In an effort to keep my loved ones, I have got them penned, as it were, in my bedroom. The hard core is by friends and family, from grandfathers to children, and some of them have lost their spines in the rough and tumble of life in a hanging bookcase. They are all precious, of course, but too many to go into here. They include *Park Top: A Romance of the Turf* by Andrew Devonshire, a book that reveals as much about its author as it does about the famous filly, bought for him as a bargain yearling in 1965 by his friend and trainer, Bernard van Cutsem. And there's *A Fine Old Conflict* by Jessica Mitford. When she was working on this autobiographical book, I asked my sister what its title was to be. 'The Final Conflict', she replied. I wasn't listening properly and thought she said 'A Fine Old Conflict', which is what she decided on.

The others are a motley lot and all prized. I made a list of a few some years ago: *Fowls and Geese and How to Keep Them*; *Book* by Lady Clodagh Anson and *Another Book* by the same author;

What Shall We Have Today? by X. Marcel Boulestin; Priscilla Napier's autobiography, *A Late Beginner*; *Another World*, the first twenty years of Anthony Eden's life; *The Secret Orchard of Roger Ackerley* by Diana Petre; *The Prince, the Showgirl and Me* by Colin Clark; *Rio Grande's Last Race and Other Verses* by A. B. Peterson; *The Best of Beachcomber*; Thomas Hardy's *The Woodlanders*; *The Anatomy of Dessert* (1933) by Edward A. Bunyard; *The Curse of the Wise Woman* by Lord Dunsany; *Peter Rabbit*; *Ginger and Pickles*; *Small is Beautiful* by E. F. Schumacher, and Peter Guralnick's *Last Train to Memphis: The Rise of Elvis Presley*.

There are also the essentials: *The Definitive Edition of Rudyard Kipling's Verse*; *The Collected Poems* of A. E. Housman and *The Oxford Book of English Verse* (1922 edition). The latter is inscribed 'Unity Mitford from Uncle George, Asthall, August 1925', with '11 years old' added in childish writing. Some years later, Unity wrote in it again, 'U.V.M., St. Margaret's, Bushey' – the school she loved and from which she was sacked. Since my sister's death, this volume, printed on India paper, has been my travelling companion. 'Lament of the Irish Immigrant' by Helen Selina, Lady Dufferin, which brings tears to this day, has been eliminated from later editions. Why?

The list has inevitably grown over the years; new ones have joined my classic crowd and more shelves have been filled.

Black Diamonds by Catherine Bailey is now next to *White Mischief* by James Fox.

The Day of Reckoning by Mary Clive. Born Pakenham, and still alive at 101, she is as good a story-teller as any of that tribe of writers. She writes of the 'day-to-day surroundings of well-to-do families' in the early part of the twentieth century. The illustrations, some familiar – *When Did You Last See Your Father?*, *The Finest View in Europe*, a cover of *Chatterbox* – others of private and national events, whirl you through her life with nostalgia and joy. But don't miss the text.

Ask the Fellows Who Cut the Hay by George Ewart Evans

(1909–88) is one of a cherished series that includes *Where Beards Wag All* and *The Horse in the Furrow*. The author describes rural life in Suffolk and set about his task just in time, when there were still farm labourers who could remember working the heavy soil with Suffolk horses and all that went with it.

Notes from a Small Island. The brilliant American Bill Bryson notices so much about this country which we take for granted but are fascinated to see described as new. It beats me why he is so fond of England and its natives – it's amazing that he stayed here after arriving on a foggy midnight in Folkestone to the typical English opposite of a welcome.

I galloped through *On the Black Hill* when it came out in 1982 in order to get an impression of Bruce Chatwin's inimitable way of writing, which carries you with him to the novel's inevitable tragic end.

Heinrich Hoffmann's *Struwwelpeter*, a terrifying illustrated book for children, could not find a publisher now. My sisters and I used to think that great Agrippa, 'foaming with rage in his dressing gown' and 'so tall, he almost touched the sky', was the double of my father.

Somerville and Ross: The World of the Irish R.M. by Lewis Gifford is a biography of my Anglo-Irish heroines who wrote about life in southernmost Ireland before the boom when there was only bust.

Coke of Norfolk and His Friends by A. M. W. Sterling was a Christmas present long ago from my Uncle Jack Mitford, who could not have guessed that agriculture would be my overriding interest.

They're Away was a present to Andrew from a bookmaker. It is my favourite volume of poetry about hunting and racing, by Beatrice Holden (1886–1968), a redoubtable hunting woman of Atherstone and Warwickshire fame. Years ago I stuck her obituary from *Horse & Hound* inside the cover. It ends, 'Gallop on blithe spirit, and may you find your heaven in a good grass country.' 'A Closing Memory of Lord Harrington' is one of her best, a mysterious tale known by all hunting people. Lord Harrington's dying wish was that his hounds should meet the day after his funeral. They quickly found a fox that ran straight to their master's grave, where 'the grass was trampled and pressed / Where yesterday the best-loved man in the Midlands was laid to rest'. The huntsman took off his cap and whispered, 'Gentlemen, I am taking them Home; / His Lordship has called his Hounds.'

Primrose McConnell's *Agricultural Note-Book* (1919 edition) is inscribed, 'After my death this book is to be given to Debo. With love Conrad Russell, XII Night 1947'. The blue-eyed Somerset dairy farmer became a friend during the war when Andrew was stationed at Warminster. He made cheese, and was as clever and individual as Russells are apt to be.

Primrose was a man. His *Note-Book* is dedicated to the memory of his son, also Primrose, who was killed in the Great War. It is closely packed with facts and figures pertaining to the land. The physical work expected of a farm labourer earning pitiful wages is shocking to us now. A man was expected to pitch 4,000 to 5,000 sheaves of corn a day and a woman to milk ten cows, night and morning, for 1¼d per cow.

Out of Africa by Karen Blixen. I suppose this book is on everyone's list.

If Hopes Were Dupes (1966) by 'Catherine York'. This is by my first cousin, Ann Farrer, who wrote this sorrowful account of her nervous breakdown and total dependence on her psychoanalyst. It would send a shiver down any spine.

The Uncommon Reader by Alan Bennett. How did he do it? I wish I knew. There are copies of this book all over the house. They won't last long. My own is guarded by fatter volumes, several inches thick (*Farm Live Stock of Great Britain* and *Mrs Beeton's Book of Household Management*), which protect this little jewel.

May God preserve them all.

JOHN FOWLER: PRINCE OF DECORATORS
by Martin Wood

It is not given to many for their surname to be turned into an adjective immediately recognisable by a section of society. 'Fowlerised' meant a house transformed by John Fowler to his (and the owner's) taste. In spite of having known John for many years, I had little idea of the extent of his work and influence until I read this book. Dedicated to looking and learning, he dealt with all dates and styles of buildings through scholarship and a prodigious memory.

He was born in 1906, a one-off in an unartistic family, with talents that took him to painting furniture for Peter Jones in 1934, where he earned £4 a week. He was refused a rise in wages so he and his colleagues downed paintbrushes and set up on their own.

They struggled on until 1938, when John joined Lady Colefax. Twice his age and a fashionable decorator with a shop in Mayfair, Sybil Colefax knew the women who wanted something more than Syrie Maugham's everlasting white and mushroom, which had ruled during the early 1930s. Fashion had moved on in its inexorable way and John seized the opportunity. Through his personality and knowledge he soon became the clients' favourite. He was exempted from war service because of myopia. While fabrics were rationed, he used his ingenuity to cover sofas with old curtains, and his clients' unwanted evening dresses were cut up to make trimmings or cushion covers.

In 1944, when Nancy Tree bought into the business now called Colefax & Fowler, she and John became an irresistible force. They bickered and sparred, they flounced out and flounced back, they laughed and got angry, and through this exhausting process produced some of the most beautiful interiors in the land. They fed off each other to the benefit of their clients. The business prospered through word of mouth: Nancy's friends and relations, who happened to be the highest echelons of society, aspired to this resourceful duo. Nancy had the ideas and taught John how the famous houses were to be lived in and enjoyed through comfort and beauty. John, the dictator of the work-room, got on and performed the task, supported by his skilled craftsmen. He taught them as Nancy had taught him.

Before John came on the scene, Nancy and her husband Ronnie Tree had bought Ditchley Park, a James Gibbs house in Oxfordshire, and made it an earthly paradise. Ditchley was an inspiration to John. In 1954 Nancy (now married to Jubie Lancaster) restored Haseley Court, near Oxford, where their full-blown taste reached its zenith. The list of places John worked on reads like a dictionary of that unique English asset envied by the rest of the world – the country house. It included Blithfield Hall in Staffordshire, Radburne Hall near Derby, Mereworth Castle in Kent, Arundel Park and Syon House. Most were private houses but some opened to the public after the war. The book's index shows hardly a county without an example of his work.

In 1956 John got his first job with the National Trust at magical Claydon House in Buckinghamshire. This led to many more, including Sudbury Hall in Derbyshire. I was on the committee for its redecoration before the Trust opened it to the public. I carried John's patterns, flew up and down stairs, moved furniture ('Don't push that chair – PICK IT UP') and trudged the length of the Long Gallery time after time at his bidding. He was already mortally ill but did not spare himself or his helpers in the cold, unwelcoming rooms that turned into fairyland under his direction. His treatment of the staircase was an example of his disdain for democracy. The committee arrived one day to find that the carved balusters had been painted white and the walls a brilliant yellow. Jaws dropped, but the murmuring went unheeded and we moved on to the next thing.

Cornbury Park and Chequers, two mammoth jobs, were his last major commissions. Neither is accessible to you and me but both are mighty impressive according to the lucky few who know them.

John was two people. A tyrant to his staff, he changed into a delightful companion after work, amusing and amused. He took to gardening and saw the importance of the relationship between indoors and out. He was also a master of scale. The photographs in the book of a 'pocket' flat, the size of a double garage, give the impression of a much bigger place. He dealt with palaces and cottages with equal enthusiasm.

This book is an historic document, a reminder of times past, beautifully written with photographs that accurately depict the interiors – even the colours are right. It will be the standard reference book of taste in England during the second half of the twentieth century.

December 2007

TIARAS

What are tiaras for? They are the finishing flourish to the best evening dress, accompanied by long white gloves of thinnest suede, ending above the elbow and cleaned after every outing. They are the night-time equivalent of an Ascot hat, the female accompaniment to a man's white tie and decorations, the opposite of dressing down and the pinnacle of the jeweller's art. They are often accompanied by necklaces and brooches of a like design, a casket of delight with which to decorate a female form.

Before the last war, tiaras were worn by married women (only) at all the grand balls in London, and very beautiful they were. Some of the most striking were once-seen-never-forgotten. The face underneath was known by the helmet of diamonds, rubies, emeralds, sapphires and pearls glittering above: harsh, spiky and upstanding, or a humbler circlet threaded through the marcel waves of the hair. It was like recognising people in a country crowd by their dogs. We would have been very muddled if there had been a general swap around and the Duchess of Northumberland wore Lady Astor's and Lady Londonderry turned up in one of the Duchess of Buccleuch's. Some of the young women were fairylike in their beauty. The old and fat were not, but even they were improved by their headdresses.

The royal tiaras, some of extraordinary splendour, are familiar through being much photographed, but family jewels of lesser mortals are left in the bank and seldom given an airing. Like most

English heirlooms, the jewels belong to the man and are worn by the wives. (If things go on as they are, I see the day looming when it will be the other way round.) These women are usually too busy looking after difficult husbands and animals to bother about having their diamonds cleaned, so the royal jewels shine out, always in pristine order, and the enormous stones worn by the peeresses, happier in gumboots and strangers to the hairdresser, are apt to look dim in comparison.

Queen Mary wore tiaras like she wore her toques – as if they were part of her being. In her day, when formality and rigid standards of dress were the rule, King George wore a tailcoat, white tie and the blue riband of the Garter while Queen Mary wore an evening dress and tiara, even when they were dining alone. A favourite was a diamond bandeau, the base of a tiara given to her as a wedding present in 1893 by 'The Girls of Great Britain and Ireland'.

My grandmother-in-law, Evelyn Duchess of Devonshire, was Mistress of the Robes to Queen Mary for forty-three years from 1910. Together they weathered long hours of tiara'd evenings, including those during the fabulous Indian Durbar in Delhi in 1911. The magically beautiful but relentless programme, carried out in torrid heat, was exhausting for all concerned, and after one particularly lengthy evening Granny Evie was heard to say, 'The Queen has been complaining about the weight of her tiara . . . *The Queen doesn't know what a heavy tiara is.*'

Evelyn knew what she was talking about. The larger of the two Devonshire diamond tiaras is indeed a whopper. It was made in 1893 for Louise, the 8th Duke of Devonshire's wife. She was formerly married to the Duke of Manchester and was known as the 'Double Duchess'. The diamonds have an historic interest. They were not, like so many, bought by their owner as a result of the fall of various royal houses; they came from the Devonshire Parure. This set consists of seven monumental pieces of jewellery, which, until you look closely at them, might have been pulled out of the dressing-up box. They are a bizarre combination of antique (Greek and Roman) and Renaissance cameos and intaglios carved from emeralds, rubies, sapphires and semi-precious stones – cornelian, onyx, amethysts and garnets – set in gold and enamel of exquisite workmanship by C. F. Hancock of London. They were commissioned by the dear old, extravagant 6th Duke of Devonshire, the 'Bachelor' Duke, for his niece, Countess Granville, to wear at the coronation of Tsar Alexander II in Moscow in 1856. This tiara and its companion necklace, stomacher and bracelet are very prickly to wear. I know because I put them all on for a Women's Institute performance when I was cast as 'The Oldest Miss World in the World'.

My mother-in-law, Mary Devonshire, was Mistress of the Robes to the Queen from 1953 to 1967. Tall and beautiful, she looked magnificent when dressed for a grand occasion. The big tiara suited her perfectly and anyone who saw her in close attendance on the young Queen at the coronation in 1953 will remember the perfection of her bearing on that famous day. In the course of her duties, which included formal banquets for visiting heads of state and other ceremonial occasions, she used to fetch the jewels from the bank stowed in a Marks & Spencer carrier bag.

There can be no slouching with a tiara on your head. It makes you stand and sit up straight. In spite of combs, hairpins and kirby grips, there is always the possibility of it slipping, which makes the most dedicated teetotaller look the worse for wear. Tiaras elevate the wearer, making her look more distinguished and taller because of the unaccustomed posture (which used to be taught as 'deportment', long forgotten in this sloppy age).

The Queen Mother was a lesson to us all in this. She was not tall but her carriage was such that she would have been outstanding in a crowd even if she were not a queen. When she was over eighty, I remember seeing her sit bolt upright through an entire performance of the ballet at Covent Garden, her back never touching her chair.

Tiaras could often be 'taken down', unscrewed from their frames by miniature carpenter's tools, and fastenings screwed on to the back to make brooches. These were the ruin of many an evening dress when the pin was blunt and had to be forced through satin or silk, leaving a sizeable hole.

In the 1930s, the 6th Duke of Portland was wounded by the enormous diamond headdress about to be worn by his beautiful wife, Winnie. He went to talk to her when she was getting dressed and sat on a nearby chair. The tiara was there first and he leapt up, impaled on the platinum spikes that held the precious stones. It was hopelessly broken. 'Oh never mind,' said Winnie, not bothering about her husband's injured behind, 'I'll wear another one.' Some could be useful weapons. Two quarrelling women sprouting branched spears on their heads look for all the world like stags about to clash antlers in the October rut. A curiosity of about 1860 is a coronet of fox's teeth, mounted points upward. It belongs to the Marquess of Waterford, an Irish peer whose family has always been devoted to foxhunting. Lady Waterford tells me it is not often worn.

At a big dance in the 1950s and 1960s it was not uncommon for men to wear tailcoats and women their jewels. I remember going to such an entertainment in London in the early 1960s, by myself as Andrew had an engagement elsewhere. With unwonted confidence I wore the big tiara. It must have looked rather odd because my home-made dress of cotton broderie anglaise was definitely not up to it. When I ran out of partners and wanted to go home, I went out to look for a taxi. It never occurred to me that it might not be a good idea to stand alone in the street, long after midnight, with a load of diamonds round my neck and 1,900 more glittering above my head.

One memorable evening we were staying at Windsor Castle for a dance given by the Queen. I came down to dinner, got-up as I thought our hostess and the other guests would be, the big tiara firmly in place. To my horror none of the other women wore theirs. It is far worse to be overdressed than underdressed and I sat through dinner wishing I was anywhere else. When the dancing began, I took it off, put it under a chair and enjoyed myself enormously. I suppose Windsor Castle is the only house where you could be sure of finding the blessed thing still there at bedtime.

March 2002

AUCTION CATALOGUES

The catalogues of the big auction houses arrive here by post. They are fat and heavy and when you have flicked over the pages that tell you how to bid and how to pay (and your fate if you don't pay pronto) you reach the nub of the matter, profusely illustrated, with what you are encouraged to buy.

The number and quality of works of art that find their way to the salerooms never cease to amaze me. In spite of the vast quantity now frozen to death in galleries and museums, a big proportion of which is not shown because there is no room, a seemingly endless supply still passes through the auction houses of London, Paris, New York and Geneva – covering the whole gamut of artists and craftsmen from over the centuries.

The scholarship and meticulous research that make up the descriptions in these catalogues are a history lesson in themselves, as well as a lesson in the history of art. Specialists in each subject trot out their expertise. Details of works by familiar and unfamiliar names sometimes end with 'Thanks to . . . for the identification of the sitter' or 'Thanks to . . . for confirmation of the artist'. In these cases even the experts, in their ceaseless search for accuracy, have had to call on others for help. But suddenly your unquestioning acceptance of all this scholarly stuff, the last word in some narrow field of painting or other art, is nullified by the ignorance of much to do with birds, fruit and flowers, crops in landscapes, beasts of the field, horses, carriages, hounds and dogs.

Sporting art may be in fashion but cataloguers are often wide of the mark. They ought to be sentenced to a few months in the country before being let loose on their job. When you think of the teams of young people employed by auction houses, who are often brought up in the shires – by followers of hounds, keen shots, farmers, foresters, fishermen and gardeners – the directors would do well to ask these boys and girls to get their dads to cast a critical eye over the descriptions of forthcoming sales. This would avoid partridges being described as grouse, grouse as black game, snipe as woodcock, ptarmigan (even in white winter plumage) as grouse, hares as rabbits and vice versa. Beagles, harriers and foxhounds would no longer be muddled up. Haycocks would not be described as *corn stooks*, or haymaking as *harvesting corn*. The Scottish illustrator, Archibald Thorburn, who knew one bird from the other, wouldn't allow these untutored descriptions, so when his works are on offer they are correctly named – by the artist.

Some artists, however, are apt to muddle us. *On a Mossy Bank* may combine birds' nests and all sorts of flowers as though by chance. This is where we need a resident botanist to stop primroses being described as cowslips and an RSPB officer to stop the artists pulling nests and eggs from where they belong and dropping them in the open. The enormous canvases of Dutch flower-painters depict unseasonal combinations of tulips and roses, daffodils and passion flowers, hyacinths and dahlias, which is confusing. Did they paint the spring flowers and leave gaps till the summer ones came along? I wish I knew.

I have a sneaking feeling that when it comes to less important pictures, cataloguers may have an off-the-peg list of descriptions to fit. The figures in rural scenes are always *Peasants* or *Cottagers*. If the female peasants have got pots on their heads they will be *In an Italianate Landscape*. Any water in the way puts them into *A River Landscape*. If you can see for miles, start with *An Extensive Landscape*. Should there be a glimpse of the sea it will be *A Coastal*

Landscape or perhaps *A Rocky Coastal Landscape*. Sometimes add *With a Town Beyond* or *With a Storm Raging* or *With a Tavern*. Peasants and cottagers *carouse* outside these taverns, they are seldom just plain drinking. Cottagers' wives are quiet types who are *Gathering Flowers* or *Knitting* – especially *In a Cottage Interior* where there is a wooden cradle in front of the fire, a sheepdog lying on a home-made rag rug and Grandpa sitting in a rocking chair smoking a clay pipe.

Faggot Gatherers make up a considerable part of the rural population, and their near-relations, *Woodcutters*, provide fuel for the *Charcoal Burners in a Clearing*, who make a great deal of smoke – now illegal. These law-breakers seem to be very decent sorts of criminals, so it is just as well they are no more as I don't think they would take kindly to being shut up in prison.

Returning to sport, a favourite subject is *Ferreting* – sometimes threatened by *A Gathering Storm*. *Ratting* is the lowest of the low and unaffected by the weather. Anglers seem to be a better class of sportsmen as they cast their lines *On a River in a Wooded Landscape*. Fishermen spend a lot of time telling stories to audiences of little boys sitting on a breakwater gazing at the catch. Highland cattle and red deer are unheeding of the snow *In a Highland Landscape*. But the ubiquitous *Faggot Gatherers* are often bent double against a bitter wind as they approach their thatched cottages where, presumably, the faggots will be burnt in an attempt to warm the knitting wife, the baby and its grandfather.

At a meet of hounds all the followers are described as *huntsmen*. As every country skoolboy knows there is only one huntsman, so this is a serious mistake. When it comes to horses the cataloguers prefer chestnut to any other colour, so bays, browns and blacks are *chestnuts*. Anything as unusual as a strawberry roan stumps them; piebald and skewbald are reversed, and as for a flea-bitten grey, such a rarefied description is far beyond them. Shire horses hauling timber wagons are mistaken for Clydesdales. *Cavalry*

Charging is often just the King's Troop practising their act for an agricultural show.

This very day a catalogue has come from one of the leading auction houses. *A Thoroughbred Mare and her Foal* – the foal, as any fool can see, is an old Shetland pony. Dogs and hounds get the same treatment. An obvious Spaniel is a Setter while a Great Dane turns into an Irish Wolfhound, as does a Deer Hound. West Highland Whites are in fashion so they are correctly described, but Cairns are Scotties.

None of these yawning gaps in the knowledge of country affairs seems to matter. Beauty is in the eye of the beholding bidders, who cheerfully pay millions of pounds for their fancy.

Contemporary art is another subject altogether. The creators of these strange daubs have given up and *Untitled* is often as far as they will go – a wise decision.

There is one more twist to the ways of auctioneers. In the name of economy, two have written to me recently to say they cannot go on supplying catalogues for nothing. No wonder, when they must cost a fortune to produce. So I wrote back to thank them for past generosity and to say how much I have appreciated receiving them over the years. The surprising result is that I now receive two copies of each. I'm not complaining but it is a funny way to economise.

BUYING CLOTHES

London is becoming very odd. Shops, in particular. Wandering round the environs of Sloane Street, I saw in a window the very garment for the coming Derbyshire winter – a woolly coat one degree up from an old woman's cardigan, decent to look at and warm. So I went in, looked closer and still fancied it.

I asked the very nice but not exactly what the prime minister would call a British shop girl in a British job (sorry, Customer Service Assistant), just what colour it was. The reason for this basic question is that I have got an eye disease which muddles colours. The C.S.A. looked doubtfully at it, read a label or two and cleverly found the answer, saying very slowly, 'ELM'.

For one who cannot distinguish colours this is not very help-ful. First of all, we have – alas – been denied the sight of an elm since the 1960s when they all died. The majority of shoppers are too young to remember them but depending on the time of year they were three totally different colours: in spring the buds were brownish-pink, in summer the leaves were dark green and in autumn they turned into the purest and most beautiful yellow.

I bought the coat but I have no idea if it is pink, green or yellow. What's more, I have suddenly thought, was it the *bark* they were on about? Add silvery dark-brown with deep fissures as a fourth possibility. I would love to meet the manufacturer's colour expert and try to pin her down.

THE DUCHESS OF DEVONSHIRE'S BALL, 1897

A fancy-dress ball lasts only a few hours. Compared with other occasions for dressing up – performing in plays, ballets, operas and so forth – which are often repeated night after night, a ball is as ephemeral as a dream. Yet once they have accepted the invitation, serious grown-up people will take endless trouble – and often suffer extreme discomfort – to appear on the one-and-only night as their chosen character. The enthusiasm is infectious and the grumbling about what a bother it all is soon forgotten in the spirit of competition that goads the guests into making sure that their clothes are more beautiful, authentic, outrageous or funny than their neighbours'.

The Devonshire House fancy-dress ball held on 2 July 1897 to honour Queen Victoria's Diamond Jubilee is legendary. Until my daughter Sophy began to find out more about it for her book, *The Duchess of Devonshire's Ball*, I thought that, like many legends, it had become ridiculously exaggerated over the years. I was wrong.

In the days when a ball was given in London on four or five nights a week in May, June and July, when the now-vanished private houses of Mayfair and Kensington were going full blast, it had to be a very special entertainment to arouse much interest. The Duchess of Devonshire's ball was a very special entertainment.

It was not difficult for Louise Duchess to mobilise her female guests – they can have had little else to do but arrange themselves for such an occasion and one can easily picture the excitement and pleasure it gave. But even clever old Louise must have been surprised at managing to persuade a lot of middle-aged men to order their costumes and suffer the tedium of trying them on.

That she was able to persuade her sixty-four-year-old husband to give the party in the first place shows how indulgent he was towards her. At the time, the duke was Lord President of the Council, responsible for education and the Cabinet's defence committee in Lord Salisbury's third government. By this time he had given up frivolity and his idea of a pleasurable evening was a game of bridge with his wife and some old friends. One can only imagine how he must have groaned and sighed at the prospect of the night's entertainment. But he entered into the spirit of the thing to please his adored Louise.

Perhaps Englishmen secretly love dressing up. Perhaps, by pretending to be somebody else, they lose the self-consciousness with which so many of them are plagued. Certainly at any ceremonial occasion, whether military, ecclesiastic, academic or political, whether in the City of London or at Westminster, it is the men who wear fancy dress. They appear in cock feathers and sables, ermine and swords, lace and silk tights, and even carry posies of flowers through the streets, while their women melt into the surroundings like hen pheasants in the bracken.

Luckily for posterity, the duchess's guests submitted to the boredom of being photographed for a privately printed album presented to Louise by her friends. The expressionless faces of the subjects remind us of the long exposures necessary for photography a hundred years ago. Fashion in beauty has changed and looking at the photographs of the women (with a few glittering exceptions like the Duchesses of Portland and Marlborough), it is hard to imagine the sitters as the heart-breakers they certainly were. One could be forgiven for questioning if they even possessed a heart, or any other organ for that matter, as they seem to be made of wood or some harder material, standing set as concrete against the photographer's backcloths.

In spite of the rooms full of papers at Chatsworth, there is surprisingly little about Devonshire House itself. Rebuilt in 1733 after a fire, to designs by William Kent, it stood opposite the Ritz Hotel in Piccadilly. The 9th Duke of Devonshire sold it in 1919 but reserved some of the fixtures and fittings. Five years later it was pulled down by its new owners. Some of the doors (the ones from the billiard room had removable panels to let the smoke out) and fireplaces were used at Birch Grove, Harold Macmillan's house in Sussex. Harold's wife, born Dorothy Cavendish, was a daughter of the 9th Duke and had lived at Devonshire House as a child. For years, much of the furniture and even the silk off the walls were spread about Chatsworth. Piled high in the kitchen-maids' bedrooms were silk curtains, cushions, tassels and braids. Chimneypieces lay on their backs in the forge by the stables, while in the granary loft above were stored the London state harness of the carriage horses, extravagantly carved and painted pelmets, gilded fillets, and other grubby and tattered remains of old glory.

Just before Devonshire House was sold someone took a photograph of Billy Hartington, my brother-in-law, on the staircase. He was two years old at the time and stood on the wide shallow steps at the curve of the staircase with its crystal handrail that led to the saloon and other reception rooms. The photograph is doubly sad: the house disappeared in a pile of dust and twenty years later Billy was killed in action. The destruction of the house is one of many such tragedies of the twentieth century and it is not much comfort to think that today it would be forbidden to pull it down. The palace on Piccadilly has gone for ever and with it the elegance of the ghosts of 1897 whose everyday clothes are fancy dress now.

1985

A LONDON RESTAURANT ON TRIAL

One of the perks of being a director of a hotel is visiting and eating at the competition. The idea is to taste, look and learn. On this mission (and on the instructions of our chairman) the managing director of the Devonshire Arms Country House Hotel at Bolton Abbey, Yorkshire, and I met for lunch at one of the most famous restaurants in London. The Devonshire Arms is the proud possessor of a Michelin star, so the managing director and his chef know a thing or two about the job.

As I seldom go to London, it is an excitement to see what's what in the fashionable world. I have known the chosen restaurant* for many years but I am so stuck in my ways that I was surprised by the changes I found since last eating there. There is a black-trouser-clad lady greeter, a new role in the restaurant staff. She was one of the few females to be seen, as the place soon filled up with men – a good omen for the quality of the food (and bad for the size of the bill).

The arrangement of the tables is ideal, like a railway carriage with high divisions, so the booming voices of the confident customers discussing business and sport are contained. The decor is brown, beige and more brown. No colour. The lighting is perfect – full marks for that, as it is the hardest thing to get right. The plates are a normal size, none of those huge oval platters like dog dishes that put you off eating.

Every table was taken. The charming head waiter (French?

Italian?) answered our questions very politely. How many covers? Is there a private room? He may have smelt a rat and imagined we were from one of the many magazines that describe places to eat, or perhaps he just thought we were naturally curious country-bumpkins on an outing. My companion and I considered the overheads as we watched the young, long-legged waiters, so numerous that they were in danger of running into each other. These boys have taken the place of the middle-aged women in white overalls, with a lot of nanny about them, who used to serve the excellent, plain English nursery food in a plain English nursery way. Bread-and-butter pudding and raspberry crumble came naturally to them, as they do to the customers, all brought up on such no-frills fare. I am sorry the nannies have turned into waiters but that is because second childhood is setting in.

When the bill came my companion and I smiled and marvelled at the prosperity of this country. Stuffed with decent food, one glass of house wine and two glasses of fizzy water, we went home to write our reports for the chairman. I can't wait for the next outing.

February 2004

* Wilton's in Jermyn Street.

EDENSOR POST OFFICE

They shut our post office yesterday. For the first time in living memory there is no early morning light at that end of the ancient cottage and the little shop that goes with it. The stacks of newspapers and magazines with unlikely titles have disappeared overnight.

No longer can a letter be weighed to go to the ends of the earth. No more postmaster, one elbow on the counter, turning the thick cardboard sheets with brightly coloured stamps of all prices lurking between them, painstakingly adding them up to the right amount for a letter to Easter Island or Nizhni Novgorod. No more blue airmail stickers to speed the thing along like a migrating bird. The letter box remains, but what good is that without a stamp? It is a ghostly reminder that yet another service in another part of life is finished.

So it is into the car once more to queue in the Bakewell supermarket instead of walking down the hill, looking at the gardens and their dogs, and seeing the minibus calling for the schoolchildren. What about the old people who haven't got a car? What about the other pensioners in the village? No one cares about them because they don't stab each other after a bout of drinking and have never bothered the police or a counsellor in their long lives. They are just the nostalgic past because they behave decently. For these people, who spend most of their time alone at home, the post office was like a club. Old and young met there, people called in on their way to work to pick up a paper, as well as children on their way to and from school. They had a chat, a grumble, compared gardening notes or gave news of a former resident who has gone to New Zealand. We all knew each other, we knew when someone was ill or had gone on holiday. Now our meeting place is dark and dead.

The government don't care. They pretend to be keen on 'rural welfare'. They have invented 'community centres' and spend our money building monstrous new ones when our post office *was* one. A vital support, impossible to value in money but sticking out a mile to those of us who live in villages, has gone. Teas in the cottage remain popular but the locals don't go out to tea – they have it in their own home. Fine-weather walkers and tourists are welcome but they don't belong, their roots are elsewhere.

There has been a post office in Edensor since 1886. It was one of the first in a small village, presumably provided to serve Chatsworth. By 1892 the postmistress, Mrs Jane Bacon, dealt with two deliveries and two collections on weekdays and one of each on Sundays. The then Duke of Devonshire and his politician guests made good use of the newly installed telegraph office and the locals appreciated several other services.

A bellboy, aged twelve and a half, was the human on whom Chatsworth relied for telegrams. One of his jobs was to run the half mile to the Edensor post office to fetch and send them. His name was W. K. Shimwell. This education served him far better than sitting in a classroom, as he went on to be private secretary to the duke when he was governor-general of Canada, 1916–21, and later became comptroller of Chatsworth and clerk of works to all the buildings scattered over the thousands of acres of the Derbyshire estate, including Chatsworth itself. Sometimes it pays to leave school early.

It's all gone. There is no bellboy and no post office. Now, that horrible form of communication, email, rules. Even people in the same office send emails to each other instead of talking.

Bang go human relationships. All is sacrificed to speed. No time to ponder – bung off the email and back comes another in a ridiculous new language invented for it. With no proper signature, no envelope for privacy and paper galore, manners, spelling and grammar are out of the window. Email is cold, impersonal, demanding, unfading, invading and often incomprehensible. Like the hymn, it is immortal, invisible . . . and silent as light.

April 2008

THE ARRIVAL OF THE KENNEDYS IN
LONDON, 1938

'Coming out' had a different meaning in 1938 from what it has today. The last London season before the Second World War followed much the same pattern as it had done before the First.

For a small section of people there were three frantic months of entertainments. For eighteen-year-old girls and their young men-friends there was a coming-out dance (and sometimes two) four nights a week, and often one in the country on a Friday night (not on Saturdays, because it was not seemly to dance into Sunday morning) from early May till the end of July. The bands, led by Ambrose, Carroll Gibbons and, best of all, Harry Roy, played all night every night for our pleasure.

We took this strange state of affairs for granted; it was part of life, to be enjoyed or endured according to temperament. There were country weekend parties in the houses of debutantes' parents, race meetings – from Ascot and Goodwood to the local point-to-point – topped up in August by Highland gatherings, which included the jolliest and rowdiest of reel parties.

1938 was a vintage year for beautiful girls. Hollywood would have nabbed any of June Capel, Clarissa Churchill, Pat Douglas, Veronica Fraser, Jane Kenyon-Slaney, Sylvia Muir, Sissie Lloyd Thomas, Elizabeth Scott or Gina Wernher.

Our lives were ruled by invitations, lists of girls and young men, trying to keep up with clean, white-kid gloves, including elbow-length ones for the evening that gave such style to the wearer, and shoes that suffered from being danced in all night. I longed for another evening dress. Mine were home-made by our retired housekeeper (£1 a time) but some of the girls had enviable clothes from Victor Stiebel and mothers who were dressed by Molyneux or Norman Hartnell. Hats came from Madame Rita in Berkeley Square. We wore silk stockings in London and lisle in the country and all the extras that seemed so essential then.

It was at the beginning of the 1938 season that the new US ambassador to the Court of St James arrived with much friendly publicity. Joseph P. Kennedy, his wife and nine children were warmly welcomed to London. Such a crowd of good-looking boys and girls had never been seen before among diplomats and they made an impact that was never forgotten.

The fourth of the nine was eighteen-year-old Kathleen, called Kick. Her initiation into the English season was to spend a weekend at Cliveden where the American Nancy Astor was the most famous hostess in this country. The Astors had four sons. The two youngest, Michael and Jakie, inherited their mother's brilliant talent to amuse and were the best company for any girl lucky enough to be invited to that Thames-side palace. Kick was understandably nervous when she arrived among the typical Cliveden mixture of young and old, politicians and religious leaders from all over the world, with the Astor boys poking fun at pompous guests as only they knew how. She emerged with flying colours, having charmed the lot of them.

Kick fell happily into this frenzied social activity and became the centre of attention. She was not strictly beautiful but differed from English girls in her infectious high spirits, lack of shyness, ability to play games, as well as talk politics with the older generation. Above all, her shining niceness came through. Because of her charm and lack of cattiness, none of us natives resented her, in spite of her success with the young men who were fascinated by the American phenomenon. She had the advantage of having two older brothers, Joe junior and Jack, who could take her around with her mother's consent.

The Kennedys lived in Princes Gate, round the corner from my father's house in Rutland Gate. There was much coming and going between the houses in company with Billy Hartington, Dawyck Haig, Andrew Cavendish, Hugh Fraser, David Ormsby Gore, William Douglas Home, Charlie Lansdowne and his brother Ned Fitzmaurice, the Astor boys, Charles Granby, Mark Howard, Robert and Dicky Cecil and various Woods and Stanleys – all undergraduates at Oxford or Cambridge.

Joe Kennedy junior was handsome and dashing but he preferred more sophisticated women to us eighteen-year-olds. Jack, who was just twenty-one, already had something about him that separated him from the crowd. He was very thin, the legacy of serious illnesses, but he put everything into the moment, which in 1938 was to enjoy himself. My mother, watching him at a dance and impressed by what she saw, said to Andrew, who never forgot it, 'I wouldn't be surprised if that young man became president of the United States.'

A year later came the war. The frivolities of living for pleasure ended with a bang, and we all went our separate ways. Kick and her family returned to the States, but she had made lifelong friends in London and was soon back wearing American Red Cross uniform. Billy Hartington had been one of her crowd of suitors for some time. He eventually won the prize against all comers and, after what seemed endless negotiations over her Catholic and his avowed Protestant faith, a compromise was reached about any children they might have. They were married in London on 6 May 1944.

The double tragedy that was to follow is well known. The Hartingtons spent only five weeks together before Billy's battalion was ordered to France. On 10 September he was killed by a sniper's bullet. After four years of widowhood, the twenty-eight-year-old Kick fell in love with Peter Fitzwilliam, another of those irresistibly attractive men who loved her. They were planning to marry and were on their way to the South of France in a small chartered plane when it crashed in a storm over the Alps and all on board were killed. So a life of such promise was extinguished. Kick is buried in the churchyard at Edensor, by Chatsworth Park. On her headstone is engraved, 'Joy she gave. Joy she has found.'

To all of us who had known and loved her it was impossible to believe that she was dead, just as it was impossible fifteen years later to believe that Jack had been assassinated. The sheer vitality of brother and sister made us think them immortal. Alas, they were not.

May 2006

PRESIDENT KENNEDY'S
INAUGURATION, 1961

After the marriage of Andrew's brother, Billy, to Kathleen (Kick) Kennedy, and their tragic deaths, Andrew, his two sisters and I were treated as part of the family by the Kennedys. This was the reason for our invitation to the inauguration of John Fitzgerald Kennedy as president of the United States of America in January 1961. Andrew was intrigued by the invitation and also realised what an honour it was to be asked. I did not want to go. There were engagements I was looking forward to at home, including the last shoot of the season. But it was so good of them to think of us that we accepted and set off for this unique celebration. The British ambassador, Sir Harold Caccia, and his wife put us up. These are the notes I made at the time.

The jumble of impressions of the last three days is so thick with oddness and general amazement it's very difficult to put them in any sort of order. The utter sweetness of our ambassador, Andrew hopping about being humble and saying that his job as parliamentary under-secretary makes him a very junior minister, the deliciousness of the brekker, the warmth of the embassy, the dread coolth of outdoors, the friendliness of the Kennedys and the extraordinary informality of the most solemn moments. My word, it is an odd country.

Thursday 19 January
The first day was mercifully quiet after the journey, which was very long (we came down at Shannon for some strange reason,

257

also the plane from New York was late so we arrived at the embassy at what was 4.30 a.m. for us, having left London at 2 p.m. the day before – fourteen and a half hours).

They raked in some embassy people for lunch, so that was easy. Then it started to snow and it snowed and snowed, and although Snow Plans A, B, C *and* D were put into operation, the capital city of the USA pretty well seized up, as they are not prepared for such an eventuality. Cars were abandoned in the middle of streets; engines chuck it very easily it seems and snow gets packed under the mudguards so that the wheels won't go round.

We were given tickets for the gala performance which was to raise money for the Democrats, who are $4 million in debt after the election (seats $1,000). So we buggered off to the place called the Armory, which is about twice the size of Olympia and the same idea. The embassy gave us a car while we were there, a very old-fashioned English thing called an Austin Princess. It took two and a half hours to get to the blooming Armory. It should have taken twenty minutes but the traffic was solid and so many cars broke down in the queue to get there. Our heater broke and I had only a fur cape, my word it was bitter. Andrew panicked all the way as the tickets said we had to be there at 8.30 and the President Elect was due at 9.00. At about 10.00 he said we'd better give it up and go home but luckily we couldn't as we were hemmed in on all sides by dread cars. The cold was extreme, about twenty degrees of frost, snowing hard and a bitter wind.

We finally loomed and by a miracle arrived at a very good time, viz. about ten minutes before the Kennedys. We needn't have worried as people were coming and going all the time, which we weren't to know. I thought it would be like a royal do in England but it was far from it.

We had marvellous seats, next to the Kennedys' box and between two very grand senators and their wives, who looked slightly down their noses at two complete strangers having such good places, till various Kennedys came and were fearfully nice, especially Bobby (who turns out to be attorney general with a staff of 35,000) who hugged us. Old Joe Kennedy, that well-known hater of England and the English, was very welcoming, and to crown all Jack came and said hello, to the astonishment of our senatorial neighbours.

The performance included all my favourites: Frank Sinatra, Jimmy Durante, Nat King Cole, Ethel Merman, Tony Curtis, Ella Fitzgerald, to mention a few, also Laurence Olivier and the chief American opera singer called Helen Traubel, who sang in a huge voice some ridiculous verses about the Kennedys' baby. It was WONDERFUL, especially at the finale when they had all done their turns and they ended up doing skits on popular songs with topical words. So unrehearsed were they that they had to read their lines and somehow it *was* so funny, just like Women's Institute theatricals at home, but when one looked again, there were all those famous faces. I adored all that.

We got home at 3 a.m. The heat in the house was fantastic. I opened all windows and slept with one blanket but it was still BOILING.

Friday 20 January
Next day was the actual inauguration. Left the embassy about 10 a.m. in order to be in our places at 11. Long queues of cars as we neared the Capitol. Anyone of note – ambassadors, senators, governors of States – had their name or country on the side of the car. We were next to some ratty-looking souls from Bulgaria in one traffic block, it made one think.

Eventually arrived at the Capitol. Horrid getting out as it was *so* cold with a cruel wind. The ambassadress had given me some long nylon stockings and knickers combined, also some rubber boots to put over my shoes. It was fearfully cold *with* these things – without them, heaven knows, I think I would have frozen to death. They gave Andrew a flask of whiskey but he still shivered throughout and put his scarf round his head (like the Queen).

259

We were told to wear top hats and smart things – both absolutely unnecessary as people were dressed for the Arctic. Some women had come in ridiculous flowered hats, which they soon covered up with scarves, rugs and anything to hand.

It was difficult to find our seats, no one knew where anything was, not even the few policemen who were about. When we eventually found our places they were very good for seeing – we were on street level, immediately in front of the Capitol where the ceremony was to take place, on a large balcony, high up but all plainly visible. Our seats were wooden strips, no backs, no floor and snow everywhere. No numbers or reserved places, one just sat where one liked on forms like at a school treat. Next to us were two Pakistanis with cameras. Just in front of me was old Mrs Roosevelt who had arrived an hour before we did and must have been terribly cold. The organisation seemed so vague I was afraid it would all be very late and we would be pillars of ice but in fact it started only a quarter of an hour after the appointed time.

The balcony of the Capitol was full of senators and congress-men sitting either side of the roofed pavilion from where Jack was to speak. The Capitol is faced with gleaming white marble and looked fine against the blue sky and snow, though the dome is painted just off-white, which slightly spoils the brilliant effect. Various members of the Kennedy family arrived. The girls – Eunice, Pat and Jean – were without hats, which seemed surprising for such a formal event. One could pick out the Eisenhowers, Trumans – Margaret and hubby – old Joe and Mrs Kennedy, but they were about the only people I knew by sight. Nixon and Mrs soon joined them.

Tension was mounting for Jack's arrival but it was badly arranged from a dramatic point of view – so different from things in England. No proper path was made for him through the crowd – people started shouting and suddenly there he was. Jackie looked very smart indeed in plain clothes of pale beige; the only woman who looked dressed at all.

There was a long pause after his arrival. People were cold and were stamping their feet. The star was there but nothing was happening. Eventually, the master of ceremonies announced some tune by the band and a famous gospel singer, Mahalia Jackson, whom I'd never heard of, sang 'The Star-Spangled Banner'. Then the swearing-in and four prayers – Roman Catholic cardinal, Jewish rabbi, Greek Orthodox priest and a Protestant – all much too long and not at all moving or impressive. Nobody paid the slightest attention and even the senators took photographs throughout, moving about to get in better positions. Some people in our row didn't stand up for the prayers. My Pakistani neighbour, at the third one, gave me a wink and said, 'Let's sit this one out', which I was going to do anyway as the rug fell in the snow every time we stood up.

Jack's speech was wonderful, the *words* were so good, almost biblical. Everyone was thankful to get up and move when it was over as we could only think of getting out of the cold and wind. We were told there was a bus reserved for the Kennedy family which we were to get on, but it seemed impossible to find. No one knew anything and there was no official-looking person to ask. After pushing and shoving and, in desperation, even stopping to ask a police car, we found it at last and the relief of getting into an overheated bus was wonderful.

In the bus we found Eunice and her husband (whose Christian name is Sargent, if you please, *fearfully* nice though). We were driven to a hotel for lunch with the family and close friends. Lots of grandchildren milling about, lots of delicious buffet food. Jack and Jackie, and Bobby and Ethel had lunch in the Capitol with the Cabinet, so weren't there. Back into the bus (which had a label on it 'Kennedy Family' like 'Chatsworth Tours') and through the guarded gates into the garden of the White House, whereupon all the people in the bus gave a loud cheer, led by Eunice, and shouted 'Here we are'.

As I got into the hall of the White House, a Marine stepped

forward, gave me his arm and armed me all the way through the house to the president's stand, from where we watched the parade. Andrew and I had seats several rows back. (All the seats were marked with people's names. The Marine asked me mine, I said, 'Devonshire', so he said, 'Mrs Devon*shyer*, you are heeere.') Next to us were Mr and Mrs Charles Wrightsman, who never turned up because they thought it too cold. The box had a roof and was enclosed at the sides with perspex but it was still extremely draughty and bitterly cold, even though there were army rugs on each seat.

The stands were gimcrack and the decorations practically nil, just a few small flags. Queer for such a rich country. The diplomats were next to us, sitting on raised forms, completely in the open. The Eastern ones looked so cold I felt terribly sorry for them as there was no escape and they couldn't leave till the parade was over.

The parade itself was an extraordinary mixture of army, navy and air force with girls' bands, majorettes in fantastic uniforms with long legs in pink tights, crinolined ladies on silver-paper floats, horses from the horsy states all looking a bit moth-eaten, army tanks, dread missiles (rhymes with 'epistles') on carriers, bands everywhere. One man marching by in an air-force contingent broke ranks, whipped out a camera, took a photograph of the president and joined in again. Imagine a Coldstream guardsman doing the same at Trooping the Colour.

The television cameras and a host of other photographers were immediately opposite the president's stand. The cameras were on him the whole afternoon. The informality was so queer – the president drinking coffee and eating a biscuit as the parade marched by. But he stood there for over three hours.

After about an hour and a half a message came, Would I go and sit beside him. It was the oddest feeling I've ever had, finding myself a sort of consort, standing by this man, talking to him during lapses in the parade. The telly people were stumped by

263

the advent of a strange English lady; they knew the politicians and the film stars but not ordinary foreigners. We told Sir Harold Caccia when we got back and he said no English woman had ever done that before, so I *did* feel pleased.

Jack Kennedy has got an aura all right and he was obviously enjoying it all so much. After about three-quarters of an hour he said would we like to go with his father to the White House for tea, which I took to mean I'd been there long enough. The White House is very good inside, big rooms covered in silk, one dark red, one dark green, a huge creamish-coloured ballroom and a rather awful round room covered in a horrid blue Adam-design silk, which everyone seemed to like best. The diner is green, I'm sorry to say, painted solid gloomy green, pillars and all. Pictures of presidents all over the shop, all ghoulish.

We didn't see the president again as he was still at the parade when we left after tea. Got back to the embassy about 6.15 to be told dinner at 7.15, so I rushed to dress for the ball. Luckily I didn't take a tiara, which various people said I ought to have done, as no one wore one and I would have looked like a daft opera singer dressed up for Wagner. Mercifully only the Caccias for dinner. Afterwards we were taken by them to a party given by some cinema people. Lots of ambassadors and grandees there, a sort of after-dinner cocktail party. They don't mind the press like we do, and no wonder as they write in a very different way from ours, perfectly friendly and no sting in it.

Then back to the Armory for the Inaugural Ball. This time no traffic jam and we arrived without difficulty. All the seating at floor level had been removed and a vast dancing floor put in its place. Shown to the president's box again, where we sat until someone said there was drink and a telly in a room at the back. So we made off there and saw Mrs David Bruce, a friend of Nancy [Mitford]'s, rather beautiful and probably coming to London with her husband as ambassador. Without any warning, the president suddenly walked into the room and was taken off to a television interview next door. Meanwhile we watched his inaugural speech again on the telly.

Back to the presidential box to watch the dancing, which didn't happen because everyone stood looking up at the box, waiting for Jack to appear. When he did he got terrific applause. He didn't go down to the dance floor but talked to various people along his row. Wherever he goes he is like a queen bee, surrounded by photographers, detectives, nexts of kin and worshippers. By this time, we were sitting in the topmost tier just below the roof. As Jack came back along the first row, fenced in as usual by humans, he saw us, broke away and climbed over seven rows of seats to say goodbye, to the utter astonishment of the people sitting either side of us. A photographer who had got, as he thought, a very bad place and who had been grumbling, was now able to take the closest close-up of all.

I told Jack about Unity [Mitford]'s letter of twenty-one years ago saying how he was going to have a terrific future. I also asked him if he knew Harold Macmillan and he said he was going to see him soon. We said how we were loving everything that had been arranged for us, to which he replied that we'd stuck it well. He and Jackie then left. We waited till some of the crush had dispersed and thought we'd leave too. Andrew went out into the bitter night to look for the chauffeur – no sign of him. Eventually he was found, the car had broken and there we were with no hope of getting home. After an hour and a half the chauffeur suggested we take Labour leader Mr Gaitskell's car and send it back for him. By a miracle we saw Gaitskell among the 10,000 people there and thankfully squashed into his car, me sitting on a drunken lady who answered 'balls' to everything I said.

Saturday 21 January
We went to the Senate the next day, taken by a new senator's wife who had lunched at the embassy. Hideous place; they each have a desk and chair, like in school. Andrew went into the Chamber

(they have a reciprocal agreement with members of certain foreign governments) and two senators immediately launched into speeches of welcome. I was sweating in case he would make one back but he only bowed. Good old Andrew.

The upshot of the whole outing is two new bodies to worship – Sir Harold Caccia and Jack Kennedy. I've written him a letter beginning 'My Dear Jack'. I do hope I won't have my head cut off for impertinence. One of the comical things was that Andrew had some secrets from Harold Macmillan to tell the ambassador and nothing was said until we all went to bed on the last night, when I heard them talking in the passage outside my room for hours. I can see that's the way things are done in high life, very odd.

PRESIDENT KENNEDY'S FUNERAL, 1963

President Kennedy was murdered in Texas on 22 November 1963 and his funeral was held in Washington three days later. Andrew and I were offered places in the plane chartered for HRH Prince Philip, who was representing the Queen, to attend the funeral. Also on board were the Prime Minister, Sir Alec Douglas-Home, and Lady Home; the Leader of the Opposition, Harold Wilson; the PM's private secretaries, Sir Philip de Zulueta and Sir Timothy Bligh; Prince Philip's valet and three girl secretaries, two of whom had stayed with us at Bolton Abbey and Chatsworth when working for Harold Macmillan. After the funeral, I made the following notes.

Sunday 24 November
Left Chatsworth with Andrew at 12.40 to drive to London airport. Found Mr Wilson in the VIP lounge. Talked to Marie-Louise de Zulueta, who had come to see her husband off. The PM and his wife arrived soon afterwards. Prince Philip arrived exactly on time. We got into the plane at 4.50 and took off at 5.10. There were headwinds of 140 mph that slowed us up and the flight took nine hours.

It was a huge Boeing 707. There were 150 empty seats behind us – something I have never seen before. Prince Philip called us up to his seats in front and asked Mr Wilson to join him for dinner. I sat next to Wilson with the Prince opposite, and Andrew sat with the Douglas-Homes on the other side of the aisle.

My lot started talking about aeroplanes (a safe subject, I suppose) in such an incredible, almost technical, way that it was
quite impossible to listen to them and I found my mind wandering. Wilson had such dirty fingernails it put me off dinner.
I wished I was with Andrew and the Homes but kept thinking
how extremely odd the company and that I ought to be interested, but it was impossible to be so. Wilson has a level, grating
voice and podgy face with a too small nose. After dinner tried
to sleep a bit.

When below was all lights on the east coast of America, the sad
reason for the journey hit me again and I dreaded arriving. We
were met by a 'mobile lounge', a vast bus-like thing with room
for many more people than we were. Our ambassador, David
Ormsby Gore, and his wife, Sissie, looking red-eyed and worn
out, the secretary of state, Dean Rusk, whose face was puffed
up, and some others welcomed us on the tarmac and joined us
on the bus.

At the terminal were the Commonwealth ambassadors,
including nice George Laking from New Zealand with whom
I'd had tea on my last visit. Television cameras and lights, then
a procession of about six cars with police sirens at front and
rear. Twenty-two miles into Washington and no stopping at red
lights. It was a strange feeling arriving at the embassy. We had
a drink and short talk in the drawing room before, thankfully,
going to bed.

David said that Bobby Kennedy was taking the brunt; not only
was he bitterly sad himself and having to deal with arrangements
that were chaotic because of everything being at such short
notice, but also he was the one person who could comfort Jackie.
He said that General de Gaulle was the only head of state who
had demanded to see Jackie, so she said she would see them all.
Jack's belongings have already been removed from his office and
bedroom and the White House has taken on a deserted look.

Sissie said that Mass at the White House for friends and the

Catholics who worked there was the most tragic thing she ever saw – everyone crumpled with grief.

Monday 25 November
Prince Philip, the prime minister and David left for St Matthew's Cathedral before we did, as they were to walk in the procession from the White House. Andrew and I, Sissie, and Prince Philip's ADC left at about 11 a.m. Brilliant sunshine, frosty day with bright blue sky. We arrived at the Cathedral without a hitch. It is not very big and has only about 2,000 seats. We were all seated separately as the pews reserved for friends were already full. I was on an aisle, having arrived late, and the people already in the pew moved up for me. Prince Philip seemed very far towards the back of the church. Apparently he had no seat and the Douglas-Homes had moved to make room for him.

When I could bring myself to look round, I saw Jayne Wrightsman and behind her Fifi Fell, as beautiful as ever. There was no music for a long time. I never saw so many sad faces and when Jack's great friends came in – Bill Walton, Chuck Spalding, Evelyn Lincoln, Charles Bartlett, Arthur Schlesinger, MacGeorge Bundy – it was too much. Then the family arrived with Jack's two little children. Rose Kennedy looking small and hunched and Bobby too. Eunice, Jean and Pat with no veils but wearing black-lace mantillas, their faces set and staring and so so sad.

The coffin was carried by eight soldiers. It was impossible to believe that the vital, fascinating and clever person was shut up in that box. Quite impossible.

The service, luckily, was incomprehensible and the cardinal faced the altar most of the time. No agonising hymns, so it seemed far away and impersonal. There was Communion in the middle and quite a lot of people besides the family went up to the altar. On our way into the church, the Scotch pipers had played very fidgety music, as had the military band. We heard afterwards that it was because they do not do a slow march here, so it does not sound nearly as solemn as in England.

On the way out of the church, the overseas visitors stopped several times and for a full minute General de Gaulle stood next to me. He has the strangest appearance I ever saw – very tall, yet collapsed somehow and a long ugly nose. Haile Selassie looked fine – small and beautiful. The rest looked as they do in their photographs.

Our car arrived wonderfully quickly and we followed the procession to the cemetery. When it began to go at a slow pace, the secret service men – who were guarding Prince Philip, Alec Douglas-Home, De Gaulle and the Canadian prime minister, Lester Pearson – all got out and walked three-a-side of each car. There were crowds all the way for the three miles to the cemetery, which is on the side of a hill and beautiful. We arrived just as the last part of the service had begun. Aeroplanes flew overhead, including the president's plane that we'd seen at Lincolnshire airport in June when Jack came to Chatsworth. Prince Philip was jostled to the back again, behind a lot of soldiers, so he was not among the foreign visitors when they came away from the grave. The Russians were completely enclosed by secret service people. I saw Colonel Glenn and that ghastly Queen of Greece with her dangling earrings, and many famous faces mixed up with police and hangers-on, who were all ambling about in the bright sun waiting for cars. Jackie looked tragic, with tears glistening on her veil, and Rose so very pathetic. The Kennedys are so good when things are going well but they are not equipped for tragedy.

We drove back to the embassy through thinning crowds. There was a great sense of sorrow and emptiness everywhere. We drank a lot of tea. I was very tired, as were all – we had left at 11.00 and got back about 4.00. Andrew went up to change and pack. Prince Philip went to Lyndon Johnson's reception at the White House. We watched it on television and, as usual, De Gaulle hogged the limelight. He arrived late so there was much speculation as to where he was and, when he did arrive, all was focused on him. The TV commentator was not too nice about Prince Philip or Sir Alec. Andrew and the Prince left for New York in an air-force jet and then on to London on a scheduled flight, Mr Wilson in tow.

The Canadians came for dinner – Ambassador Charles Ritchie with his talkative wife, Lester Pearson and his wife and their foreign secretary, Paul Martin, who had to go to the lav in the middle of dinner. David and Sissie looked slightly better, I thought. The very fact of having to have people in the house is probably a good thing; having to go on with ordinary life, though the outlook here is very bleak for them. They came and talked for ages in my room. Very, very sad, but we talked about other things. I wonder so much what David will do. No doubt he will have to stick out another year as ambassador here, which must be an awful prospect. It will be very difficult working with the new administration – no intimacy, no shared memories and no jokes.

Tuesday 26 November
The prime minister went to see Lyndon Johnson and came back saying he was friendly, tried to make a good impression and said that he would carry out Jack's foreign policy, etc. David said the White House was completely changed. Jackie had wanted to move by today but has put it off till Friday.

I went over to Eunice and found her perfectly extraordinary, laughing almost as if the thing had never happened, yet talking about everything in the past tense. We walked round her house about twelve times. How awful to live in a place where you can't go for a proper walk. Horses and dogs everywhere and one little boy aged about three. Bill Walton came for lunch, so nice, and both were wonderfully cheerful and talking about a memorial for Jack and what it should be. They suggested a long street from the White House to the Capitol, paved in different colours and with graded heights so people could see processions etc.

It seems Jackie has been extraordinary, planning everything with Bobby to do with the funeral. She was even laughing about going to see Johnson as the widder woman with lowered eyes and asking him to carry on various things Jack had been interested in. She is going to live in Georgetown it seems.

I left with Bill, having telephoned Bobby who said I could go and see him. His house is near the road and had a few sloppy policemen outside it. A man opened the door in his shirtsleeves. Jack's special assistant, Kenny O'Donnell, was there. Bobby and Ethel have built on a big drawing room, a lovely room, where there was a cot for the new baby. Ethel came in looking about seventeen – it's impossible to believe she has eight children. She's so terribly nice and good. I love her. Then Bobby arrived in a dressing gown which did not reach his knees and all hairy like an animal from top to bottom, but a v. lovable face and stout legs. I did not stay long. The house was in turmoil, telephones going everywhere.

Back to the embassy. Much chatting with Elizabeth Home, who is cast in the same mould as Dorothy Macmillan – a large reassuring body and great niceness pervading all. Johnny Walker, director of the Washington National Gallery, and his Scottish wife came for drinks. Then the Russian ambassador, Anastas Mikoyan, suddenly turned up with interpreters. An odd roomful.

For dinner came Joe and Susan Mary Alsop, Ted Sorensen – Jack's special counsellor – and his girlfriend and Bill Walton. Sorensen scarcely spoke all evening. Sissie says he is one of the worst affected of all. I sat next to the prime minister. He says his brother, William Douglas-Home, has written a play about a peer who gives up his title to become PM. What a surprise. Had a talk with Joe Alsop after dinner about Mollie Salisbury and Pamela Egremont and their different roles in life. Everyone left quite early and we went to bed because of the early start. Somehow the atmosphere has lifted a bit but I would not stay here for *anything* and long to get out of it.

Wednesday 27 November

Called at 6.45. Quick breakfast downstairs with everyone. Sissie and David came to the airport in an overheated mobile lounge and suddenly the atmosphere was like that at our arrival. Did not say much. Felt David so overwhelmed again with pent-up emotion. He kissed me goodbye – something he has never done before. I feel a strong bond with him. He loved Jack so much and saw the funniness better than anyone.

I do not know what I remember most about these strange two days, which is all it was though it seemed like three months. Perhaps it was three-year-old John Kennedy leaving the church, touching the flag on the coffin and being led away by some huge man, followed by a sobbing nanny; or General de Gaulle standing just by me as he waited for the heads of state to leave the church; or Prince Philip's stern blue look as he stood in the same place while tears poured down my face; or Dean Rusk all crumpled when he came to meet our PM; or Chuck Spalding and Bill Walton as they arrived at church; or Fifi Fell's beautiful face in a trance at the end; or David and Sissie, blotchy and thin – I came away feeling so terribly sorry for them that words were impossible. The light has gone out for so many people and for David and Sissie it has been a hammer blow.

Besides the secretaries, there were only the Douglas-Homes, Liberal leader Jo Grimond and me in the PM's vast chartered plane on the way home. Went across the aisle to talk to Mr Grimond, who is charming and woolly and hopeless but sees the point, very quick. The four of us had lunch together. It was dark outside because of the time change. Any strain there may have been soon wore off. We had a friendly talk as politicians do with people of opposing convictions, yet there sat the man, Grimond, who is probably going to do-in any chance Home has of getting back at the next election. Sir Alec's sweet string vest showed through his shirt. He has a strange, saintly streak, so quiet and calm and good. When Elizabeth Home and Jo Grimond were talking, the PM said he had wanted to make David OG foreign secretary but Rab Butler had said he wouldn't serve unless he was given the job. Home evidently has a tremendous regard for David. His patience is extraordinary.

About half an hour before we were due into London, a message came to say there was fog and that we would have to land at Prestwick or Manchester. I said do let's go to Manchester and all come to Chatsworth for the night. They politely said they must get back to London whatever happened. In the end we made for Manchester. I repeated my invitation and sent messages for cars to meet us.

We arrived at Chatsworth at about 11 p.m., after what seemed an endless journey. House floodlit. Dennis, Bryson and Henry standing at the door. It all looked warm and welcoming. The only sad thing was no flowers in the rooms. Jo Grimond, Harold Evans – the PM's public relations adviser – Timothy Bligh and Philip de Zulueta all turned up. Sir Alec said if he crept into bed and lay very still we would not have to change the sheets for Princess Margaret who was coming the next day.

I so wished they could have stayed the weekend but they were called at 6.30 and to catch the 7.24 train. They arrived and left in the dark.

'THE TREASURE HOUSES OF BRITAIN'
EXHIBITION IN WASHINGTON

On 31 October 1985, I was lucky enough to go to the National Gallery of Art in Washington for the private opening of 'The Treasure Houses of Britain: 500 Years of Private Patronage and Art Collecting'. It was the culmination of nearly five years of planning for the organisers. The director of the gallery, J. Carter Brown, is a young man of great energy and knowledge, both directed at the success of his gallery. He has a love of England and English things and has long been fascinated by what he has seen in houses here.

In summer 1981, Carter Brown and his wife stayed at Chatsworth for a weekend and later he told me that the idea for the exhibition came to him then. He wrote to Andrew soon afterwards to enlist his support and no doubt also wrote to many other owners, most of whom were willing to lend. One of the difficulties was the timing. Nearly all the houses are open for six or seven months of the year and could not spare their best things during that time, so Carter Brown was limited to the winter months for his show.

A sponsor was soon found in the Ford Motor Company. The two governments provided the horrendous sum for insurance and the plan was under way. The masterstroke of the organisers was the appointment of Gervase Jackson-Stops, the National Trust's architectural adviser, as chooser and collector of the works of art. He came to Chatsworth many times in search of what he called 'D.O.'s', Desirable Objects, and each time he added something he said he MUST have. No doubt he did the same at Burghley House, Castle Howard, Woburn Abbey and the rest. Such is his charm, with an appalling stammer that he does not give in to, and his unrivalled knowledge and memory of what is where, Andrew found it impossible to refuse him anything. He would be the best burglar ever. He and Carter Brown commuted between Washington and England for months, choosing and persuading the owners till they got (very nearly) everything they wanted.

When they had completed the list of D.O.'s from Chatsworth, Andrew got a letter saying Thank you very much, it is very kind of you to lend so much but they are all dirty and lots are broken, so will you please have them cleaned and mended before they go? No, I will not, answered Andrew. You can either have them as they are or you can't have them at all. I believe other owners answered in the same sort of way, so poor old Gervase was in a bit of a fix. I don't know how he and Carter managed it but in the event the Getty Foundation paid for cleaning and restoration. The glowing condition of the D.O.'s will make the pairs to those returning look a bit glum.

You have no idea (but I'm sure you have) of the time it takes to pack and send such an extraordinary collection of objects, varying in size, make and shape, from Canova's *Three Graces* from Woburn Abbey to a Fabergé snuff box from Luton Hoo, not to mention Lady Lambton's tiara and the colossal marble foot from the Chapel Passage at Chatsworth. The great packing began in July 1985 and the last things left Chatsworth in early October. Each had its own box or packing case, made to measure and lined with the sort of thing I wish my mattress was made of, so they reclined in luxury and safety while crossing the Atlantic until unpacked with tender care by the white-gloved lads at the National Gallery. We were given photographs of what was taken and these were put up where the missing objects belong, with a notice saying 'This Work of Art . . .' to explain their absence.

Meanwhile the National Gallery nearly lost its director. When Carter Brown was driving from Chatsworth to Castle Howard in the summer of 1984, he went the wrong way down a dual carriageway of the A1 and had a head-on crash with a lorry. He was badly hurt and spent weeks in hospital in York. Fortunately, he made a good recovery but it left him with a lot of pain from broken bones.

I happened to be in Washington six months before the exhibition opened. At the time, Gervase and the Gallery's brilliant designers were working from models of the proposed rooms, with all the objects cut out to scale. The part of the Gallery set aside for the exhibition was then just high white walls without a hint of the transformation that was to take place during the summer.

As time drew near for the private view, the organisers set themselves another fearful task – as though they hadn't already done enough. They planned a dinner at the National Gallery for the lenders and, more complicated still, they arranged for us all to be entertained at dinner the following night in private houses in Washington. Now Washington hostesses are famous, as we who are old enough to remember the musical *Call Me Madam* will know. I would not have wanted to be the person to decide who dined with whom and I believe the lobbying for bagging the more so-called glamorous of the English guests was interesting.

A tour of Virginia houses was also arranged, which lasted several days, and this was taken up by many of the lenders and was greatly appreciated and enjoyed by all who took part. One thing which delighted me was that it never stopped raining all the time we were there. I shall never feel guilty again when our American guests find they have hit a wet spell in this country.

To return to the exhibition, I went round at leisure four times. I should have liked to see it forty more. It is the best exhibition

I have ever seen, really faultless. It isn't often you can say that about anything. Inside that ultra-modern building, the designers recreated rooms from Tudor times till now, embellished with things familiar and unfamiliar. They chose not only the great works of art, known by all interested in such things, but curiosities and very private possessions – a number of which had been most generously lent by people whose houses are not open to the public. I say that, and underline it, because it is obviously good for a house like Chatsworth to be represented, but for someone like Lord Halifax, for instance, to lend his superb Titian, *Portrait of a Young Man*, is very public-spirited indeed. I remember seeing it in his human-sized drawing room in Yorkshire. It gives you the shock of recognition of genius. Nothing can compare with the way the Young Man seemed to be not just on canvas but in the room and ready to talk with the rest of the company. Such pictures on exhibition always start a spate of enquiries from people wanting a special visit to a private house, besides which there is security to be considered.

There is no charge to go to the exhibition but visitors pass through a turnstile so numbers are known. You enter a huge modern building with one or two shockingly ugly mobiles floating overhead. Then the first room takes you straight into an atmosphere of Hatfield House or Haddon Hall or Penshurst Place. The jewel-like beauty of the Elizabethan portraits and the extraordinary *Lumley Horseman* (carved in oak and painted in oils, with stirrups, bit and axe made of iron – the earliest known equestrian statue, from Lumley Castle, Durham) silence the crowds who seem to have wandered into church.

The next room is redolent of Hardwick Hall or Parham Park – a Long Gallery faithfully reproduced. The windows are leaded; the ever so slightly tinted glass was made in Germany. There is matting on the floor, admittedly not rush but the nearest thing to it, and the portraits of royal people, explorers and other worthies in the extravagant clothes of the time warrant going all the way to Washington to see. Of all the rooms in the exhibition perhaps this Long Gallery reminds you most of the real thing.

From here you pass into a sort of giant silver-cupboard dominated by a glass-fronted wall of shelves, laden with incredible objects, from the jewelled Beaufort garter badges from Badminton to the vast Burghley wine cooler – a silver bath of fearsome proportions which was one of the extravagances the press fastened on in their reviews.

Every now and again I came across something familiar in these most unfamiliar surroundings and I began consciously to look for Chatsworth things while other lenders looked for theirs. It reminded me of before the war when it was the fashion at smart weddings to display the presents. On one occasion my mother had been much amused by an old couple going round tables covered in grand things saying, 'Where's our blotter?' Listening to the English voices was just like that, only it was, 'Where's our Rembrandt?'

When we reached the early to mid-eighteenth century, I felt more and more at home as Lord Burlington's loved possessions seemed almost to take over with the Grand Tour and what the guidebook refers to as 'Souvenirs from Italy'. Some souvenirs these! There is a room devoted to Lord Burlington and the Palladian Revolution, which has several pictures of Chiswick Villa with furniture and other designs by William Kent, Burlington's distinguished friend. Most of these are now at Chatsworth.

You progress to an Adam room. Not my favourite period with its small, finicky and ladylike designs, but I know I am in a minority and I have to admire the skill of its execution. Here one is impressed once more by the meticulous attention to detail of the designers. As in all the rooms, the cornices and other architectural details are faithfully reproduced. Some of the furniture is on plinths a few inches high, which gives them importance and ensures that they are not kicked by passing feet.

But the cleverness is that the plinths are made of polished boards of the same wood that was used for floors at the time when the furniture was made – oak in the earlier rooms, wide boards and other woods as we progress through the centuries. This little touch gives authenticity to the piece; it rings true. I don't think I noticed it the first time round but then it impressed me as much as the specially made silk on the walls, woven in Suffolk. The compilers of the catalogue are too modest to describe all that they did and there are no photographs of their 'rooms', but I hope somewhere all their huge efforts are documented. It would serve as a pattern for anyone trying to do something similar in the future.

All that is missing in this perfection is evidence of the *désordre britannique*, the hallmark of the English country house. A couple of toys (one broken), a sofa covered in newspapers, stray novels, an old dog flopped down by the fireplace and the smell of wet macs would have nailed any of the rooms as having been well and truly lived in by the same family in the same way for generations.

One of the two things in the show that attracted the most attention (along with the Burghley silver wine-cooler) is the bed from Calke Abbey. The bed is English with Chinese hangings – embroidery of coloured silks and gold thread, close-covered on an oak and pine framework. It has been illustrated in colour in *Country Life* and is striking because of its intricacy of detail and brilliant colours. (Some of the trimmings look as if they ought to be on a ball dress rather than a piece of furniture.) It's the very opposite of today's fashion for pastel colours and is very refreshing indeed. It was found in packing cases at Calke, having arrived probably in 1734, and was never set up – which accounts for its immaculate state of preservation.

I happened to be in the room with the bed while Henry Harpur Crewe of Calke was being interviewed by an American television company. It was as good as a play. His questioners were earnest and polite, so unlike their English counterparts who are neither. 'Is it true that this bed arrived in your house two hundred and fifty years ago and was *never unpacked*?' 'Yes, absolutely true.' Pause. 'Why was that?' 'Well, I suppose they had other things to do. Oh no, they didn't *unpack* it.' As though it was perfectly ordinary, which of course it was at Calke. I couldn't resist saying, 'Henry, do get into that bed.' And then the television people knew they were among a lot of loonies.

And so you progress to the Rotunda, designed to show sculptures, through the Regency furniture and on to Victorian pictures where there are Landseers, including the dogs' *Trial by Jury* from Chatsworth, and a marvellous giant Edward Lear of a Corsican forest from Beaufront Castle. There is some amazing furniture from Osborne House, made from antlers and even stags' neatly divided slots (hooves), produced in Germany and belonging to the Queen.

Then on through Edwardian portraits by John Singer Sargent, John Lavery and Alfred Munnings. In Munnings' portrait *The Princess Royal on Portumna* (1930), the princess is painted on the grey horse given her as a wedding present by 'The Hunting Women of Ireland'. The artist and sitter had three consecutive sittings during the Craven meetings at Newmarket. Munnings described it as his 'best equestrian portrait', adding, 'The conditions under which I worked, including the weather, were the best I have ever known.'

In *Sybil Cholmondeley, Countess of Rocksavage* (1922), a late work by Sargent, the sitter wears a copy of a sixteenth-century court dress specially commissioned from Worth, which cost over £200. Artist and sitter had a 'month of sittings in the fog', after which Sargent announced, 'Sybil is *lovely*. Some days she is positively green', a compliment apparently.

There is a brightly-lit showcase with four tiaras and a library, which by its nature is almost impossible to reproduce satisfactorily, but the designers have made a good stab at it with some open books in showcases. The first day the exhibition was open to the public, I heard an English reporter ask a group of women what they liked best. Without hesitation they all said the tiaras. There is no accounting for taste. The doll's house from Nostell Priory attracts a great deal of attention; it is a wonder of its kind. I think the selectors began to lose heart after this and the present day tails off sadly, saved by some nostalgic photographs of house parties at Cliveden and elsewhere.

Not surprisingly, the exhibition had rave reviews from the press, with a few predictable exceptions. To give nothing but praise is more than journalists can bear and some papers had to be different. My son went on to Kentucky, to the centre of the American racing industry, and there an Irish-American paper had some rough stuff to say about the wicked English aristocrats grinding the faces of the poor to enable them to show off to one another by their extravagant purchases of works of art. The *New York Review of Books* gave a depressingly negative account, mostly directed at the owners because even that paper had to admit the quality of the exhibits. *American House & Garden* was scathing about the lenders in a tiresome, gossipy kind of way, but on the whole the reviewers gave it its due. Several have harped on the value of the exhibits and have hinted that because they have been chosen to go to Washington, their value has increased by 20 per cent (how they arrived at that figure I don't know) and that some owners will be inclined to sell, having had this unrivalled opportunity for inspection by American antique dealers and collectors. Time will show if these journalists are right.

As well as being generously entertained in private houses, as only Americans know how, we were also given tea at the White House by Mrs Reagan. This outing had its comic side. Among the heaps of paper with itinerary and invitations was an instruction that some other form of identification, as well as the invitation, must be produced for entry into the White House. Few of us had read or even noticed this, so we queued up at a lodge in the pouring rain while bemused guards had to decide if the motley crowd really were the Duke and Duchess of This-and-That or assassins. No one minded queuing or the rain – all are very used to both – but it was very funny indeed to see this rather bedraggled crowd of English grandees. One or two did look unlikely customers, chiefly Lord Neidpath who is always oddly dressed. For Mrs Reagan's tea he wore a dirty white suit with a broad black stripe, a high wing-collar and gym shoes, and he hadn't shaved for three days. However, he must have satisfied the police because I saw him at the sandwiches later on.

When we got to about tenth in the queue to meet Mrs Reagan, we were stopped by a policewoman who showed us how to shake hands – something that has never happened to me before, but now I know just how to do it. We all managed and the First Lady stood patiently as we filed by. Then we could wander about the rooms as we liked. They are most beautifully kept; everything in spanking condition and just as it should be, flowers, carpets and curtains all gleaming.

The dinner at the National Gallery was an eye-opener. In my long and spoilt life I have seen many wonderful entertainments but this had an originality which made it memorable. About four hundred people, I believe, all dressed in their best, which once in a while is a pleasure to see, were seated at round tables for eight. The tablecloths were made of flowery cotton – a nod to English chintz. Then something clever, which I have never seen before: on the tables, instead of the usual little bouquet of flowers of just the right height so you can see the people opposite, there were tall, narrow vases on plinths with a huge high arrangement – perfect for the immensely high space we were in. You couldn't call it a room, it was a sort of first-floor hall which goes to the roof.

The waiters in Washington are said to be out-of-work actors. I don't know whether this is so but they certainly act being waiters very well. They are handsome, smiling young men, apparently enjoying themselves as much as the guests and it is extraordinary how this atmosphere pervaded the whole place – a gala if ever there was one. I sat next to one Mr Schultz, who I suddenly realised was the foreign secretary, and on the other side Mr Petersen, the managing director of the Ford Motor Company.

The memory of all this excitement will remain with me. In tangible form there is the catalogue. 'It weighs as much as a salmon and is as difficult to hold,' someone said. True. It is also a work of scholarship, of utter fascination – history distilled through works of art. I cannot recommend it too strongly as a book to turn to for minutes or hours; every item is illustrated and it is beautifully written. Expensive, I know, but worth every penny.

March 1986

In 1995, dear good Gervase Jackson-Stops died. The unforgettable experience of this exhibition was due to him, more than anyone. I hope he realises, when he looks down on us who remain, how we all revelled in his creation.

MARBLE MANIA

'I have made several journeys into Italy, and at Rome the love of marble possesses most people like a new sense.' So wrote the 6th Duke of Devonshire, the 'Bachelor Duke', in his *Handbook of Chatsworth and Hardwick* of 1844.

On his first visit to Rome in 1819 he was indeed possessed. He soon translated his new passion into reality, and marbles, both ancient and modern, arrived at Chatsworth by the dozen. His first purchase, for £2,000, was of two alabastro cotognino columns which he described as 'the most beautiful in the world'. The now familiar story of an embargo on the export of antiquities put a stop to the transaction (Pope Pius VII claimed them for his new gallery at the Vatican) but the experience only increased the Bachelor Duke's desire for these wonders.

As always with the duke, friendship with an artist fuelled his wish to own some of the artist's work, and he held the charming Antonio Canova in high regard. He was introduced to the sculptor by his stepmother, Elizabeth Duchess of Devonshire (Bess Foster of the famous *ménage à trois* was his father's mistress and also the beloved friend of his mother, Georgiana). The widowed Bess lived in Rome where she organised and paid for what is now called a 'dig', which revealed the surrounding road and pavement in the Roman Forum as well as many fragments of antiquity.

The duke was often to be found in Canova's studio and before long he had acquired the seated figure of Napoleon's mother,

Madame Mère – 'The old lady herself used to receive me at Rome, and rather complained of my possessing her statue, though my belief is that it was sold for her advantage'; a bust of Madame Mère; a bust of Petrarch's Laura – 'entirely formed by his own chisel'; *Hebe*, bought from Lord Cawdor – '*Hebe* came on springs by post from Wales'; and a colossal head of Napoleon – 'Canova kept the large bust of Napoleon in his bed-room till his dying day. He finished it from the study of the colossal statue, now in the possession of the Duke of Wellington.'

The duke's favourite statue, *Endymion*, was commissioned by him from Canova. He was on tenterhooks when its arrival in this country was imminent, and his sister said it was no good talking to him, he could not concentrate and was beside himself with anticipation and worry. 'What anxiety for its voyage to England! A cast of it, sent from Leghorn to Havre, was lost at sea: it was to have been copied in bronze at Paris.' Often the long and hazardous sea voyage was too much for the safety of the precious cargo. Thorvaldsen's *Venus* arrived broken in three places – 'A bracelet, hiding the fracture of the arm, is one that the Princess Pauline procured when she went into mourning on the death of Napoleon, and she gave it me for this object.'

After Canova's death, which affected him greatly, the duke concentrated on other sculptors working in Rome, many of them pupils of Canova; he bought works on their merit but also perhaps to reflect his friendship with the master. Thomas Campbell took fourteen years to complete the seated figure of Princess Pauline Borghese – 'She was no longer young, but retained her beauty and charm . . . Campbell used to bring his modelling clay to a pavilion in her garden. The little luncheons on those occasions were delightful; for the Princess Borghese, when compelled not to talk about dress, was extremely entertaining and full of the histories of her time.'

At Chatsworth the duke's love of stone begins to show in the long wing that he added to the house in the 1820s. It was built by Wyatville and includes the Sculpture Gallery, designed to display his new passion. There is marble in every shape, colour and form: pillars, vases, plinths, urns, tazzas, table-tops, heads, bodies and legs of men, women and children, mythological wings supporting mythological horses, dogs, babies and snakes, in every pattern of salami, brawn, liver sausage, galantine, ballantine, pâté, ham mousse, veined Stilton cheese, Christmas pudding and mincemeat known to the buyer for a delicatessen.

In the crowd of gods and goddesses, emperors and vestals, you will find works by Kessel, Gibson, Tenerani, Thorvaldsen, Schadow, Albacini, Trentanove, Bartolini, Westmacott, Rinaldi, Campbell, Finelli, Tadolini – and a greyhound bitch and her puppies by Joseph Gott, 'the Landseer of marble'. But Canova remained the favourite. His tools are preserved behind a glass panel and are 'certainly the last he employed'.

So much for the Bachelor Duke's modern sculpture, which is such a feature at Chatsworth, admired again today as it was when first acquired. He was also an ardent collector of antiquities. At Smyrna in 1838, his catholic taste made him buy the Greek bronze head of Apollo, c. 470 BC, Chatsworth's most important antique sculpture. It is now in the British Museum, having been taken for death duties in the 1950s. Wisely, he kept ancient and modern apart. Under a draughty stone arch at the entrance to the garden, he arranged the bits and pieces of architectural and other fragments collected on his journeys. When we cleared an impenetrable mass of rhododendrons in the garden in the 1980s we found a Greek altar from the island of Milos – mentioned by the duke in his *Handbook* and hidden for a hundred years. Each piece held a particular memory for him of a place or person and he wrote their detailed descriptions in his *Handbook*. Many came from Canova's own collection, including a group noted by the duke as being 'rich, busy and pleasing' – words which conjure up the writer himself.

The most impressive and powerful of all are the two Egyptian figures of Sekhmet, goddess of war and strife, half-woman half-lion, hewn from dark granite, 'sent home by a famous traveller and purchased by me in the New Road'. These massive creatures are from the Temple of Mut at Karnak and date from *c.* 1360 BC. I can't make up my mind whether their powerful presence is malign or benign, but they certainly dominate the Chapel Passage.

Taste in works of art is notoriously susceptible to fashion and none more so than the neoclassical pieces in the Sculpture Gallery. Andrew's Granny, who reigned at Chatsworth from 1908 to 1938, detested them and tried to lose them by scattering pieces around the house and even in the garden. She considered them to be so much bulky trash. A nadir was reached in the 1950s when an inventory valued the whole collection, including six works by Canova, at under £1,000. The sculptures have not changed – taste has.

October 2001

BRUCE, MARIO, STELLA AND ME

In early summer 1995, the photographer Bruce Weber was working on Long Island with our granddaughter Stella Tennant, who is a model. Bruce was planning to come to England and asked Stella if she knew of a house, perhaps in the country, which would make a good background for pictures of her in the next season's clothes. So Stella telephoned to ask if they could come to Chatsworth. Bruce liked the idea of taking family pictures in a family house, so the plan was made.

The 'shoot', when Stella arrived with Bruce and his eleven assistants, was of a very different kind to when King Edward VII and Queen Alexandra came to shoot at the beginning of the last century. Pheasants were the target then and photographers were kept at bay.

The nursery was used as headquarters and in no time big trunks of clothes from some of the most famous fashion houses in Europe and America were unpacked and their contents hung on the portable rails usually kept near the entrance hall for people to hang coats when they arrive for charitable events. Three tables were covered in pairs of shoes of all colours of the rainbow, with the highest heels I ever saw. Bruce's team wasted no time in getting to work and Stella was soon sitting in a chair being made up.

Chatsworth has been much photographed and it is difficult for someone who has never been before to find a new site, but Bruce saw at once where he was to work and chose original places for

Stella to pose. Stella's parents (our daughter Emma and son-in-law Toby Tennant), brother Eddie, sister Isabel with her two-year-old baby, Rosa, Andrew and myself were all brought into the 'shoot', as well as another granddaughter, Jasmine Cavendish, and our dogs.

The teamwork of Bruce's assistants was fascinating to watch. They seemed to sense when he needed them and surrounded him with all he required – one holding the silver umbrella to shade the lens, others with extra cameras changing films at top speed. Joe McKenna, the stylist in charge of how the clothes, shoes and hats looked on Stella (who is as much at home in the lambing sheds of her father's farm in Scotland as she is on the catwalks of Paris, Milan and New York), is a master of his craft.

I have kept a few clothes I bought in Paris in the late 1950s and I showed them to Joe and his assistants. I had no idea they would be so interested. Forty-year-old Lanvin, Dior and Balmain garments were admired like Old Master paintings. They even photographed the labels as works of art in themselves.

The shape of 1950s coats and dresses has come back into fashion, as inevitably happens if you keep clothes long enough. So I was persuaded to put on one or two, while Stella wore the latest models. I am afraid the fifty-one-year difference in our ages was very apparent, but the Lanvin coat I wore at Ascot in 1959 compared well with Stella's new one by Prada. Bruce made me wear a red satin Balmain ball dress of 1960 – beautiful, certainly, but out of place at even the grandest entertainment now – to feed my chickens. The iron spoon and tin bucket were a huge contrast to the exquisite satin.

I have seldom met such a charming group of people – so hard-working, oblivious of the long hours, dedicated to their profession and to Bruce himself, who is a shining star. We were all very sad when the trunks were packed, the troupe left and the nursery was quiet again.

Stella also wrote down her recollections of that weekend.

The floor outside the nursery at Chatsworth is covered in ancient lino-leum. It has a warmth and a particular smell that always remind me of when I was young, especially the excitement of arriving for Christmas. However, I wasn't opening presents last time I visited. I was there for a fashion shoot with Bruce and his team, along with all my family. It was strange to wander through those familiar rooms and find them full of alien clothes, shoes, bags and all kinds of accessories; even stranger to think that these were the same rooms that my sister Izzy and I had roller-skated wildly round as children.

My family was amazed by the scale of the shoot, which surpassed all their expectations. The weekend was a new experience for me too – intro-ducing my family to fashion and fashion to my family. Not only did my family get an unusual insight into what my work involves, but the role reversals were hysterical – my brother in Prada! Mum in Blahnik shoes! I've never seen her in anything other than gardening trousers or knee-length tweed. Fortunately, Joe skilfully managed to put her in outfits that suited her and in which she felt comfortable.

Granny, on the other hand, has a fantastic collection of clothes. (Now that the 1950s look is back in, she is in serious danger of having her ward-robe raided by her granddaughters.) I was amused when some of the shoot rubbed off on her and, having looked through Joe's wardrobe, she has placed an order for a Helmut Lang suit. Dad isn't male-model sample size, so no orders there, but Mum's getting some Manolos for Christmas.

As well as the fun and peculiar buzz of doing a fashion shoot with my family, it will be invaluable for us to have the pictures. In The Pursuit of Love, *my great-aunt Nancy compared such family portraits to flies held in the amber of the moment . . .*

In September 2006, another famous photographer worked at Chatsworth for a day: Mario Testino, a great friend of Stella. He took the pictures at her wedding in 1999, when she married his erstwhile assistant, David Lasnet, in the Scottish Borders on a May day of freezing cold and biting wind. The French guests had come dressed for summer and rued the choice, but it was the happiest day for all concerned.

Mario Testino, like Bruce Weber, is one of those all-time charmers who has the knack of making his subjects feel happy and at home in whatever outlandish garments the magazine decrees. He seemed to take a fancy to Chatsworth, which fired his enthusiasm and produced some memorable photographs for *Vogue*'s ninetieth anniversary issue. I described his visit in a letter to Paddy Leigh Fermor later that month.

So one Mario Testino, famous photographer, came in a helicopter with a crew of makeup, hairdresser, 'fashion editor' etc from London.

I've got a really beautiful dress, grand evening, given me by Oscar de la Renta, so that was my kit. They bound Stella's legs, up to where they join her body, in tartan. A Union Jack flag hung from her waist & her top was what my father would have called meaningless.

Hair skewbald/piebald, all colours & stuck up in bits. THEN they produced 'shoes' with 6 inch heels. More stilts – she could hardly put one foot in front of the other, wobbling & toppling, and being 6' tall she turned into 6' 6".

(I forgot to say to Paddy, a prop was a big toy lamb, legs dangling as though dead.)

We looked just like that Grandville drawing of a giraffe dancing with a little monkey. I was the monkey.

Fashion is as queer as folks.

July 1995

ROMNEY MARSH AND OTHER CHURCHES

One of the great charms of England is the variety of country. You drive fifty miles and find yourself in a different world: different voices, landscapes, soil, breeds of sheep and, most noticeable, different buildings. But one feature is constant throughout the towns and villages of every county, and that is the churches and cathedrals. Not constant in date, shape, make or style but in the fact that they are there and, until not so long ago, that their towers or spires were the tallest buildings in the landscape, drawing attention to themselves as landmarks and proclaiming their importance to locals and travellers alike.

It is difficult to decide on a favourite. For myself, I so much prefer English churches to the more theatrical and dusty European ones, however magnificent their architecture. I so agree with the English nanny who was taken with her charges to Chartres Cathedral and, when they came out into the fresh air so beloved by nannies, was asked what she thought of it: 'Well, it's a bad light for sewing in there.'

The construction of these buildings seems nothing short of miraculous. Who designed them? How many people worked on them and for how long? How was it done? How and where did they get the stone? And WHY? If we ponder these questions of village churches, what about cathedrals? Ely, which makes you gasp when you walk in and look up, or Wells with its magical Chapter House stairs. In some cases the answers to these questions are known – the dates, a few facts, such as the stone having been brought from Caen in France, it being comparatively easy to bring by sea. *Easy?* Well, it depends on what you mean by easy.

What is difficult to evaluate today, and can hardly be imagined, is the faith that inspired these incredible buildings. It is this that gives them an indefinable sense of wonder. I find it intensely moving to go into a church alone, to allow the atmosphere to overwhelm me and take me for a few minutes back into the past, to drink in the peace which such an atmosphere brings. It eases the mind and puts the bothers of everyday life into perspective.

The fourteen churches that come under the Romney Marsh Churches Trust are truly amazing, from the smallest – St Thomas Becket, Fairfield, with its inspired white-painted pews, edged in black, that are unlike any other church interior – to the Cathedral of the Marsh, the vast St George at Ivychurch, which must have been too big for the community it served even seven centuries ago. Why that size? The churches are spread around Rye, on the wetlands that support the Romney Marsh sheep (which make such good eating). In our crowded country, the area is a haven of peace; the ancient roads that thread their way past dykes and through flood plains are emptier than those of the remote Peak District two hundred miles north.

Someone sent me a newspaper cutting with an article about walking on Romney Marsh next to an article about walking in Derbyshire. What caught my eye was the grumble of the Marsh walker when he came to a ploughed field on his way to a church, and sticky grey earth piled on to his boots, thus inconveniencing him. More space was given to the mud on his boots than to his description of the church. I wonder how he would have reacted to the slightly bigger inconveniences which must have beset the builders and congregations of centuries ago.

I think it is simpler when you're old. I suppose long experience of the trivia of life makes one glad to be able to absorb the other sort of experiences, to be able to consider the wonder of buildings, of their builders, of the generations of preachers and lay people who guarded their sanctity and the centuries of prayer that have left their mark. How else can you explain what one feels?

When my sisters and I were children at Asthall, in Oxfordshire, the churchyard was almost in our garden. Although we weren't allowed to, we used to watch the funerals from the nursery window, fascinated. My sister Jessica and I fell into a newly dug grave once and our much older sister Nancy pronounced fearful bad luck on us for the rest of our lives. We must have driven the grown-ups mad, writing Greta Garbo and Maurice Chevalier in the church visitors' book. I've since read in John Piper's brilliant piece in the 1937 *Shell Guide to Oxfordshire* that 'the inside of Asthall Church is like a church furnisher's catalogue', and that 'there is a fourteenth-century canopied effigy of Lady Joan de Cornwall'. All very fine but lost on me at the age of six.

Later we moved to Swinbrook, a few miles from Asthall, still on the River Windrush. It has a church of great beauty which contains the amazing early seventeenth-century monuments of the Fettiplace family – stone men lying full-length on their sides, heads supported on their hands, elbows resting on stone pillows – described by John Piper as 'intelligent, wicked looking former lords of the village, lying on slabs like proud sturgeon in enormous wall tombs'.

There is also a big wooden board in the church at Swinbrook with the Ten Commandments painted in a beautiful script. Another board announces that in 1617, £10 15s 9d was left by a benefactor with instructions that the income from this sum be used for 'charitable purposes' for the poor of the parish. But the last sentence dashes all hopes for the unlucky poor. 'This money is now lost,' it states.

My father used to take the collection at services and would pass round the plate twice to our aunt, his penniless sister. This happened every Sunday and the second time round she used to frown at him. He would remain in front of her looking hopeful until she slapped his hand, which set us off on the peculiar agony of church giggles.

I suppose there is no church in the country that does not have a memorial to its sons killed in the two world wars. Sometimes whole families of young men are listed as having died. If one of several brothers survived the Great War to father a son, as like as not that son's name will be among the dead of the last war. These memorials set one wondering what this country would be like now had those wonderful people, many of them just boys when they died, survived.

We know that regular congregations of churchgoers are getting smaller (except, I must say, at our village church in Derbyshire where I believe the church is full for two reasons: firstly, because the vicar is loved and, secondly, because he uses the 1662 Prayer Book and King James Version of the Bible). But the milestones of life – christenings, weddings and funerals – are still celebrated in church. The people who do not go regularly to church but who *use* it, as it were, for these purposes take it for granted that it will be there when they need it and would be dismayed if it suddenly wasn't.

Even more surprising are the memorial services to people who made a point of *not* going to church all through their adult lives. Yet when they die their relations feel they must arrange a memorial service in church. There seems to be a deep necessity for saying the final goodbye in the safety and sanctity of such surroundings. Humans have a need for a faith in which they can immerse themselves, even for a short time, to celebrate or to mourn. When the mind is all over the place, the Church provides something ancient and lasting – a feeling of stability that nothing else can equal.

1996

SASSOON: THE WORLDS OF PHILIP AND SYBIL

by Peter Stansky

Describing these two shining stars from the East who arrived in
this country apparently by divine providence, Peter Stansky has
quoted from their many friends. Luckily the people who knew
the Sassoons were famous themselves, so their thoughts are in
diaries and memoirs from before the First World War until
Sybil's death, aged ninety-six, in 1989.

Their ancestors were devout Jews from Baghdad who settled
in Bombay, traders who dealt in opium and skins. Six Sassoon
brothers arrived in England in 1858 and immediately made their
mark. Abdullah, soon to be Albert, was the first Jew to receive
an honorary Freedom of the City of London and was made a
baronet in 1880 as reward for good works. Albert's son, Edward,
married Aline de Rothschild and so the fortunes of the two
great Jewish families were joined and, in due course, came to
their children: Philip, born in 1888, and Sybil, six years younger.
Their exotic background stayed with them for all to see and
enjoy. They were at the core of what used to be called 'society'
and set a standard of luxury and elegance slightly foreign to the
old English families, who delighted in glimpses of a glamorous
way of life which they did not go in for themselves.

Philip went to Eton. When his house was on fire he poured a
bucket of eau de cologne on the floor of his room. Osbert Sitwell
was his fag so presumably had to clean up the mess. In 1912, he
became the youngest MP (aged twenty-four) winning Hythe,

a seat he held for twenty-seven years. He was ADC to General Haig from 1915. Eyebrows were raised about a man of his age being safely on the staff while his contemporaries of promise were cannon fodder. After the war he passed, apparently effortlessly, as parliamentary private secretary to Haig's loathed Lloyd George, a chameleon-like feat. He served both masters loyally.

At Trent Park north of London, at Port Lympne overlooking Romney Marsh in Kent and at 25 Park Lane, he lavishly entertained politicians of all persuasions, the royal family, writers, actors, musicians and artists, from Charlie Chaplin to the Prince of Wales – via the Sitwells, John Singer Sargent, T. E. Lawrence, Lytton Strachey and Noël Coward – to Mr and Mrs Baldwin and Lloyd George and his mistress. All were delighted to luxuriate in his company and eat his superb food, surrounded by works of art shown to me later by Sybil with the words, 'These were my brother Philip's things, they are the best of their kind.'

In 1924, his love of beauty led him to reface the sombre-looking Trent Park with rose-coloured bricks from the demolished Devonshire House, and to people it with statues from Stowe. At Lympne he took his guests up for a spin in his own aeroplane, to the fish market in Folkestone (in his constituency) where the fishmongers crowded round him; then polo, followed by a swim in the sea and a memorable dinner. His energy was frenetic.

The red-headed radical Labour MP Ellen Wilkinson recorded his arrival in the House of Commons, with 'that fascinating lisp of his', and continued, 'If he would tuck up his legs and sit on the Big Table behind the Mace, with one finely carved hand on each brass box, he would make an appropriate Eastern altar-piece.' In the 1930s, his service in the air ministry was dear to his heart, since he was himself an aviator. It was followed by the perfect appointment for him – the Office of Works.

Philip, the perfectionist, loved life and made the most of his glittering opportunities. In Rome he had audiences with the Pope, Mussolini and the King; he preferred the exquisitely dressed Pope's 'white flannel and sapphire'. His Holiness 'kept me over an hour and rocked with laughter . . . so thankful to be with a heathen & not to talk *Shop*'. But in spite of the trappings, Philip, described so often as 'oriental', remained an exotic outsider – solitary in his invited crowd.

His adored Sybil ('she is the most charming person in the world. I love her so much. I can never marry, she sets me too dizzy a standard') must have made the stuffy 'society' of 1913 sit up when she married Lord Rocksavage to become mistress (and saviour) of Houghton Hall, from 1919 until her death.

In both world wars Sybil held high office in the Wrens. Years later I watched her, well over eighty, pulling on miserably thin blue gumboots for a day's shooting on the frozen Norfolk plough. 'Naval issue,' she said, proudly. She was the best woman shot I ever saw, as easily in tune with the Houghton keepers as with the aesthetes of Kensington Palace Gardens, the Cholmondeleys' London house. Her fifty-five-year marriage to the handsome Rock Cholmondeley, Lord Great Chamberlain, was a total success. She had a parade of would-be lovers, including Sir William Orpen ('Old Orps' as she called him), but Rock, her children and Houghton were the solid background of this fascinating creature who spread her aura over all lucky enough to know her.

If you want to escape from war, sex and shopping, join Philip and Sybil on their magic carpet and read this book.

April 2003

ANIMAL PORTRAITS

I wish James Lynch, a living Somerset artist whose work I love, would turn his attention to poultry. His three gouache pigs – a Gloucester Old Spot, a Middle White with fat cheeks and squashed snout, and a sleeping Tamworth – have been joined more recently by a Hereford bull in my bedroom at Bolton Abbey in Yorkshire.

Dog paintings are now high fashion. There is a goodly number at Chatsworth as the Bachelor (6th) Duke of Devonshire adored his dogs and had several of them painted, some by Sir Edwin Landseer. These paintings are a continual joy to me. One shows the duke's Sussex spaniel, Tawney, by the Colosseum in Rome – said by his owner to be Tawney's favourite resort.

I have added to my collection by buying at Bonhams' 'Dogs in Art' sale, which takes place every January. Some of these pictures are in our Devonshire Arms Hotel at Bolton Abbey, where one of the sitting rooms is called the Dog Lounge. There is a pair of eager old-fashioned fox terriers, their studded leather collars giving away their date. The regulars seem to like them as much as I do.

I am a sucker for a sheep or a Shire horse. I remember Shires at work when I was a child. The smell of the leather harness mixed with that of sweat and new hay, and the feel of their coarse manes and tails, are such a part of my childhood that I delight in their likenesses now. I came across the crudely painted portraits of two turn-of-the-century beauties: *Ditchford Princess* and *Lockinge Bay Leaf*, with their irresistible manes and forms, standing four-square in their Warwickshire yard, a feathered leg at each corner.

And then there's the work of Lucy Kemp-Welch. Carthorses with hemp halters and huge, patient heads – these are all that the heart could desire. Lucy's illustrations for *Black Beauty* are extraordinarily moving, taking me back to being read aloud to and having to stop the reader when the tears came. I was lucky enough to get her watercolour, *In Double Harness*, which shows Black Beauty and his friend Ginger, every detail of the harness shining in pre-Great War perfection. In the same gallery hung its companion, *It Was Ginger* – the chestnut, her head hung low after long hours between the shafts of a hansom cab, has just been recognised by her old companion Black Beauty. Much as I would have loved to have both watercolours, *It Was Ginger* would have had to be kept out of sight, it is so sad. I wonder if anyone had the courage to buy it.

Pictures of sheep by Millet and Rosa Bonheur, which have been given to me as presents, complete my bedroom farmyard. A cheerful party to wake up to.

Surrounding myself with these things is a way of expressing my long-standing love of the subjects. Fancies change with the years but I am still delighted by them. The regrets are always for the opportunities that were missed.

February 1992

MOTORWAYS

In Derbyshire's bleak midwinter it is a comfort to come indoors for good at 4 p.m., out of the half light and off the sodden grass, knowing that – chickens fed and dogs, alas, dead – I need not go out again till morning. Staring into the fire and wondering what next, I read a masterly review of a best-selling book on commas (name too difficult to remember). It set off thoughts of words and how oddly they are used or misused.

Motorways, part of everyday life for car owners and lorry drivers, have a language of their own, invented by whom I do not know. Such roads are wider and faster (until bunged up) than little roads, but it would be easier, especially for foreigners, if their vocabulary were the same.

The part you drive on is called the 'carriageway'. This is a misnomer because carriages are not allowed to use it. Nevertheless, carriageway is repeated *ad infinitum* down the length of the three-car-wide tarmac. Roadworks are part of the fun of a long drive, making little diversions from the dull old slog. After you have wriggled sideways, guided by cones standing shoulder to shoulder, and faced oncoming traffic uncomfortably close for several miles, you are ordered to 'rejoin the carriageway'.

You begin to wonder if you will meet a four-in-hand, the coachman sitting high up in his many-tiered cape, top-hatted men travelling outside and crinolined ladies inside. At the service station there is a special place allocated to them clearly signed

'Coaches Only'. Four fresh horses await the express coach to take it to the next stage. They are put to as in a scene painted by James Pollard, a barking terrier prancing round their feet in the atmosphere of excitement as the horses are changed in double-quick time, like the tyres on a Formula One car at a pit stop. Perhaps a phaeton will appear, one of those C-spring creations of delicate beauty, or a pair of Norfolk Trotters drawing a shooting brake. Black Beauty and Ginger trot past Junction 29, followed by Victorias and hansom cabs. Hackneys and Cleveland Bays are recognised as the elite of draught animals, while honest van-ners pull vehicles with drop sides that provide all kinds of wares for sale in neighbouring villages. But this is all imagination as carriages are not allowed on the carriageway.

The next words to learn are 'hard shoulder'. This is an import-ant part of the road, running parallel to the carriageway but a sort of poor relation. It is meant to be a place to stop in an emergency. It is indeed hard but I can't understand where the shoulder comes in. If it were a soft shoulder you could at least cry on it, which would help when in despair. It is no good leaning on this sort of shoulder as the police will move you on. If you lean long enough you risk being sectioned. Don't try to sleep there. In spite of notices that crop up frequently saying 'Tiredness Can Kill – Take a Break', sleeping is against the rules.

You will be picking up the language quite well by now, but just wait. Suddenly a sign introduces another word, 'chevrons', with 'Watch Your Distance – Keep Two Chevrons Apart'. It is followed by upside-down Vs painted on the road. Chevrons is not a word used every day so you stop on the hard shoulder to get the dictionary from the bowels of the boot in order to know what they are on about. The *Shorter Oxford* says a chevron is 'a beam or rafter; especially in plural, the couples of the roof which meet at the ridge; a charge on the escutcheon, consisting of a bar bent like two meeting rafters, thus Λ; a distinguishing mark on the sleeve of a non-commissioned officer, policeman'.

Those who are not builders by trade may hesitate for a moment or two while they imagine how the beams and rafters of a roof meet. Having assimilated this (not too difficult but it does distract you from keeping your distance), you are then faced with the mysterious language of heraldry. 'A charge on the escutcheon' might be crystal clear to the compilers of *Burke's Peerage* but rather obscure to the majority of lorry drivers. People over eighty who lived through the war may remember the marks like meeting rafters (or a charge on the escutcheon) worn on the sleeve of a non-commissioned officer – three for a sergeant, two for a corporal and one for a lance corporal – but the vast majority of the population have never seen them.

So that is the language of the motorway. I am thankful there are no hard shoulders or chevrons on the way to Bakewell and that the road is not a carriageway. Should you wish to travel by horse and cart you can.

MEMORIAL SERVICES

Memorial services have swum into fashion. I don't know why because most of those remembered (with some notable exceptions) did not go into a church after they grew up, except possibly for their first wedding. The reason may be that, as death is against the rules now, the sight of a coffin at a real funeral is too much for the sensitive.

These gatherings used to be arranged only for prime ministers or for men who had spent their lives in public service. Now they happen for every Tom, Dick and Harry, and have spread to Thomasina, Ricardia and Harriet. They cause a lot of anxiety. There is doubt as to whether you should go to the funeral, which is sometimes for family only but is apt to include some friends, or wait for the inevitable memorial, or both. Do you count as a great enough friend to intrude on family-only grief or not?

I have never been to a memorial service that has reminded me of the deceased. They seem to be an exercise in social behaviour, the congregation meeting out of duty in the hopes of pleasing relations rather than from a wish to bring back the memory of the person whose name is on the service sheet. Often as not the officiating clergyman does not know the person but has to carry on as if he did and put on the sad face learned for such occasions at his theological college. The one who did know Harry/Harriet is the unhappy victim chosen by the family to give an address. For weeks this friend has struggled with what to say, how honest to be, or whether he should just deliver a eulogy and leave the intimates to think about what the deceased was really like. If the speaker makes jokes it can be acutely embarrassing. If he does not, there is no relief from the solemnity and he may leave out an important part of his subject's character.

A grandchild, deeply fond of the departed and overcome by the occasion, the surroundings and the unaccustomed lectern, reads. Watching and listening can be as painful for the congregation as it is for the performer. Sometimes there are several readings. 'Jabberwocky' is fashionable just now. The old and deaf can hardly believe what is left of their ears.

Then there is the music. It has been chosen with great care by the nearest and dearest, and includes an anthem, which is a splendid chance for the little boys in the choir to show their skill and sing the high notes before their voices break. The anthem ensures you are in for a lengthy sit. There is no knowing how long it will last. The dangerous word is 'Alleluia', which is spun out far longer than you can imagine possible when you see it written down. What is more, it is repeated again and again. 'Lo' can rattle on a bit, but 'O' is the worst offender. Even when it has dropped its 'h' this single letter goes on and on, up high, down low, fast, slow, back to where it started, then up and down once more till you wonder what can ever stop it. In spite of the anthem, the service eventually comes to an end and you meet the family and friends on the steps of the church. 'That was very beautiful,' you hear yourself say, when you are thinking of lunch or the train.

Compare it to the burial service of the 1662 Prayer Book in Archbishop Cranmer's magnificent language, moving and comforting — 'For we brought nothing into this world, and it is certain we can carry nothing out' — and the time-honoured ceremony ending in the churchyard, accompanied by sun, wind, rain or snow — 'all ye works of the Lord'. We are reminded that golden lads and girls and chimney sweepers, and those of us in between, are not immortal. The coffin is lowered into the grave accompanied by the final farewell, 'Man that is born of a woman hath but a short time to live, and is full of misery. He cometh, and is cut down, like a flower; he fleeth as it were a shadow, and never continueth in one stay.'

Isn't that good enough? Please, no memorial service.

OFTOF

We constantly read about the organisations that are meant to keep things straight for the benefit of those who use the relevant industries. OFCOM covers communications; OFGEM gas and electricity (but not jewellery); OFWAT, well, water of course; the aptly named OFRAIL; OFT, poetic for the Office of Fair Trading; and OPRA, nothing to do with music, pensions more likely.

Now we come to the latest and most far-reaching of all the OFs – OFTOF. The idea is to ensure that Old Etonians looking for work are seen off before getting to the interview stage. OFTOF will have already succeeded in blocking their progress to Oxford or Cambridge. Sometimes, in spite of this obstacle, the lads are accepted for an interview by a prospective employer. Then the pantomime begins.

It is against the rules to ask a prospective employee what colour they are, if they are married, have children or if they are a terrorist, yet it is allowed to ask if they've been to school and even to narrow it down and ask which school. Narkover* is all right, of course, and Fettes, but if the word Eton should slip out, OFTOF is summoned immediately and the candidate is told to push off and on no account to reapply for the job under another name because the ghastly truth will out.

The OFTOF man may himself be a public schoolboy, even an Old Etonian, and be up to all the ruses learnt there. He will also know of the despairing parents who have scraped and saved to pay for their lad to get a good education, have sweated down the M4 for various school celebrations for five years only to realise that OFTOF has the whip hand and there is no hope of the boy finding gainful employment.

February 2004

* Narkover, the school in Beachcomber's *Daily Express* 'By The Way' column, specialised in gambling, racing and extortion.

Since this article was published, the OFTOF officials seem to be slipping as one or two top jobs have been landed by Old Etonians. What next?

CONSERVATIVE?

How contrary the British people are and how we hate change.

When British Rail was just British Rail it was a joke, like mothers-in-law and piles. Now that it is 'threatened' with privatisation, it has suddenly blossomed into a loved institution bordering on heritage. Flowers have appeared on platforms and stations have been repainted as they were in the olden days. One London terminus even has a porter. Suddenly it must no longer be laughed at or, if it is, it must be in the indulgent way of a parent with a favourite child. Snow and autumn leaves on the line are excused as something to do with the environment and therefore sacrosanct.

It is the same with the Health Service and Education. They were hopeless, people said, until their ministers tried to improve them. Now the cry is, leave our hospitals alone and don't interfere with the schools.

Who says we are not conservative?

September 1993

DEBATE AT THE CAMBRIDGE UNION

In autumn 2003, to his surprise and delight, Andrew received an invitation from the president of the Cambridge Union to take part in a debate. He accepted without hesitation. The rather curious motion was: 'This house would rather be an aristocrat than a democrat'. He was asked to speak for the aristocrats. The old warhorse in him smelt an agreeable battle ahead.

Years ago, he had taken part in another debate at the Union and remembered the atmosphere as antagonistic – to say the least – towards someone like him and he expected to find the same again only with knobs on. Imagine his surprise when the president wrote with the final arrangements – times for drinks and dinner, and dress *black tie*. That such an outfit should have shaken off its mothballs and re-emerged at a student debate was a huge surprise. Where are the jeans of yesteryear? What has precipitated such a change? Instead of missiles – from soggy bread-rolls indoors to more serious weaponry in the street – he found nothing but good manners and a student dinner-companion of such charm he has been talking about her ever since.

You will be surprised to hear that the motion was carried by the democrats, the poor old aristocrats biting the dust as usual. Andrew abstained. I am told by someone who was there that when he finished speaking the applause was loud and prolonged.

'So what did you say?' I asked. 'Oh, I can't remember.' But the audience had laughed – and that was the point.

February 2004

CHANGING LANGUAGE

In 1994 I wrote a piece for *Country Life* about changes in our language on rural matters: country turning into countryside, hedges into hedgerows, bogs into wetlands and so on. Weather forecasters have changed the age-old Scottish 'hills' of poets, shepherds and sportsmen into 'mountains'. 'Home is the hunter from the mountain'? Surely not. The new words are longer and sound more important but the additions are unnecessary for meaning.

We know that language changes. Sixty years on, who would say *Great Scott*, *By Jove*, *vamp*, *scram*, *mannequin*, *blighter*, *shut-eye*, *copper* (or *Bobby* for that matter)? Many would not even know what the words mean. *Swank*, *spiffing*, *pansy* and *top-hole* have gone with the wind. So have those dressing-table necessities *cold cream* and *vanishing cream*. *Capital*, *conked out* and *topping* have also disappeared. Cars don't have *chokes* any more (they hardly have gears and their windows have given up winding down).

Shoot used to mean a cheery gathering of friends bent on a day's sport. If pheasants are the quarry, it will take place during the darkest season of the year; if partridges, it is likely to be in October; if it's in August, you'll be on a grouse moor. But whatever the weather, you go. Today a *shoot* can mean a crowd of curiously dressed young men and women, one of whom is king of the camera. In spite of being armed with huge silver umbrellas they don't go out in the rain, so in this part of England there is

315

a lot of waiting about. It makes for frayed tempers as there is a deadline to be met for the fashion magazines. Nothing could be more different from the other kind of *shoot*.

A *stalker* was, and still is, a man whose name is likely to begin with Mc. He wears a fore-and-aft hat and crawls on his stomach over bog and rock, spying for a stag, and he is often in charge of an amateur behind a rifle. Today he is also someone who takes a fancy to (usually) a woman and can actually be arrested for his trouble. *Stalking* is now a criminal offence.

There is a new vocabulary spawned by technology, most of it as ugly as *blog*. A *web* is nothing to do with spiders (or lies) and is used a thousand times a day by all. The same goes for *net*.

Technology apart, change gallops on. Words are as much driven by fashion as are hats. The chosen ones are done to death till they lose their impact. *Icon*, for instance. *Icons* are everywhere, chiefly actors and actresses or television people. *Iconic* describes anything desirable till he, she or it falls from grace because of a scandal to do with money or sex (though the latter sometimes adds to the fascination). The dictionary says an *icon* is 'a representation of some sacred personage, itself regarded as sacred, and honoured with a relative worship'. I suppose this is how those people and objects are seen, but everyday use has devalued the word and no doubt we shall soon hear of a new one to describe 'anything venerated or uncritically admired'.

Consumer is a funny one. It seems we are all *consumers* not just of food and drink, which you can understand because we have to consume them to stay alive, but of everything we buy. How can you *consume* a sofa? Or a string of pearls, a car or a cruise? Perhaps an obese person could open a vast mouth and cram in a piano or two before sending for the fire brigade to recover them, but it is unlikely. We must all give it some thought. Meanwhile lunch is ready and I will *consume* it.

Market place and *workshop* worry me. I think of the former as where Bakewell Market happens every Monday – cattle and sheep at one end and at the other a thrilling mixture of kitchen gadgets, stuff by the yard, household goods, clothes, fruit and veg, all under dripping canvas and cheaper than in the shops – cheerful bargains on every stall. I am wrong. *Market place* applies to where anything is bought and sold, including the antics of City traders in their shirtsleeves yelling at each other down telephones without a cow or sheep in sight – and certainly not in mind.

Surely a *workshop* is a shed where carpenters in aprons and other talented men make something. Saws, hammers and chisels hang in neat patterns on the wall and the floor is deep in wood shavings and sawdust. But the word has been bagged by the ubiquitous actors and actresses who speak of a *theatre workshop* – the next best thing to an oxymoron, to my mind. There are theatres and there are workshops but they don't go together.

An *issue* is as common as an *icon* and is beginning to replace a *problem*. I don't like the sound of it, conjuring up as it does the woman in the Bible with an *issue of blood*. Politicians are very keen on them. There is usually more than one and they can't make up their minds as to what to do with them. They spin out the time, unresolved, till a more urgent *issue* comes along, which is almost at once.

You can't hide behind *transparency* because you can see through it. Mr Blair was as *transparent* as they come and full of *issues* which you could also see through. Everything has to go through a *process*. A *peace process* is the favourite, perhaps because there are so many wars. The United States is enduring an *electoral process* and I am about to get out of bed and follow a *dressing process*. Quite a business and one that involves a *strategy* as well. Generals used to be the ones for that, conducting a campaign and manoeuvring an army. Now *strategy* is used instead of 'plan', I suppose because it sounds better, more urgent, with a warlike ring to it.

Don't forget *scenario*. Back to the theatre: 'An outline of a dramatic work scene by scene', says the dictionary. It is dangerously close to *strategy*, both words used to enliven dull sentences and brighten up dull lives by constant reference to the stage. If you don't look out you'll be back in that *theatre workshop* where you can deal with *strategic scenarios* in the company of *icons*.

When I was a shopkeeper I was forever *sourcing* things. Unwittingly, though; I thought I had just found them. The source of the Thames is there all right, mysterious and romantic, but it is quite different from trudging down the aisles of *Consumer Goods* at Trade Fairs, yet I was *sourcing* the day away on that ploy.

Rooms are *spaces*. You can't fill them with consumer goods because they must be minimalist, i.e. empty. A drawing room, once a withdrawing room, is no longer. It must be just a *space* – there is nowhere to withdraw to. It cannot be a *drawing space* because that is a studio, which has another meaning. The unhappy tenant of a studio is not a draughtsman but just a person who has been squashed into a very small *space* by a greedy landlord.

Bureaucrats love *putting things in place*. I think it means starting something – but that is often an *initiative*. So you put your *initiative in place*. This is after it has been vetted by a few committees, some planners and a panel of experts. The whole thing is soon forgotten. Even so, it could become an *issue* before you've had time to ask an *icon* to open it.

Watch out for *initiative*. Don't, whatever you do, use your own. You'll break the law and bring Health and Safety running. It is better to quash it before the *process* begins or you will be branded as a menace to society. The mere idea of doing anything without consulting consultants is too risky even for a risk assessor to *put in place* and *drive forward*. And a *road map*? Oh, PLEASE . . .

If you mind any of this, never fear, it will be all change soon and we can rest in peace.

DEPORTMENT

After spending a day in Oxford during term time, I have been wondering what has happened to deportment. Isn't it high time it was brought back as a compulsory class at school? I suppose there would be a riot and the Narkover-type pupils of today would knife the teacher before the lesson could begin.

If only the girls could see themselves in their expensive, creased jumble, slouching about, faces hidden by curtains of hair, compared to how they would look if they carried themselves like Edwardian beauties. There would come about a change which would cheer things up no end wherever young people congregate.

The girls are just as pretty as they always were but they go to amazing lengths to hide it. Yet they spend fortunes on make-up and tragic coverings, which can hardly be described as clothes.

I think they must be longing to sit on juries, for we are repeatedly told that anyone who is clean, tidy and stands up straight is objected to for jury service without further reason.

June 1986

319

CHRISTMAS AT CHATSWORTH

Little was made of Christmas at Chatsworth in the eighteenth and nineteenth centuries as, strangely enough, there were no Cavendish children there for nearly a hundred years. It all came to life early in the twentieth century when the newly refurbished theatre became the scene of home-made entertainment of the most sophisticated kind. Professional singers and amateur members of the week-long house parties sang and acted sketches, with King Edward VII and Queen Alexandra heading the guest list at the regular annual shoots of the 8th Duke of Devonshire and his German duchess. The audience was magnificently dressed and glittering in diamonds.

In 1908 Victor (9th Duke) and Evelyn arrived with their large family. In due course they had twenty-one grandchildren, who made the Christmases of the 1920s and 1930s memorable. The parents came with their maids and valets, the children with their nannies, grooms and ponies (they hunted with the High Peak Harriers on Boxing Day). Some of the nannies were keenly aware of the status of their charges. My sisters-in-law remember being told to sit on their luggage in a passage while their nanny demanded the best night-nursery, already occupied by Stuart cousins who had arrived earlier. On the insistence of Nanny, the cousins were ousted in favour of the preferred Cavendish girls.

Granny Evelyn had a famous cook, Mrs Tanner, who trained under Escoffier no less. She left books of receipts which show that the Christmas food was rich and rare – so were the menus, which seemed to go on for ever. The dining room, schoolroom and nursery all had different menus. The unlucky children had to eat the hateful bland food thought suitable for their ages. Even the Christmas puddings were made of different ingredients according to where they would be eaten. Those for the staff were mostly suet and breadcrumbs mixed with stout and milk, whereas Mrs Tanner's 'Best Christmas Pudding, Buckingham Palace receipt' included French plums, stoned raisins and half muscatels, plus half a bottle of brandy – underlining the great unfairness of life.

With my own family in Oxfordshire it was different. Seven of us children were a solid start. My mother gave a tea party for the Asthall and Swinbrook schoolchildren on Christmas Eve, with the parson as Father Christmas. She bought and wrapped a toy and a garment for each child and took infinite trouble over the list of ages and sexes. One year she settled on penknives for the boys. Today these innocents would find themselves in the police station.

Christmas Day routine never varied for us. Early-morning opening of stockings, church, undoing presents ('the festival of paper', my mother called it), lunch of turkey and a plum pudding with sixpences, bachelor's buttons and other anti-Health and Safety charms embedded in it, and, after dark, a card game so simple that the youngest and stupidest of the children (me) could play. Fancy dress in the evening – anything to hand was seized on. My sister Nancy was always the most imaginative. My father's only concession was to wear a red wig. He took the group photograph so was never in it. My mother must have been thankful when it was all over.

It starts in October now. The Chatsworth Farm Shop is packed with things to eat and people to buy them, its reputation having spread since its quiet start in 1976, when we had planning permission to sell only hunks of freezer meat. The hampers are sent

hither and thither to corporate and private buyers galore. Some, I'm glad to say, prefer ours to those of the famous London shops. The butchery counter is crammed with 745 turkeys, 50 geese, 400 hams and a goodly show of our own beef and lamb.

Our children, grandchildren and fourteen great-grandchildren come to stay in alternate years. It is odd having middle-aged grandchildren, and some of the greats are getting on. The change in them in two years is fascinating to see. The five-year-old, who told an enquiring schoolfriend last year that he was going to a public house for Christmas, will probably give a dissertation on Euclid next year when he is seven. Stone passages apparently constructed for roller-skating come in useful when it is wet. There are hazards which make it more exciting, like a long ramp where you get up the speed to crash into the door of the boiler room, hundreds of yards and two staircases away from the comparative safety of the nursery.

For the intervening Christmases come old (very) friends – ninety-two is the oldest this year – plus a wheelchair cousin who will be whirled up and down the corridors by a nine-year-old, I hope with some notion of safety.

It's no good sinking into a chair after lunch. Whatever the weather the hens must be fed. The midwinter light soon disappears and no sensible hen stays out of doors after dark or the foxes, which our government adores, would get their all-time Christmas dinner.

In 2001, the spectre of foot-and-mouth caused havoc at Chatsworth. Andrew suggested the house should stay open till Christmas to recoup the losses, and so it has remained. People come from all over England to see it decorated and lit by candles (yes, *candles*) and the house-shops turn into fairyland. No one from outside advises. The house staff do it and seem to be inspired, so the result pleases all who come.

Well, nearly all. One year I got a letter saying how awful the tinsel wreaths round the heads of Roman busts were ('tacky') and what frightful taste I have to allow such a travesty. So we can't please everyone, but I think Christmas without tinsel, however Roman the heads, would simply not be Christmas.

October 2005

THE FALL AND RISE OF THE
STATELY HOME
by Peter Mandler

'Aristocracy', says the dictionary, means 'government of a state by its best citizens'. All over now – more's the pity – and the so-called aristocrat, now powerless, is hardly the word to describe the latter-day villains of this book. As builders of the stately homes, they started off quite well. Hatfield, Penshurst, Burghley, Haddon, Hardwick and Co. were all open to the public in the eighteenth century. A hundred years later the railways brought big crowds and it was still considered the people's right to be shown round these houses, romanticised by the Victorians. Entry was free.

It was a shock when Lord Sackville, a crusty old chap who disliked his fellow men, closed Knole in the 1880s. There was a near-revolution in Sevenoaks where the tradespeople depended on the trippers. One or two owners began to charge to reduce numbers but it was the 4th Earl of Warwick who, in 1886, actually set about turning his castle into an asset rather than a liability. His family continued to do so till 1978, when they eventually succumbed to a tempting offer from Madame Tussaud.

Peter Mandler lumps owners together as if they were a breed of dog when, in fact, they are as individual as their houses. It is their problems and interests which are the same. The Lords Warwick get the publicity, but for one of them there are dozens of steady people who look after their inheritance, as well as carrying out endless local duties, which the author finds too boring to mention. The silent majority still *in situ* seem to me to have ridden out the storms of punitive taxes, recurring agricultural depressions, wars, pestilence and Lloyd's, with judgement and rectitude.

Mr Mandler seems to be unaware that the statelies have attendant cottages, farm roads and buildings, and endless outgoings that must be paid for, as well as the upkeep of the houses themselves. Pensions? Not mentioned. Forestry is deemed to be an asset. In all the years I have lived near trees they have been a constant drain on estate resources. The author often mentions, but fails to understand, the Englishman's deep-seated love of his land.

The unfortunate owners can't do right. If, like Lord Montagu, they try and make a go of the place, they are greedy. If they are forced by taxation to sell up, they are running away. If they sell what is loosely called a 'work of art' to pay for new lead on the roof, they are 'threatening the integrity of the house'. But if holes in the roof allow the Old Master drawings and rare books to get wet there is not much integrity left.

He is surprised that little was done about country houses in the 1940s. Had he been in England then, he would have noticed that the minds of government and owners were on other things. He might look at the names on war memorials in village churchyards – few landowning families were spared the deaths of men of military age.

In the 1950s, taste descended to a nadir and the author is right in saying that few English people wanted to live – and fewer wanted to work – in a big house. There has been a gradual change in attitude which has gained momentum in the last twenty years. Television programmes have sharpened people's interest in works of art, and concern for conservation of the best buildings and their contents is driven by 2,300,000 members of the National Trust.

The author can hardly bear it when things begin to look up for

326

some owners but, alas, many houses are still vulnerable and will inevitably come on the market to be sold, and almost immediately resold when the buyers discover they don't fancy their new responsibilities and have bitten off more than they can chew.

Hoping for a word of encouragement in the summing up, I find French chateaux cited as an 'instructive comparison'. Oh PLEASE. You can't compare them. There are two basic differences between French and English attitudes to country houses. Frenchmen who have the choice would rather live in Paris than in the country, whereas the opposite holds here. The Code Napoléon has split up estates and emptied the chateaux of their contents, while primogeniture has been the saviour of what is left in this country – and a great deal is left.

The academic-eye view cites reasons for visiting houses as nostalgia and snobbism. Nowhere can I find the word 'beauty' to describe a house or garden, and I believe that to be the reason you and I enjoy seeing the wonders that are available to us. There are mistakes in facts and figures and little which is constructive but, living over the shop as it were, I read it with intense interest.

April 1997

COLD HOUSES

Anyone of my age is qualified to write about cold houses. Staying away in the 1930s for Pony Club dances before graduating to hunt balls taught me many a lesson in how to survive when the liberty bodice was overtaken by an off-the-shoulder evening dress.

Friends' parents usually made a big effort to warm the house on the evening of the entertainment but for some strange reason no one feels cold in his own house, besides which they always started too late. Beatrice Lillie's song, 'Oh, For a Night in the Ballroom' – 'fires in the bedroom at four' – said it all. The hostess, always an outdoor creature, was bound to be doing something with her dogs till the winter sun went down. The host was apt to be out hunting, so serious stoking didn't start till they got in.

The best moment was a hot bath before dinner. In a big house you might have quite a trek to reach this haven of warmth and if someone else got there before you it was bad luck. You had to retrace your steps down the draughty passage and face the fact that the hot water may have run out. Twice I suffered the cruellest cut of all: hot water gushing beautifully from its tap and empty silence from the cold tap. Nothing for it but, undressed and shivering and making a fog of steam, to leg it back to the bedroom, disappointed and unwashed.

If the dance was in another house, there was the drive in the car to contend with. No one under fifty remembers cars before heaters. My mother's car had wooden floorboards with big gaps between them so you could see the road rushing along under your feet. All the rugs in the world couldn't keep you warm.

Back to bed in the strange house to find perfectly ironed sheets, which are at once the coldest and the most luxurious things going. You slid between the icy, shining linen only to gather up your feet into a place made warmer by the rest of you.

But all that was long ago and at Chatsworth things aren't too bad. A new heating system was installed when we moved in and it works pretty well. Even so, the wind can penetrate huge old window frames which don't fit exactly. In September we go round with rolls of sticky brown paper to stop the gaps. When the front door is open and people with luggage dawdle, all our part of the house feels the blast so we've cut a small door out of the big one and you have to enter at speed. There are zones of intense cold, seldom visited in winter: the Sculpture Gallery, State Rooms and attics, where a closed-season search for forgotten furniture can feel colder than being out of doors.

Nothing is so bad for pictures painted on board, furniture and leather bindings as central heating; even the modest temperature of the rooms we live in does some damage. Humidifiers have been recommended but they are so hideous that I don't think I can bear to live with their sharp, white, metallic presence and horrible ceaseless noise. Anyway, they don't work. Perhaps a kettle or two perpetually on the boil would do the trick and be homelier.

No one has suggested air conditioning. There I draw the line. I prefer hit-or-miss English heating to waking up with swollen feet and fingers about to burst, like cows' udders at milking time, which happens after a night in an air-conditioned hotel. Or when in the tropics you need a fur coat to wear at dinner in an over-cooled restaurant.

After years of trial and error I've got my bedroom at Chatsworth about right, but there are the dogs to consider. When it was whippets, it seemed unkind to open the window at all. Then there was an old collie who would search for a cool spot, and for him the window had to be wide open. Labradors are accommodating as long as they aren't in a draught, and one slept under the bed. The springs made a noise that went through my head whenever he turned over.

It is far less risky to stay away in the winter now. Things have changed since Andrew and I spent two unforgettably cold January nights in an official house in Northern Ireland some years ago. We were given an enormous room with a single-bar electric fire (which I drew life-size in a letter to a sister). And yet you were expected to wear a décolleté dress in the evening.

Standards now get ever higher and when people talk of 'warm hospitality' I reckon they mean hospitality *is* warmth.

January 1987

RECOLLECTIONS OF DITCHLEY AND NANCY LANCASTER

I had a letter from Nancy suggesting I write what I remember of Ditchley. I said I would try. The next day came a postcard saying, 'I don't want a eulogy . . .'

After many years, does memory play you false? Do you look back on events, people and places in a slanted sort of way, slanted to summers being fine, friends always there, jokes, laughter, pleasure and entertainments galore, untouched by responsibility and living for the moment in a cheerful, hopeful sequence of exciting exploration? Perhaps you do, and perhaps it is lucky that adolescent discontent and the humdrum things which occupy most days are lost or are run together in a vague mist of recollection, and the special times remain, leapfrogging the rest. When I think of Ditchley all those years ago and the profound effect it had on me – and must have had on everyone who went there – it is impossible to write anything but a eulogy.

When I was a child we lived at Swinbrook, eleven or twelve miles away. I loved fox-hunting above all else and it was out hunting that I first saw Nancy. The meet of the Heythrop hounds was near our home, the unfashionable side of what was then an unfashionable hunt. The field consisted of people who lived in the Heythrop country, enlivened in term-time by wild undergraduates from Oxford riding unruly hirelings. Smart folk hunted in the shires. I can't imagine what Nancy was doing at Ford Wells on a Saturday.

I was trotting along on my dock-tailed pony when a big chestnut horse came thundering by. It was ridden on a loose rein by an elegant woman on a side-saddle wearing the Heythrop green livery, faultless top hat and veil – the smartest thing imaginable. 'Who is that?' I asked our old groom. 'Mrs Tree from Ditchley, on a blood 'orse.' He didn't have to tell me *that*. Later, when we passed the few horseboxes there were in those days, I saw her second horseman, a cockade in his top hat – something I had never seen before. I don't know who made the greater impression, I only know that I have never forgotten them.

I first went to Ditchley when I was sixteen or seventeen, having got to know Nancy's sons, Michael and Jeremy, out hunting. But I had seen the house before Nancy and her then husband Ronnie Tree bought it – empty and desolate, the park full of rabbits and sad white grass, at the time of the agricultural depression of the early 1930s. When Nancy and Ronnie arrived, it came to life and there they created perfection. On looking back, I realise that Ditchley taught me an invaluable lesson and that was to notice, to look, and try to absorb and remember what I saw that was beautiful. It was certainly the first time I became aware of such things. I suppose it was because of what Nancy gathered together under her roof, and the way she arranged the house. Whatever she touched had that hard-to-pin-down but instantly recognisable gift of *style*, arresting in its originality and satisfying to the spirit.

The house itself and its fixed decorations, together with much of the original furniture, was a wonderful start. But her genius (and that is no exaggeration) was her eye for colour, scale, objects and the dressing up of them, the stuffs the curtains are made of, their shapes and trimmings, the china, tablecloths, knives and forks; the things you see in all houses, but O the difference between Nancy's way with household necessities and anyone else's. Even the bathrooms were little works of art. Warm, panelled and carpeted, there were shelves of Chelsea china cauliflowers, cabbages, tulips and rabbits of exquisite quality. (A far cry from the cracked lino and icy draughts to which I was accustomed.) I had never seen such huge, square, down pillows as she went in for, nor the Porthault sheets decorated with carnations or trailing blue flowers of M. Porthault's imagination, and scalloped edges of the same colour. Nor the puffed-up eiderdowns covered in pale silk with tiny bows where a stitch held the cover in place. The tea tables, which came and went at the proper time, had no cloths but were painted brilliant Chinese red. Easy enough, anyone could have done that – but no one else did.

The rooms and their delectable contents were only part of the story. All that beauty could have been set up and people would have delighted in it, but the whole of Ditchley reflected the personality, the aura if you like, of Nancy herself. She was the star on the stage she created.

I can see her now, sitting bolt upright at the end of the dining-room table on one of the high-backed yellow chairs with Ronnie's initials embroidered on its cover, wearing something enviable with her own signature of a brilliant bit of colour somewhere, taking over the table so that people stopped to listen and laugh, making a comical mountain out of an ordinary molehill – a top-of-the-bill entertainer as well as a generous hostess.

The Trees were supported by a staff of servants no less talented at making their guests comfortable and happy than the hosts themselves. Mr Collins, the butler, was an extremely handsome man who was as polite to a seventeen-year-old girl as to a head of state. This invisible asset of perfect manners continued down to the housemaids, the kitchen staff, the grooms and the gamekeepers. These last were father and sons by the name of Starling, as neat and chirpy in their buttoned gaiters as the partridges they looked after. Cheerful Sunday morning visits to the chef and the stables were a pleasurable feature of staying at Ditchley.

In my mind's eye there is Mr Collins, tall and splendid in his tailcoat, piling coal on the hall fire on a Monday morning when most people in his profession would thankfully leave such a task till the next invasion of weekend guests. But at Ditchley you were made to feel they actually regretted your going. Rare enough. I have known two other houses where you have that feeling – Houghton with Sybil Cholmondeley at the helm and my sister Diana's Temple outside Paris.

Nancy and Ronnie were innovators in the garden, leaders of fashion outside as well as in. It was they who began the renaissance of old-fashioned roses, edging and designs in box, and so much else which has been copied *ad infinitum* in the last forty years and is so common now that you could be forgiven for forgetting who started it all.

After the war began and there was no petrol, I used to drive over from Swinbrook in a pony trap, fetching the pony out of the field and draping its second-hand harness over it to jog along the empty roads. On arrival the stud groom fetched it from the front door. Going home the next day the pony looked very different, shining all over, hooves dressed with oil and the harness and trap polished as never before.

When Winston Churchill used the house for weekends away from the bombing in London, I was delighted by Jeremy Tree's yawns and sighs and evident longing to go to bed when the PM started – and went on – talking till the early hours. (My own children did just the same years later when Harold Macmillan came to Chatsworth and talked till the cows came home.) At Ditchley we would have preferred to listen to Nancy.

I have no doubt that, as in every other family, you only had to scratch the surface to find worries, dramas and sorrows not far away. But such was the atmosphere created by the Trees and the magic of the place that, as a young girl, I found unalloyed pleasure in my visits there.

How short a time this oasis of perfection lasted. I count myself very lucky to have seen it. In my life I have been to many beautiful places and met many fascinating people but I have never seen the like of Ditchley and Nancy. 'I don't want a eulogy . . .' she said. Sorry, but how could it be otherwise?

HOME TO ROOST

I lived in the friendly palace that is Chatsworth for more than half my long life and, at eighty-five, I was the oldest person by far in that unusual house, where one of the many luxuries was that you never had to look at anything ugly because you were surrounded by the best of everything from four centuries. Chatsworth is unusual because of its size, beauty, fame, contents, garden, surroundings and staff, and the fact that it is visited by about 600,000 people every year. Under its roof is a kind of university of knowledge. Art historians, educationalists, cooks, needlewomen, accountants, plumbers, electricians, lodge porters, joiners, security guards, cleaners, retailers, lecturers, night watchmen, firemen, a photographer, a silver steward, a computer man and archivists mingle, their roles sometimes blurred and melting into the next profession. They make up an organisation unmatched in this country. That is the house I have left.

My new house was once the vicarage for the parish of Edensor, surrounded by a park wall and a ha-ha wide enough to deter the most athletic deer from invading the garden. The house is old and curiously constructed, having been altered many times since the eighteenth century. It has been enlarged, made smaller and enlarged again. We found windows in what is now an internal wall, and a stone gatepost, with a hinge for hanging a gate, at the bottom of the stairs – apparently holding up the first floor. Another surprise awaits upstairs where the landing and one of the bedrooms has a stone floor seven inches thick and therefore extremely heavy. No explanation has been discovered for these oddities. In another bedroom the builders removed some plaster from an internal wall to find it lined with reeds, the flowers still attached to the ends of the stalks. They have put a glass panel so you can see this pretty and practical kind of insulation.

Bits of house stick out at angles. The dining room and the bedroom above have three outside walls, causing the last tenant to retreat to a bedroom over the Aga. For me it is an unheard-of pleasure for the kitchen to be just two steps away and for it to be two steps the other way into the garden. At Chatsworth both destinations meant an expedition. Time to cancel the glossies and order the *Smallholder*.

One luxury has backfired badly. My new film star's bathroom has got a hand-held spray fed from the bath taps, something I have always wanted. Delighted, I tried it out. The beastly thing took control as if possessed of a devil and leapt about in my hand, soaking the much-too-pale film star's carpet and all else in its path with scalding water. I won't try that again.

Forty-six years and a month is not so long to stay in a house in these parts. There are a few ancients around who still live in the house where they were born. Nevertheless, nearly half a century produces a staggering accumulation of what my daughter calls 'glut' and decisions as to what to take from the quart jug to fit into the pint pot filled my waking hours and sometimes woke me when most people were sleeping.

A few precious things are lost in a move but many are found. Lurking unseen for years in a bookshelf was a Roxburghe Club volume, whose title I won't mention for fear of offending the donor. Given to Andrew by that elite company of bookworms, it was sitting there between *Fowls and How to Keep Them* and a slim volume to delight the heart of any teenage boy entitled *Studies in the Art of Ratcatching: A Manual for Schools*, published by John

Murray, no less, in 1891. I must ask the present bearer of that distinguished name if it was a best-seller.

At Chatsworth, clothes were hung far into a cupboard the size of an ordinary room in any normal house. Some French numbers of the 1950s and 1960s still hold their own in any company: quality incomparable; style timeless. One of the unwanted bedrooms in the Old Vicarage has become home for these beautiful garments. A granddaughter looked as if she had been poured into the simplest, best-cut, pitch-black evening dress – long sleeves, long skirt, no fuss, no decoration, made of some magic material between satin and thick silk. A dress to wear and to keep for her daughter now aged fifteen.

Trickier than pictures and clothes when it comes to a new home are ornaments: bits of china, stopped watches, presents from six-year-old grandchildren made with deepest concentration, hideous and easily broken but well remembered by the manufacturer and important for them to find still there. The boxes used by publishers sending books for our shops are invaluable at this point.

For weeks I felt like Edith Somerville, the Irish writer, who, aged eighty-eight, left her home of sixty years for a smaller house. In despair, she wailed to a nephew, 'Under everything there is something.' I pity people who have to move to the north of Scotland or Cornwall or, worse still, abroad. Being only a few hundred yards away, I can at least – like the Swiss Family Robinson – 'go back to the wreck' for a vital hammer or a pearl necklace left behind.

Decisions as to what to keep and what to throw are curiously wearing. Every scrap of paper, every ornament brings back its history with it. You pick them up and put them down, wondering. There is no doubt that throwing away is a kind of cleansing and you feel better afterwards. But you immediately want the thrown thing back and have to dig in the bonfire box. The drawer of my bedside table contained a horrid, ancient, floppy leather cover for a book. It held my mother's ABC Railway Guide and now encloses private papers from the lawyer. The ABC was a remarkable source of pre-war, pre-Beeching information to do with trains, their timetables of long ago – all, alas, irrelevant now – including the Early Closing Days for every town where there was a station.

My new house is spacious and sunny and has all the attributes beloved of estate agents. But the great thing about the Old Vicarage is its atmosphere. It is benign, serene, welcoming, good all through. Is the feeling left by the holy men who lived here? Do other Old Vics have the same legacy – intangible, but invaluable and very apparent? In 1838, the incumbent was Francis Hodgson, who went on to be Provost of Eton. He was a friend of Lord Byron and had his likeness in a marble head by Thorvaldsen. This somehow found its way to Chatsworth, but I am glad to say it is now back at the Old Vic. In 1856, the Reverend Joseph Hall was the vicar and remained in that office for fifty-one years. He must have known the place fairly well, a comforting thought in the restlessness of the 2000s. When the Reverend Harry O'Rorke arrived in 1908, the house was enlarged to accommodate his family of seven children and eight indoor servants. The widow of the last vicar to live here, Mrs Iola Symonds, is hale at ninety and often comes to see her old stamping ground. She had twenty-two rooms to look after. I have planted a tulip tree in the middle of her tennis court, which makes me feel guilty of desecrating the old playground.

The old vicars lived well here. The garden and outbuildings cover nearly two acres. A table to seat twenty would easily go into the dining room. There were fourteen bedrooms till 1972 when, wisely, the house was split to become the first semi-detached Old Vicarage in the country. There it has remained and I am the lucky tenant of what could be described as a rambling family home. The view to the west is lovely and gloomy. It reminds me of a hymn which fascinated my sisters and me as children: 'Within the churchyard, side by side, are many long low graves.' A few Jacob sheep are penned there, doing service as grass keepers. Joseph Paxton's memorial is far grander than those of the Dukes of Devonshire and makes a good shelter for the lambs, all in the shadow of Sir George Gilbert Scott's enormous 1868 church. The nearness of the churchyard underlines the fact that this life is finite and 'in the twinkling of an eye . . .'

March 2006

NEWLY LAID

'UNCLE MATTHEW' AT *THE LADY*

You could not imagine a more unlikely candidate looking for a job at *The Lady* than my father, David Mitford. He had just survived a bullet wound in the Boer War, which destroyed a lung.

In 1902 he had been thrown on an ox cart and covered with corpses when someone noticed a hand slowly winding and unwinding fingers. 'There is someone alive at the bottom of that heap,' shouted the keen observer.

He was indeed alive and joined the wounded – although no one expected him to live. Three or four days later, he was deposited at the hospital in Bloemfontein from where he began the long voyage home and his even longer convalescence.

Shortly after his return from South Africa, my father proposed to my mother, Sydney Bowles. But he had first to ask the permission of her father – and my grandfather – founder of *Vanity Fair* and *The Lady*, Thomas Gibson Bowles.

'How do you propose to support her?' Gibson Bowles had asked.

'I've got £400 a year, and these,' my father answered, holding up his hands. They married on 6 February 1904 and lived in London, in a tiny house in Graham Street, Pimlico.

I believe Mr Bowles gave them a three-month cruise on his yacht as a honeymoon and found his new son-in-law work at

The Lady, without the formalities of form-filling beloved by the bureaucrats of today.

My father reported for work accompanied by his pet mongoose, whose job was to get rid of the rats in the nether regions of *The Lady* building. He immediately became not only popular but loved by the staff, from cleaners to editors, always acknowledged by him as his equals.

I do not know if Thomas Gibson Bowles explained to him what were his responsibilities as deputy general manager, but I imagine he had to study the fashions of women's clothes in 1904 and presumably had to peruse the many classified advertisements from governesses and nannies to gardeners and nursery maids, and from rooms-to-let to corsets. (Holiday cottages were yet to be invented.)

Mr Bowles never asked my father for a job description. Had he done so the answer would have divided his time thus – cheering on his mongoose in the course of his mongoose duties 80 per cent, all the rest 20 per cent.

My sister Nancy was born on 28 November 1904 – the first of six disappointments. My mother was longing for six boys, but girls appeared one after the other, only punctuated by one boy, Tom.

My father was tall and handsome. Nancy nicknamed him Great Agrippa from *Struwwelpeter* ('so tall he almost reached the sky') when he announced around tea-time, 'I am going to get out of my good clothes', and came back in a dressing gown looking just like the figure in the book.

He was the originator of all the jokes in our family. Nancy picked these up and exaggerated them for the character of 'Uncle Matthew' in two or three of her novels and my father was also the model for 'General Murgatroyd' in another.

My father was a great ally of my sister Jessica and myself. When we complained about the horrible lunches served at the day school we went to in Beaconsfield for two terms, he took matters in hand at once. Believing in going straight to the top, he entered the headmistress's study armed with nothing more than his blue eyes and irresistible charm. He won. He got what he, on our behalf, wanted – which was to be excused the unrecognisable scraps of old cow steeped in a stew of their own juice – and henceforth a banana was our lunch.

My father was adept at taking on that formidable female, who insisted on having 'For those in peril on the sea' sung at every assembly, in honour of her brother, even though he was safe and sound on his ship with no sign of war to interrupt his naval career. Such determination must have proved useful with some of *The Lady*'s doughty readers with whom I imagine he had to deal.

He never wrote anything for the magazine himself. That was not his talent. He just got on brilliantly with the female staff and most of *The Lady*'s readership.

I have often wondered if he had to answer some of their letters criticising aspects of the magazine. I rather hope not, because his idea of women (unless they were beautiful) was less than sympathetic. My mother once asked him why he had to be so early at the Army & Navy Stores when he went to do his shopping. He used to leave his dogs outside and wait patiently until the doors opened at 9 a.m. 'If I am any later I am impeded by inconveniently shaped women,' he replied – 'inconveniently shaped' because of the parcels they were carrying. He was too polite to push and shove, so he had to be there first.

On the rare occasions when my mother invited a friend to lunch, if he did not like the unfortunate woman, my father would say, after she had gone, 'Why did you invite that meaningless piece of meat? She was a dismal, worthless sort of creature . . .' These remarks never reached *The Lady* or Mr Bowles might have had second thoughts about my father's suitability for the job.

My father was unread, because in early life he had read

White Fang, by Jack London, and loved it so much he did not ever want to read another book. My triumph of last week was getting a copy of it from the internet for £2. I felt I had landed a big fish and was so proud, but I expect I shall be like my father and will never want to read another.

When the war broke out in 1914 my father joined his old regiment, the Northumberland Fusiliers, so his time at *The Lady* came to an end. But he had learned a lot about publishing from his father-in-law's firm, which I am glad to say survived his decade there and has gone from strength to strength.

THE BALLAD OF THE CAPPOQUIN
BOATHOUSE

In 1932 Lord Charles Cavendish married Adele Astaire. She was at the very top of her career as a singer and dancer with her brother Fred, but gave all this up when she married Charlie.

I do not know how much it meant to her to drop her acting career, but it was final and she never went on the stage again. Fred, as we know, went on to make ten films with Ginger Rogers as his partner that were acclaimed by all who saw them.

Lismore Castle, its garden, farms and woods covering thousands of acres in County Waterford were given to Charlie Cavendish as a wedding present by his father, Victor, 9th Duke of Devonshire.

Very sadly, Adele and Charlie lost the three babies born to them and Charlie suffered from alcoholism which hastened his premature death at the age of thirty-eight in 1944.

Adele remained at Lismore Castle, but Charlie Cavendish's will stipulated that the castle and estate should go to my husband Andrew if Adele married again, which she did in 1947. This was a wonderful gift to Andrew because, as the second son of a duke, he had not expected to inherit any of the family property.

Andrew and I were married in 1941 and had no idea of the tragedy to come when his elder brother, Billy Hartington, was killed by a sniper when leading his men into a village in

348

Belgium in September 1944. Suddenly Andrew was his father's heir.

This totally unexpected series of events was then added to by the equally premature death (aged fifty-five) of my father-in-law, Eddie, 10th Duke of Devonshire, in 1950. So Andrew assumed responsibility for all the Cavendish family properties including Lismore Castle and it became my job to look after the decoration, furnishing and housekeeping of these amazing houses.

However, all this was in the future when the youthful Richard Baldwyn visited Cappoquin with a touring theatre company and encountered Charlie Cavendish in a manner familiar to all who knew him.

With the author's kind permission I quote his letter as I found it:

Dear Deborah Devonshire,
. . . There are one or two 'overlaps' in our lives and one in particular that I feel might amuse you. It concerns Lord & Lady Charles Cavendish and Cappoquin [a charming village a few miles downstream on the river Blackwater from Lismore Castle]. *To tell the brief story I am enclosing a few paragraphs from a book* I wrote of incidents in my life . . . I was a 17-year-old actor in a company touring Southern Ireland in 1938.*
With admiration and all good wishes,
Richard Baldwyn

Cappoquin was certainly one of the more unusual venues of that summer. Stunningly beautiful, it was only a village with a river running through it. The 'theatre' was the boathouse and the auditorium was where the boats were stored in the winter and repairs carried out.

For our visit, the area had been cleared and some eighty

chairs installed. The lucky eight in the front row had just enough room to sit with their knees just above the level of the eighteen-inch stage.

The actors had to use the whole width of the building — there was no room for 'wings'. Entrances therefore had to be made either through a door stage right straight on to the bank of the river, or through the only other door stage left which opened straight on to the river itself.

A boat, therefore, had to be moored alongside so that actors could leave the stage in as dignified a way as possible, stepping out into a somewhat unsteady craft.

If the playwright had insensitively arranged for the actor to make his next entrance from stage right, he would have to ferry himself round the back of the boathouse to the bank. I can't remember how the dinghy then got back to its vital mooring – perhaps there was a spare one.

For our last performance on the Saturday night, we were all very excited because Lord and Lady Charles Cavendish had booked all eight chairs in the front row. Lady Charles Cavendish had been Adele Astaire, Fred Astaire's sister, and had left the stage when she married.

We had been warned that His Lordship was a very heavy drinker but we had not expected to find him asleep when the curtains parted. Even worse, he was snoring and, only two minutes into the play, he stretched his legs on to the tiny stage so that we had the choice of going round them or stepping over them.

Despite these little difficulties, the evening went well and we learnt later that not only Lady Charles Cavendish but all Cappoquinians would have been surprised – even worried – had His Lordship behaved in any other way. He would be awoken at the end of each act and would join the applause before making the most of the intervals and then returning to his slumbers for the next act.

We had our usual quota of practical jokers in the company and it was inevitable that one of them would indulge on that evening . . . It happened just before the end of the play when a male member of the cast had to make a dramatic exit left. He opened the door and swept off. There was a loud splash. The boat had been removed.

Fortunately it was a comedy that night and laughter was in the air. The audience knew exactly what had happened and even His Lordship had removed his feet from the stage at the final curtain as rapturous applause and calls of 'encore' echoed through the village.

Those on stage were desperately trying to be professional and control their laughter as the curtains parted for the first call. The audience insisted on more calls, shouting for the missing member of the cast. Eventually the victim, soaked and dripping with river, crept on stage to join the line but even then the mob wasn't satisfied. He had to take a solo call before the rest of the cast returned for the final curtain.

The Cavendishes insisted on staying and plying us with drink from the local bar as we struck the set in preparation for our departure in the early hours of Sunday morning. His Lordship regaled us with stories of the number of touring shows he had slept through in the boathouse.

* Richard Baldwyn, *Only Yesterday – Times of My Life* (Kendal & Dean, 2008).

BEAUTIFUL CHICKENS: PORTRAITS OF CHAMPION BREEDS

by Christie Aschwanden, photographs by Andrew Perris

The telephone rang and it was Mark Amory. You could have knocked me down with a feather when he asked me to review *Beautiful Chickens*. I said yes at once. I already had a copy of the book, given me by the staff of Heywood Hill as a Christmas present, so I knew the fun I was letting myself in for.

The chickens are beautiful indeed. The Frizzle, for instance – a spoilt lady coming out of the hairdressers where they have forgotten to comb out her curls – is truly surreal. But not as surreal as what I overheard a woman telling a friend at the Reading Poultry Show many years ago, long before political correctness had been invented: 'I put my little Japs in the bath.' She was staying in a hotel, so what the chambermaid must have thought I cannot imagine. Obviously her Japanese Bantams had to be in pristine shape before they went in front of the judge. The fragility of their tails, which are longer than their bodies by miles, must cause anxiety to their owners.

Some of the birds appear to be in fancy dress. The long-legged Modern Game, standing proudly on stilt-like legs, looks for all the world like Monsieur de Beistegui, who gave the ball of the century in Venice in 1953. So as to be easily recognised as the host, he stood on stilts to greet the onrushing convives. The feathers of the Sebright can be gold or silver, set off by a brilliant red wattle and comb. There you have Jacques

353

Fath, ultimate couturier, whose extravagant costume for the ball was lavishly embroidered with silver and gold.

Another in fancy dress is the Rumpless Tufted Araucana, whose claws are awesome. Her shocked expression makes me wonder if her tail has been plucked out by a rival in the fashion stakes. The black and brown Faverolles is a smart French lady guest and the Scots Dumpy, short in the leg and heavy in the crop, is a kilted friend of mine. A bit of a frump, her stubby legs, with no ankles, go straight into her feet.

The photographs in the book are fantastic and the poetic descriptions, eloquently written by a poultry expert, are instructive and repay careful reading. I would have liked even more about the chickens' varied personalities. Each one has its human counterpart. Welsummers are so shy they disappear into the corners of the poultry yard. But their eggs, dark brown like the tweed made from Black Welsh Mountain sheep, make them well worth the trouble.

Not illustrated in the book are my favourites, the despised crossbred Warrens. They make charming companions, lay an egg nearly every day and are the friendliest, cleverest birds you could ever wish for. There is no such thing as equality in the feathered world and Warrens are perfect examples of the pecking order. When the new, point-of-lay pullets arrive the best and most beautiful of them immediately establishes herself as chairman of the lowly Warrens and never relinquishes her post. She is always first at the trough and remains there until her crop is full to bursting. This self-appointed leader clings to her post for life. I know several of her human counterparts who seem to have done just that.

I would like to add to the description of the Appenzeller Spitzhauben. I think I was the first importer of this decorative Swiss bird, which flies like a pheasant and wears an Ascot hat. In the mid-1970s, my sister Pam came back from Switzerland to live in England and wanted to bring some of these intriguing creatures with her. I wrote three times on her behalf to the Ministry of Agriculture, as it then was, to get permission to import some hatching eggs. I never received an answer so took the law into my own hands and brought a dozen back with me after a visit to Pam. I stopped on the way home to stay with my sister Diana in Paris, where her matchless cook spied the eggs in my luggage and unpacked them for an omelette. I rescued them just in time, put them into my incubator when I got home and delivered them to Pam when the chickens were old enough to live happily without a warming lamp.

The last few pages of the book show scenes from the National Poultry Shows at Stoneleigh and Lanark. In close-up some of the birds look more like hawks than hens and remind me of the old men who haunt the tables at Monte Carlo. With their furious eyes and terrifying beaks, they seem ready to grab the chips and hoard them under their wings until the croupier calls *faites vos jeux* once more.

In contrast to the meticulously coiffed birds, photographed as though they were supermodels, the exhibitors look like the real experts they are. Totally focused on their beloved show birds, they are highly competitive and as delighted with success as if they had won the Derby. Some of the trophies are almost as splendid as those from the racecourse.

I used my strongest magnifying glass to scrutinise the beautiful birds illustrated in this beautiful book. It has been an honour and a pleasure to review it.

ACKNOWLEDGEMENTS

Counting My Chickens

The pieces in this book, sometimes in different forms, first appeared in *Daily Telegraph, Telegraph Weekend Magazine, Sunday Telegraph, Sunday Times, Country Living, Historic House Magazine, Illustrated London News, Woman and Home, Spectator, British Goat Society Yearbook, Chatsworth Staff Newsletter, Books and Company.*

Home to Roost

My grateful thanks are to Stella Tennant, Ian Hislop, Ben Heyes and Henry Wyndham for their help. Will Topley's drawings are a great addition and near the heart for me. Charlotte Mosley has done her inimitable job as editor. Helen Marchant: I'm running out of adjectives to describe her role in this and my other books; I can only thank her again for her support and understanding. As for Alan Bennett, words fail . . .

The following pieces were delivered as talks or appeared in the publications below, sometimes in a different form.

The Land Agents' Dinner, talk delivered in January 1983

Foreword to *The Small Garden* by C. E. Lucas Phillips (2006 edition)

The Organ Recital, *Daily Telegraph*, 9 August 2008

The Farmers' Club Dinner, talk delivered on 3 December 1991

Derbyshire, *Illustrated London News*, February 1982

Review of *Flora Domestica: A History of Flower Arranging* by Mary Rose Blacker, *Spectator*, 22 July 2000

Book Signings and Literary Lunches, *Spectator*, 19 September 2007

Review of *The Tulip* by Anna Pavord, *Daily Telegraph*, 21 December 1998

Review of *John Fowler: Prince of Decorators* by Martin Wood, *Spectator*, 11 December 2007

Tiaras, *Daily Telegraph*, 17 March 2002

Foreword to *The Duchess of Devonshire's Ball* by Sophia Murphy (1985)

A London Restaurant on Trial, *Spectator*, 7 February 2004

Edensor Post Office, *Spectator*, 2 April 2008

The Arrival of the Kennedys in London, 1938, *Spectator*, 31 May 2006

'The Treasure Houses of Britain' Exhibition in Washington, talk delivered to the Friends of Chatsworth, March 1986

Marble Mania, *Daily Telegraph*, October 2001

Bruce, Mario, Stella and Me, *Italian Vogue*, July 1995

Romney Marsh and Other Churches, talk delivered to the Romney Marsh Historic Churches Trust, 1996

Review of *Sassoon: The Worlds of Philip and Sybil* by Peter Stansky, *Spectator*, 12 April 2003

Animal Portraits, *Country Living Magazine*, February 1992

OFTOF, *Spectator*, 7 February 2004

Conservative?, *Daily Telegraph*, 2 September 1993

Debate at the Cambridge Union, *Spectator*, 7 February 2004

Deportment, *Spectator*, 14 June 1986

Christmas at Chatsworth, *Country Life*, October 2005
Review of *The Fall and Rise of the Stately Home* by Peter
    Mandler, *The Times*, 17 April 1997
Cold Houses, *Harper's & Queen*, January 1987
Home to Roost, *Daily Telegraph*, 25 March 2006

The unpublished pieces, unless otherwise stated, are new.

Newly Laid

Once again, I am deeply grateful to my son-in-law, Will
Topley, for creating wonderful drawings to illustrate the
newest pieces in this book. However, this has also been a
chance to revisit the pictures he did for *Counting My Chickens*
and give them the space they deserve. I thank Richard
Baldwyn for introducing me to the marvellous story of Charlie
Cavendish in his ringside seat at the Cappoquin boathouse. I
shall always be indebted to Richard and his account has now
been added to the Chatsworth archive. I also thank my friend
Ron Duggins, who came out of retirement to cheer me up on
a dismal winter day with his skill behind the lens. He has
photographed Andrew and me for more years than any of us
care to remember and at all manner of local events, but none
better than his brilliant photo for the cover of this book.

*Two of the three pieces have previously appeared in publications as
below.*

' "Uncle Matthew" at *The Lady*', *The Lady*, 15 February 2011
Review of *Beautiful Chickens: Portraits of Champion Breeds* by
    Christie Aschwanden, *Spectator*, 5 March 2011